Archaeology, Society and Identity in Modern

C000093430

This bold and illuminating study examines the ro
modern Japanese nation and explores the processes
by national social and intellectual discourse. Leadii
argues that an understanding of the past is a central c
tities and modern nation-states and that, since its en. ᴊ ... ᴜ. ᴜ uistinct academic discipline
in the modern era, archaeology has played an important role in shaping that understanding. By examining in parallel the uniquely intense process of modernisation experienced by
Japan and the history of Japanese archaeology, Mizoguchi explores the close interrelationship
between archaeology, society and modernity, helping to explain why we do archaeology in the
way that we do. This book is essential reading for anybody with an interest in the history and
theory of archaeology or modern Japan.

KOJI MIZOGUCHI is Associate Professor of Archaeology in the Graduate School of Social
and Cultural Studies, Kyushu University, Japan. He is the author of *An Archaeological History
of Japan, 30,000 BC to AD 700* (2002).

CAMBRIDGE STUDIES IN ARCHAEOLOGY

Cambridge Studies in Archaeology aims to showcase the very best in contemporary archaeo-logical scholarship. Reflecting the wide diversity and vigour of archaeology as an intellectual discipline, the series covers all regions of the world and embraces all major theoretical and methodological approaches. Designed to be empirically grounded and theoretically aware, and including both single-authored and collaborative volumes, the series is arranged around four highlighted strands:

- *Prehistory*
- *Classical Archaeology*
- *Medieval Archaeology*
- *Historical Archaeology*

For a list of titles in this series please see the end of the book.

KOJI MIZOGUCHI

Archaeology, Society and Identity in Modern Japan

CAMBRIDGE
UNIVERSITY PRESS

CAMBRIDGE UNIVERSITY PRESS
Cambridge, New York, Melbourne, Madrid, Cape Town,
Singapore, São Paulo, Delhi, Tokyo, Mexico City

Cambridge University Press
The Edinburgh Building, Cambridge CB2 8RU, UK

Published in the United States of America by Cambridge University Press, New York

www.cambridge.org
Information on this title: www.cambridge.org/9780521187794

First published 2006
First paperback edition 2011

A catalogue record for this publication is available from the British Library

Library of Congress Cataloguing in Publication data
Mizoguchi, Koji.
Archaeology, society and identity in modern Japan / by Koji Mizoguchi.
    p.   cm. – (Cambridge studies in archaeology)
Includes bibliographical references and index.
ISBN 0 521 84953 5 (hardback)
1. Title.   11. Series.
DS815.M5347   2006
903.107052 – dc22   2005032566

ISBN 978-0-521-84953-1 Hardback
ISBN 978-0-521-18779-4 Paperback

To Hiromi

CONTENTS

FIGURES

TABLE

PREFACE

This volume is as much about applied social theory as about archaeology, because its ultimate objective is to consider the nature and character of the particular field of social practice/communication that is called archaeology by investigating how it has been and is situated in society as a whole.

To be more concrete, the volume attempts to critically portray the constitutive elements and characteristics of contemporary archaeological practice and the problems which they generate. The contention to be put forward is that they derive from a specific form of generating and maintaining sociality and social institutions, called modernity, which is fundamentally different from its predecessors, i.e., pre-modern social formations. The difference between modernity and pre-modern social formations is multi-faceted, and hence demands a multi-faceted approach. However, according to the late German sociologist Niklas Luhmann, it can be tackled most effectively by investigating the intrinsic nature of human communication and the difference between the way in which human communication is made possible in modernity compared with pre-modern social formations. The way in which human communication is made possible has evolved through the history of the human being as the size of the basic unit of social integration and its complexity has increased, but it was not until the coming of modernity that the human being entered the stage in which every communication was bound to be critically and reflexively commented upon by other communications and effectively relativised; before that moment, communications could be determined/fixed in their values/meanings by referring to something *outside* the realm of human communication, such as the divine and god-given order (of social hierarchy, for instance). This change has had far-reaching effects upon the existential base of the human being and human relations. This change, as this volume will illustrate, was connected to the emergence of the nation-state, which still functions as the basic institutional, cognitive and physical framework and which, to a significant extent, determines our life-course today.

The change transformed the way we identify ourselves and the way we connect ourselves to the world. This change, after all, resulted in the emergence and disciplinisation of most modern scientific disciplines, including archaeology, which began examining both the world and the way human beings related themselves to, and made sense of, the world. That means that the project to be undertaken in this volume cannot confine itself within the disciplinary boundaries of archaeology. Rather, the author will draw heavily upon the fruit of sociological investigations into the characteristics and consequences of modernity. Sociology, in a way, is the epitome of modernity; it attempts not only to make sense of the contemporary world but also to comprehend how we make sense of the contemporary world. In other words, sociology is the epitome of reflexivity; sociology not only comments upon the contemporary world but also comments upon the way in which the commentary upon the contemporary world is made. By sociologising archaeology, the author hopes not only to problematise and relativise the taken-for-granteds in doing archaeology in modernity but also to contribute to the general social-theoretical endeavour to better capture the realities of social life, i.e., the ways in which we cope with socially generated difficulties in the contemporary world. In this sense, the volume is written for social scientists in general as much as for archaeologists and those who are interested in the way archaeology is situated in contemporary society.

It is widely felt nowadays that modernity is experiencing a fundamental transformation. For some, modernity has already come to an end and we are now living in post-modernity. Either way, effects of the transformation of modernity have become strongly felt in archaeology, and the atmosphere can be captured by some buzz words in the literature: fluidity, fragmentation, globalisation, multivocality, identity, and so on. Each of them can be connected to the sense of crisis and new opportunity in a distinct manner; they evoke a sense of indeterminacy, which contradicts the essence of the conventional definition of science as the pursuit of *Truth*, but they also raise hope for the beginning of new types of science more relevant to what is going on in the contemporary world. The ambivalence and confusion are also acutely felt in archaeology, and they are felt the world over, as 'globalisation', a significant consequence of the maturation of modernity, is taking its hold. At the same time, the sense of indeterminacy, the very source of the ambivalence and confusion, should also be taken as a source of hope for archaeology; it is this investigation into how to cope with it that will push the discipline forward.

I have been talking so far about the scope of the volume. Now let me touch upon its objectives. This volume is not an attempt to solve once and for all the above-mentioned problems. Rather, it suggests a way to cope with the difficulties by *avoiding* some of the predictable dangers that the problems lead to. Many of these dangers have already become quite visible and apparent to careful eyes, but their harmful implications have not been fully contextualised and appreciated, in archaeology in particular. A contention to be put forward will be that we have to live with the dangers and problems; first of all, the dangers are the consequences of the maturation of modernity which we cannot possibly discard altogether, and secondly, we need to be able to anchor and fix our identities in the past in various ways, in this world of indeterminacy and fluidity, but *relying upon* the past inevitably comes with some risk, that leads to the drawing and deepening of various sorts of social divisions. The task of archaeologists is to carry on communicating about those dangers which derive from the use of the past at the same time as continuing to produce images of the past; we cannot stop doing archaeology altogether, even if doing it implies innate dangers deriving from its unique relationship to modernity.

The investigation and argumentation of this volume will be undertaken by studying what has been and is going on in Japan and Japanese archaeology. Japan is the only country that has managed to 'modernise' and 'industrialise' itself without experiencing colonisation, and that has made the Japanese experience, particularly concerning archaeology, unique the world over. The investigation and argumentation will go back and forth in a cyclic manner between the intrinsic nature of (a) communication, (b) modernity, (c) archaeological communication/discourse, and (d) the unique ways in which communication is reproduced that are connected to the constitutive characteristics of modernity. Each chapter will tackle this 'quadrangle' and the problems generated from this tight and fundamental network from a different perspective. In that sense, each chapter can be read as an independent piece. However, the volume follows the following logical flow. Chapters 1 through 3 are designed to sketch the phenomena to be tackled, outlining the theoretical framework and the procedure of investigation and argumentation. Chapter 4 covers the phase from the modernisation of Japan to the 1970s when the transformation of modernity became tangible, and Chapter 5 covers the period spanning from the 1970s to the present, during which the phenomena variously described as late-, high-, or post-modern have become widespread and the problems and possibilities deriving from them have emerged and become widely felt. Chapter 6 will summarise and conclude the volume.

In all, I should like to reiterate, the volume is designed to portray and elucidate the core nature of the difficulties anyone interested in and working on contemporary social issues related to the formation and maintenance of social boundaries of various sorts is faced with, and in that sense it should be read not only by archaeologists and those who are interested in the relationship between society and archaeology, but also by sociologists and social scientists in general.

I began formally writing the volume back in 2001, but the (sometimes unintentional) preparations began much earlier, possibly as far back as 1998 when I wrote a short article on Anthony Giddens and Niklas Luhmann. The works of these two giants in the sociological exploration of modernity are heavily cited in the present volume, together with some implications of their views on sociality and social reproduction for archaeology. Since then, I have written a number of tentative pieces, some of which I have presented orally at a number of conferences and small gatherings, both in Japan and in Europe, where many individuals have given me invaluable comments, advice, and encouragement. Among them, I would specifically like to thank the following.

Cornelius Holtorf provided me with the initial motivation to write this volume by inviting me to the session entitled 'Philosophy and Archaeology' which he and Harkan Karlsson organised for the Fifth Annual Meeting of the European Association of Archaeologists held at the University of Gothenburg, to give a paper entitled 'Anthony Giddens and Niklas Luhmann'. Back then, I was utterly unsure about what to do with what I had learnt from my five-year-and-four-months-long study at Cambridge, when I became able to detach myself from the taken-for-granteds in doing archaeology in my own country, Japan. Returning to Japan in 1994, I suddenly realised that the environment in which I had to survive as an academic felt strange and alienating. In other words, I had become different from my former self, and I had to renegotiate my position in my own country. By 1997, I had become mentally exhausted and felt I could not carry on any longer. Giving that theoretical paper, which, back then, had no chance of being taken seriously in Japan, to a like-minded and supportive audience helped me accept that I had to find a way to feel comfortable with what I had become.

Ian Hodder, Julian Thomas, Stephanie Korner, and Colin Renfrew gave me inspiration and moral support throughout the germination and the writing of the volume in various ways. Ian Hodder and Colin Renfrew read early versions of the manuscript and gave me useful advice. Stephanie Korner invited me to a number of sessions she had organised and encouraged me to develop some core ideas for the current volume. Julian Thomas criticised my conference papers in a characteristically constructive and helpful manner, thus helping me prepare the theoritical framework for the current volume.

Conversations with Nobiru Notomi and Ikuko Toyonaga were vital in consolidating core ideas in this volume during the initial stage of the planning. Discussions with Tada'aki Shichida of the Saga Prefectural Board of Education about his experiences at the Yoshinogari site, where all the problems and challenges which contemporary Japanese archaeologists face come together, were most valuable. I would also like to thank wholeheartedly my colleagues at Kyushu University ('Kyu-dai'): Yoshiyuki Tanaka, Shozo Iwanaga, Kazuo Miyamoto, Takahiro Nakahashi, Ren'ya Sato, Jyun'ichiro Tsujita, and Takeshi Ishikawa, and my present and former students for having priovided me with a supportive and stimulating environment.

I also have to express my sincere gratitude to two Simons. I thank Simon Whitmore of Cambridge University Press for his support, advice, and wit all the way from the day when I sent a draft manuscript to him. Simon Williams of University College London carefully read the typescript (twice!), and skilfully (and educationally) corrected my English.

Finally, my wife, Hiromi, has always been on my side. She believed in what I was doing when I myself was not sure if it was worthwhile, and supported me when I felt that the whole world was hostile to what I was doing. She even took the trouble to read Luhmann and Giddens herself to understand what I was talking about. For that reason, I dedicate this book to her.

Fukuoka, May 2005

1

Archaeology in the contemporary world

1.1 A scenario of contemporary archaeology

A cluster of pristine-looking wooden structures suddenly appear in front of those who approach a low-lying hill sticking out of the heavily wooded mountain range rising steeply from the rice paddy-covered terrain. The flood plain, stretching to the south until it meets the Sea of Ariake, a large Inland Sea famous for its large tidal movements and unique marine life, is dotted with hamlets, small factories, and occasionally, heaps of industrial waste. What you see is typical contemporary Japanese countryside, where the rural is gradually eroded by the ever-expanding urban and industrial. Against this background, the Yoshinogari Historical Park, which consists of a number of 'reconstructed' archaeological features, an on-site museum, and a huge visitor centre with large car parks, looks like a gigantic theme park pretending to be an exotic ancient fortress in a setting most unusual and at the same time most mundane (Figure 1.1). These pristine-looking wooden structures are 'reconstructed' Late Yayoi period buildings. The Yayoi period was the first fully fledged agrarian period in Japanese history.

The park is the first of its kind designated by the state, and under the care of, interestingly, the Ministry of Land, Infrastructure and Transport (MLIT: www.mlit.go.jp/english/index.html), not of the Agency of Cultural Affairs (ACA: www.bunka.go.jp/english/2002-index-e.html), which is in charge of scheduling and protecting 'cultural properties' including archaeological sites and monuments, both tangible and intangible. The MLIT's legislative responsibility is 'to utilize, develop and conserve land in Japan in an integrated and systematic way; develop infrastructure necessary for attaining those goals; implement transportation policies; promote the progress of meteorological tasks; and maintain marine safety and security' (Article 3 of the Ministry of Land, Infrastructure and Transport Establishment Law). The above suggests that the protection, care and utilisation of this particular site is taken by the state to be an issue as to how to 'utilize, develop and conserve' the land of Japan. By doing so, the state unwittingly but effectively reveals that it reserves the right to choose, when it regards it necessary, between the mere protection and utilisation of the cultural properties that it recognises to be of particular importance. It also means that when it chooses the latter, the state works as a stakeholder, competing with other entities, both private and public, which also develop and utilise the land of Japan. As we shall see later in the volume, the manner in which the state differentiates what is important from what is not concerning things to do with the

Figure 1.1 The Yoshinogari Historical Park (Photographs by the author).

Figure 1.1 (*cont.*)

past is a direct consequence of the unique history of the modern nation-state of Japan (see Chapter 4).

The land now incorporated in the park,[1] owned by the state and the prefectural government of Saga, was once a mixture of forests, arable fields, tangerine groves, farmsteads and a local shrine. Back in June 1982, a plan was drawn up by a prefecture-led committee to turn the area into an industrial complex.[2] The existence of 'buried cultural properties' had been known throughout the area well before the decision was taken, and a series of test-trenchings was carried out between July and November of the same year, with another series between January and March 1986, which confirmed the dense distribution of archaeological features and artefact depositions. As a result, it was decided to preserve four pieces of land, where the distribution of archaeological features was particularly dense, about 6 hectares in total, tiny considering the size of the area to be destroyed, as 'cultural property greens', and to develop the remaining c. 30 hectares of land with known buried properties. The huge rescue work commenced in May 1986, with the plan being a three-year rescue dig and two additional years of post-excavation work (Saga PBE 1994, 18–24).

[1] 117 hectares (1,170,000 square metres), see Saga PBE 1997, 1.
[2] Saga PBE 1994, 18; Notomi 1997 provides precious first-hand accounts and thoughts of a member of prefectural personnel directly involved in the series of events described below.

Figure 1.2 Yoshinogari site under rescue excavation (permission for reproduction obtained from Saga Prefectural Board of Education).

What the excavation revealed, however, exceeded everyone's wildest expectations (Figure 1.2). It was almost the first time that a large Yayoi settlement with the characteristics of a regional centre, or 'central place', had been subjected to a large-scale excavation by stripping more than a couple of hectares, let alone literally tens of hectares, at one go. The sheer number and scale of features and the number of artefacts which suddenly emerged from the soil simply overwhelmed, first, the archaeologists, and subsequently, when the discovery was made public, the general public (Saga PBE 1994, 45).

The feeling of 'everything-happened-at-one-go' due to the stripping of the vast area seems to have determined the course of what has happened since then, both to the site and to the discourse which the site has generated. The initial stage of the rescue work revealed that the site was continuously occupied, at different scales and in different manners, at each phase (Figure 1.3), throughout the Yayoi period. This period, dating between c. 600/500 BC and AD 250/300, witnessed the introduction and

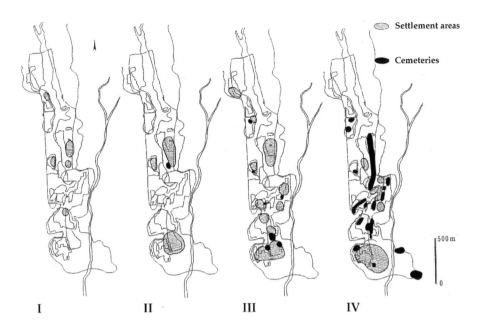

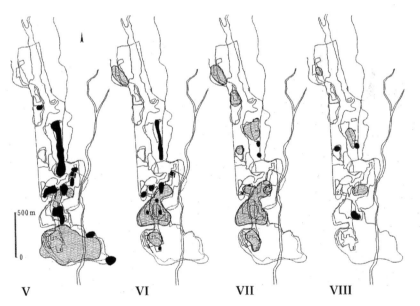

Figure 1.3 The formation process of the Yoshinogari phase by phase (modified from Saga PBE 1997).

establishment of systematic rice paddy-field agriculture in the archipelago of Japan (cf. Mizoguchi 2002, Chapter 5). Naturally, the features constituting the site and the spatial structure they made up underwent a number of changes (Figure 1.3) (Saga PBE 1997). However, the complexity of these spatio-temporal 'differences' needed to be 'reduced' in order to enable the general public make sense of and appreciate the importance of the site. The support of the general public was desperately needed in order to stop the planned destruction. This simplification had to be guided and guarded by the principle that the narrative, or way of talking about and describing the site, should be coherent, attractive and persuasive, and so a powerful narrative line was chosen. It functioned as the principle by which to differentiate what is and what is not desirable to be retained in the simplified version: selecting features, regardless of the phases they belonged to, and comparing them with what are depicted to have constituted the court of the famous Queen Himiko, the figure recorded in the Chinese official imperial chronicle of Weizhi. The queen, Weizhi records, was chosen to reintegrate the polity of Wa, thought to have covered wide areas in the western and parts of the eastern portion of the archipelago, in a momentary turmoil sometime during the earlier half of the third century AD (cf. Wada and Ishihara 1951, 37–54). The story of Queen Himiko contains many 'riddles', such as the location of Yamatai, the polity where she reigned, the location of her court, effectively the capital of the polity of Wa, how she was chosen, and the nature of the religious practice Weizhi recorded she conducted. These questions have attracted immense public attention and curiosity, and the quest for answers has developed into a popular and highly marketable genre in the publishing world in Japan. We will return to the issue concerning the cause of the popularity of the Yamatai discourse later (Chapter 4). What is important to note here is that the selection of the excavated features, to be presented as most appropriately exemplifying the character of the site, was made, despite their different dates of construction and use, because they fitted into the description in Weizhi of the residence of Queen Himiko (Wada and Ishihara 1951, 37–54). These were

(1) outer and inner moats/ditches (the former dug in the late Middle and early Late Yayoi and the latter Late Yayoi),
(2) the structures situated where the inner moat/ditch protrudes, inferred to have been 'watch towers' (the validity of this inference is strongly disputed),
(3) a rectangular-shaped tumulus containing a number of jar burials many of which contained a bronze dagger and some other grave goods (dating from the early Middle Yayoi: cf. Mizoguchi 2002, 142–147).

In spite of their different dates, they have all been 'reconstructed', and today stand as if they actually constituted a unified entity that was the Yoshinogari, the embodiment of the story of Queen Himiko (Saga PBE 2000, 2003, 1; Sahara 2003, 302–306).

In other words, the significance of the site was represented as being mediated by a type of *origin* narrative, the origin narrative of the Japanese nation in this case (cf. Saga PBE 2000, 1; see also Chapter 4.3 of the present volume), and was packaged by tacitly ignoring the flow of time during which the site underwent a number of changes and transformations.

The stripping of a vast area in one go revealed an 'archive' of the traces of human activities accumulated through time and enabled the selection of features which fitted a specific narrative line. In other words, the depth of time through which the site was formed, and the timelessness of the site as a phenomenon situated in the present/now, came together, deliberately confused, and was all used to promote of the importance of the site.

Once the initial outcome of the excavation, packaged with the above-mentioned narrative, was released to the media, the reaction by the general public was literally explosive: within two months of the press release, a staggering one million people had visited the site (Saga PBE 1994, 45). Both the importance of the site and the human drama behind the struggle to protect the site from imminent destruction to make way for an industrial park attracted media attention. This even included TV coverage of the family life and family history of Mr Tada'aki Shichida, who was in charge of the excavation (cf. Notomi 1997, 56), adding a sense of humility and contemporaneity to the movement. (We shall come back to the involvement of such human drama in the reproduction of the typical image of the archaeologist shared by the general public in Chapter 5.3.) Overwhelming pleas for the preservation of the site came from academic communities and various other sectors. Finally, the then prefectural governor decided to halt the planned construction of the industrial complex (cf. Saga PBE 1994, 45; Sahara 2003, 301–338).

It is as if the rescue excavation worked as a theatre production in which various interest groups, each with its own value judgments, both economic and emotional, played mutually affected parts, and created a drama which particularly well reflected the conditions in which we live. First of all, there was a group which tried to revitalise the local economy by constructing an industrial complex on the land. Retrospectively, the idea of stimulating the stagnant agriculture-based local economy by simply introducing production industry had come to the end of its currency by the late 1980s; the Japanese economic structure had been transformed from production-industry based 'heavy capitalism' to service and high-tech industry based 'light capitalism' (cf. Bauman 2000b) between the 1960s and 1980s (e.g. Tomoeda 1991, 139–149), and the wave of relocation of production lines to developing countries with much cheaper production costs was about to begin. Nowadays, those local governments which are running successful industrial complexes, or industrial parks, are investing large sums of money for the improvement of the environment in which the factories/laboratories function efficiently in terms of welfare for workers, access to main transportation routes, and so on. In other words, the construction of a new industrial park, by the late 1980s, had become a high-risk choice which inevitably incurred a large investment. Meanwhile, once approved, local government-run projects are notoriously difficult to halt, even if an objective calculation reveals that it will not generate wealth efficiently. The Saga prefecture, where the Yoshinogari is located, had already had previous experience of constructing industrial parks, some in the vicinity of the

Yoshinogari itself,[3] and that would have made the stoppage of the project even more difficult.

Interestingly, the above-mentioned transformation from heavy to light industry in Japan coincided with a transformation in the logic used for the protection of cultural resources ('cultural properties' in Japanese terminology) from a Marxist-oriented logic (see Chapter 4.2 below) to a logic appealing to the rather naïve sentiment of the general public. The former condemned the destruction of cultural properties as the exploitative destruction by monopolistic capitalist corporations of the heritage of the nation in socio-economic, in other words fairly hard, often academic, terms, and the latter evoked the sense of attachment to threatened sites/cultural properties by depicting them as the heritage from 'our' ancestors in a soft, non-academic, narrative style. We shall come back to the implications of this transformation in Chapter 5. What seems to me of particular importance for the current argument is that the narrative created by the archaeologists, another interest group involved in arguing in favour of the protection of the Yoshinogari, exactly embodied this trend. This narrative, regardless to what extent it was consciously designed as such, evoked a sense of attachment to the site by depicting it as one to which the origin of the Japanese nation, whose culture is widely regarded as being fundamentally based upon rice agriculture, could be traced back (Saga PBE 2000, 1). It also depicted those who were involved in the rescue, and the protection movement for the site, as slightly eccentric local heroes, men of the earth in the world of deindustrialisation, struggling for the sake of the threatened heritage of the nation inherited from *our* ancestors. No need to say that, in the narrative, *our* ancestors also were the people of the earth toiling to make ends meet by cultivating the land.

What is most remarkable about this narrative is that, initially created for the promotion of the importance of the site, it came to actually influence the way the academic discourse of the site was constituted. What you see at the Yoshinogari today are mostly reconstructed features which either date from the time of the recorded reign of Queen Himiko, i.e. the late Late Yayoi, or which do not date from that time but fit into the description in the record, the Chinese imperial chronicle of Weizhi. The buildings had to be reconstructed from mere postholes, their configuration, sizes and structures, artefacts excavated from and in the vicinity of them, and their function inferred from their reconstructed structure and location in the site. The argument is bound to be circular, e.g., inference (A) from the configuration of the postholes the building would have been like this, and inference (B) if the building had been like this, the configuration of the postholes would be understood to fit the structural demand (cf. Kensetsu-sho 1997). Without inferential/speculative reference to ethnographic data or other sources such as documents like Weizhi, this circular argument cannot be resolved. From this, it can be deduced that there were only two choices for those who are involved in the presentation of the site: (1) do not do any reconstruction on the grounds that no reconstruction supported by convincing evidence and reasoning

---

[3] The construction of one of them resulted in the destruction of the important Yayoi cemetery site of Futatsukayama, yielding a number of burials with grave goods: Saga PBE 1979.

is possible; or (2) reconstruct, admitting that the outcome is speculative, and adding an explicit description of the way the speculation was made.

In the case of the Yoshinogari, the latter was chosen and the choice was made with certain conviction: a series of volumes have been published which list the sources referred to in the reconstruction of buildings, including ethnographic parallels, figurative depictions on artefacts, excavated architectural parts, documents, and so on, and a number of experts in individual subjects were involved in the compilation of the volumes and in reasoning the references and decisions taken (e.g. Kensetsu-sho 1997, 2000). What has to be noted here, though, is that the involvement of a large number of expert scholars and the meticulous listing of numerous pieces of relevant (or inferred to be relevant) information does not itself ensure the validity of the speculative inferences, although that might enhance the *authoritative* value and aura attached to the inferences (e.g. Kensetsu-sho 1997, 12).

Tada'aki Shichida, the prefectural government officer who played a vital role in the rescue excavation and the movement for the preservation of the site, and has been a key figure in the management of the site since it was designated as a national historical park, informed me that from his perspective the reasoning behind the reconstruction at the Yoshinogari site went thus: without reconstructing them in one way or another, further argument cannot be generated concerning how they could be better reconstructed or amended in future, or indeed how the site itself should be taken care of (Tada'aki Shichida pers. comm. March 2004).

His comment sounds as if it is inspired by reflexive sociological theory or theory of communication; should the horizon of uncertainty, which leads to various attempts to make sense of it, not be generated, communication could not and would not continue (e.g. Luhmann 1995, Chapter 4; and Chapter 3 of this volume). In other words, Shichida is justifying what has been done to the site by claiming that without *problematisation* there would be no research progress. This sounds reasonable enough, provided problematisation is undertaken by making clear the limitations and potential shortcomings of the work, e.g., listing as many potential referents for the reconstruction of an archaeological phenomenon as possible, checking how/to what extent the reconstructed picture is coherent, and examining how well the picture fits the configuration of the archaeological evidence available. However, in the case of the Yoshinogari the work does not appear to have been conducted in this way. Instead of listing possible referents, the description in Weizhi was used as the dominant framework by which the range of the referents used for the inference was determined, and other possibilities and indeterminacy were either ignored or not mentioned. Of course, other types of knowledge such as architectural history, the ethnography of other rice paddy-field agricultural communities in Asia, and archaeological evidence from elsewhere were mobilised (Kensetsu-sho 2000). However, when no substantial clue is available, the Weizhi description appears to be prioritised and referred to as the 'last instance' (e.g. Kensetsu-sho 2000, 54, especially bullet point 3: 'Documental evidence').

The media, yet another interest group/stakeholder, and newspapers in particular, invariably covered the matter by quoting the similarities between the site and the Weizhi description of the residence/court of Queen Himiko. It is a well-proven fact that Himiko- and Yamatai-related stories sell very well, and the comparison by archaeologists of the site with Weizhi was most welcome from the media's point of view; or rather, it is most likely that the archaeologists, who knew it quite well, utilised this tendency of the media in order to arouse public interest.

Immediately after the initial decision was taken for preservation, criticisms concerning the accuracy and validity of the comparison began to be expressed (e.g. Oda 1990), many of which touched upon the difficulty of reconstructing standing structures from postholes, and the validity of reconstructing the features on the areas where the inner ditched compound protrudes as 'watch towers' depicted in Weizhi in particular (Oda 1990). These criticisms were expressed in a rather muted manner from fear that expressing them out loud might reduce the effectiveness of the campaign for the preservation of the site. However, it is important to note that, at that stage, the boundary between utterance for the sake of preservation of the site and that for the development of archaeological knowledge was acutely felt and sharply drawn. Ironically, the fact that the site was worth preserving, even if some potentially erroneous over-inference had to be made, made the archaeologists aware that it was of vital importance to clearly draw the boundary between what *could* and *could not* be said 'archaeologically' with confidence. When necessary, things which could not be said with confidence had to be told to the public for 'strategic' reasons, and in such cases the potential damage needed be minimised by maintaining the credibility of the discipline in the form of fully grasping what could and could not be said.

However, as time has gone by, this boundary appears to have become blurred. In particular, once the reconstructed buildings came into existence, the subject of debate inevitably shifted from how the preserved site could be better represented to how good or bad/accurate or inaccurate the reconstructed features were, and because the range of referents for the reconstruction had already been determined to be within what was written in Weizhi, the debate naturally came to concentrate on the appropriateness of the 'reading' of the referents, i.e., the reading of Weizhi, rather than on examining the validity of the range of the referents chosen. Consequently, the discursive space generated and reproduced around the site has ended up being dominated by arguments about Weizhi and Queen Himiko, regardless of whether the opinions expressed were to promote the importance of the site or to advance archaeological knowledge (Kensetsu-sho 2000, 22–25).

The most interesting thing about all this is that the majority of those who took part in the reproduction of this discourse appear to have been aware of its problematic nature in one way or another. A number of criticisms on specific points of the reconstruction and on the understanding of the character of the site have been put forward (e.g. Takesue 1990, 25–27). However, they are neither put together to form a coherent alternative narrative which can replace the present one nor are they uttered *within* the discourse itself. In other words, the mainstream Yoshinogari discourse can carry on unscathed despite the number of criticisms hurled at it. There even seems to exist an atmosphere in which those who are not involved in the Yoshinogari project and who criticise elements of it are labelled irresponsible bystanders. It is as if the discourse generated and reproduced around the Yoshinogari has come to form a protected, autonomous domain in which people are obliged to conform to a rule of communication unique to the domain. Outside it, people communicate about the Yoshnogari quite differently and sometimes harshly criticise the way the Yoshinogari discourse reproduces itself, but they never do so when they are within the domain itself.

What is tacitly but widely recognised to matter most here seems to be how to *continue* the discourse *without disruption* even if it might imply the reproduction of erroneous remarks and understandings. The risk of losing the discourse altogether appears to be judged more serious than the risk of continuing it with errors and mis-understandings, perhaps because the errors and misunderstandings can be amended later as long as the discourse continues. This can be described as the tactic of delay-ing judgment and avoiding the catastrophic termination of the dialogue, which is one of the viable choices; at least a much better choice than closing down the dia-logue altogether and making amendment impossible for ever. We shall come back to the implications of the issue of not terminating a dialogue/discourse throughout this volume.

The above observation of the formation and reproduction of a site-specific dis-course suggests that archaeology as a discipline is no longer a *unified discourse* seek-ing a unified goal but constitutes a *discursive space* accommodating various interest groups. In the perception of those who define themselves as archaeologists, a unified goal may still exist for archaeology as an academic pursuit/practice. However, those who do not define themselves as archaeologists and yet become involved in social practices dealing with matters regarded as 'archaeological' are dramatically increas-ing in number and have come to have certain impacts upon the way archaeological practice is perceived as well as conducted. The impacts the latter have brought to archaeology, in that sense, are ontological and operational, and they are intercon-nected and interdependent.

As mentioned earlier, and we shall return to it in Chapter 4, Marxism, one of the 'grand narratives' generated in and constituting the modern world, used to provide archaeologists with a type of 'ontological security', by which I mean a sense of knowing why they are doing things in the world the way they do. The sense was underpinned by the feeling (retrospectively described by many as illusion) that a unified goal existed in the practice of archaeology: the construction of a better society by reflecting upon the ills inherited from the past, the ills being of a politico-economic kind. Therefore, around the 1970s, at the peak of the destruction of sites due to a sustained spurt in Japanese economic growth, one of the most loudly expressed archaeo-political slogans was to fight against the unchecked activities of the mono-polistic capitalist by interpreting the past as the root of social inequality and injustice from Marxist perspectives (NKK 1981, Chapter 1; also see Chapter 4.2 of this volume).

Naïvity in connecting the past and the present in this manner, in retrospect, is undeniable. However, the logic appears to have fitted the reality of the contemporary society. Income-based social inequality was still a dominant social issue back then (e.g. Tomoeda 1991, 139–149), and the division between the haves and the have-nots was connected to the ideological division between socialism and capitalism, epitomised by the Cold War. In such circumstances, it would have felt natural that the rights and wrongs could be determined by the difference between the good and bad application of Marxist theory. This was seen in terms of coherence in the articulated connection between the theory, the data, and the problems of contemporary society, if a given archaeologist's stance inclined to the socialist half of the dichotomy. Such concern as to how appealing the interpretation was to the general public would have not felt so important; if the interpretation were correct and real, it was believed, the general public would accept it in one way or another because the problem was shared by everyone. If the general public could not appreciate the importance and relevance of the interpretation, it was widely accepted that they had to be educated and enlightened (we shall come back to this point in Chapters 4.2 and 4.3).

Now, this type of bold self-confidence has long gone as reality has changed from one which was deeply embedded in economic concerns to one which is concerned more with broad cultural, and hence fluid, matters such as lifestyle, fashion and health, a characteristic phenomenon of the social formation described as late- or high- or post-modern, and the feeling of uncertainty prevails: what I utter by believing in its validity could be criticised in any way by those who have different views and beliefs from mine. And we just hope our utterances will be met with some response in order to prevent unbearable silence. Otherwise, we feel as if we are lost in identifying ourselves; when there is nothing fixed and universal with which to identify oneself, such as a fixed, and believed-to-be universal value system or social class, the only viable way to confirm one's identity is to engage in a dialogue and see how others respond. In this circumstance, what matters most, it is widely felt, is how we style our utterances in order to enable the continuation of such a dialogue. And considering that it is individuals, faced with the above-mentioned difficulty, that reproduce a discourse, the finding is also applicable to archaeological discourses.

The Yoshinogari today stands amidst such ongoing discourses, that do not aim to reach anywhere specific but just to continue, hopefully in lively fashion and mak-ing (cultural and economic) profit. The discourse concerning the reconstruction of intangible features is well packaged in order to carefully avoid giving any *definite* conclusion, in curious contrast with the imposing and definite material existence of the reconstructed features and buildings in the middle of typical contemporary Japanese countryside (Figures 1.1 and 1.2). This experience is not confined to the Yoshinogari; the Japanese countryside is dotted with archaeological sites with 'recon-structed' features and buildings, though many of them are on a much smaller scale than the Yoshinogari, and more or less identical sorts of tales can be heard from those who are involved in those site reconstruction projects. The concern they share most widely is not the academic credibility of the reconstruction but the decline in annual visitor figures: as long as reconstructed sites are situated in the node of different, often contradictory, interests concerning, without exception, economic matters, albeit to differing degrees, they are bound to be *consumed*. It seems as if there is a sell-by date attached to each of these sites, and those sites that fail to 'renew' their appearance and/or visitor attractions begin to bore the general public and be forgotten. At the Yoshinogari, despite the national park project being ongoing with new reconstructions and small-scale excavations constantly in progress, the annual visitor figure is in steep decline (Tada'aki Shichida, pers. comm. 2004). It is extremely difficult to sustain site-specific discourses in the face of public apathy and the relativisation of the value/meaning of reconstructed sites.

1.2 Uncertainty, archaeology and the world we live in

The above observations of experience surrounding the protection and subsequent utilisation of a site as a cultural property/resource reveal that we have come to the point in the history of Japanese archaeology where a significant number of those who do, or are interested in, archaeology feel that there is no such thing as the 'definite', singular past. Regardless of whether or not one believes in the possibility of some day reaching the definite, i.e., *perfect*, reconstruction of the past, almost all of us accept, tacitly or explicitly, that the past is something to be continuously *disputed*. In other words, as suggested, archaeology has become widely regarded as a kind of designated arena, or *discursive space*, in which only how to negotiate one's position with others within the limit without disrupting the continuous presence of the arena matters.

Various 'stakeholders', including archaeologists, the state, politicians, developers, property dealers, local residents, farmers, factory owners, and environmental activists, are involved in the continuation of negotiations/dialogues that constitute a socially accepted, and state-funded, discursive space, or a *discipline*, called archaeology. They each negotiate their own position and try to maintain or enhance their own, often mutually contradictory, interest. However, they can do so only as long as the discursive space continues to exist. Therefore, a self-regulatory code of the way in which they negotiate, or a self-discipline (although this is far from what the term was originally supposed to mean), becomes naturally generated, and even a scholastic opinion sometimes seems to be formed through the process of negotiation and self-regulation (see Chapter 5.3).

Here, the reader might immediately notice some intriguing similarities between the phenomena illustrated above and what is elegantly reported by Ian Hodder to be happening around the ongoing research project at the Neolithic site of Catalhoyuk, Turkey (e.g. Hodder 1999, Chapter 9; 2003). There are, of course, many differences, the most significant of which is that Catalhoyuk has, from the very beginning, been an intentionally experimental, long-term research project, whereas the Yoshinogari began accidentally as a rescue dig without any anticipation of ending up as a large, partially state-financed, research, conservation, and utilisation project. Besides, the Yoshinogari is situated in a location which is typical of a developed/industrialised nation, as Japan is a member of the so-called G7 industrialised nations; in contrast, Catalhoyuk is situated in a typical so-called developing country. However, we should not overlook the similarities that do not appear to be coincidental. Both are concerned with and influenced by various financial matters (Hodder 1999, Chapter 9), they both have, admittedly to different degrees, a multi-disciplinary outlook. They both function as discursive spaces in which it is accepted, tacitly in the case of Yoshinogari and explicitly and intentionally in the case of Catalhoyuk, that various stakeholders will negotiate their position and their interpretations will be influenced by their own interests and made fluid.

What do those projects, so far apart in terms of physical distance and context, share that makes these similarities emerge? The word 'globalisation' might spring to mind. It is treated in Hodder's account as a keyword with which to capture the nature of what is going on in contemporary archaeology (1999, Chapter 9). Globalisation means different things to different people, but it can be summarised as the cluster of phenomena resulting from the inundation of the world by a developed ('hyper-') capitalism including not only the *homogenisation* of cultures but also the articulation/rearticulation of, predominantly cultural, *differences* in order either to continue generating profit or to react, at times violently, against the homogenisation and reproduction of the misdistribution of wealth/resources resulting from hyper-capitalism (Bauman 2000a).

What underpins this most significantly, particularly in developed, industrialised nations, is the shift in the source of socially shared issues, satisfaction, and discontent from predominantly economic to cultural/symbolic (Jameson 1991, Chapter 1). We shall come back to this point in Chapter 5, but briefly touching upon the matter, the general rise of living standards and the end of the Cold War transformed the tangible differences internally dividing a society from economic to cultural/symbolic ones. This resulted in the replacement of competition over the allocation of material wealth with competition over cultural/symbolic capitals (Jameson 1991). One significant situation which has resulted from this phenomenon is that there is no party policy or epistemic stance which can claim the transcendental position *outside* this field of competing and clashing, predominantly cultural/symbolic, interests, and that has led to a crisis of self identification. Without something transcendental/fixed by which rights and wrongs are judged, it is difficult to decide how to act in certain circumstances in a stable, predictable manner, and not knowing/being unable to decide how to act means you are unsure about what you are and what you stand for. This has also resulted in the situation in which any criticism against other parties/positions can come back to haunt those who made it, because any interest/position generated in this field of clashing interests is inevitably embedded in the working of hyper-capitalism which *relativises everything* in order to create and recreate differences for the continuation of profit-making. For example, a new fashion, which has emerged by claiming that the old one is boring, is destined to be *engineered to be boring* and to be replaced by a new one in order to sustain/increase the profit level (Bauman 2000b, 85). We might add that any culture/symbol-based social claim/demand is bound to be either challenged or relativised simply because there are many cultures coexisting as autonomous value systems in contemporary society, which is sometimes characterised as 'multicultural.' In other words, no one can claim ultimate victory, moral, scientific, or otherwise, over others unless one quits the game of relativisation, i.e., continuing to operate in the sphere of hyper-capitalistic social formation, yet quitting is almost impossible. Both the Yoshinogari and Catalhoyuk are firmly situated in that sphere which reproduces itself, along the line of the dichotomy between making and not making profits in the last instance.

In such circumstances, one instinctively comes to know that the only possibility left to those who still wish to do some good in the world, not definitely knowing what that good is, is to *carry on* arguing. 'To carry on' is the second-best, and only realistic, choice. Then, the most urgent, realistic question becomes: what to argue, and how? Accepting this as a matter of fact, not only for life in the contemporary world but also for the archaeological practice situated in it, this volume examines the background against which this 'attitude' has become inevitable, how such a situation has emerged, and, drawing upon the outcome of the enquiry, considers how to answer these 'what' and 'how' questions, i.e., what to argue about in archaeology, and how.

In order to begin this undertaking, we need to start by considering again, but this time more deeply, the characteristics of the world we live in. The name given to the world we live in and do archaeology in, whose symptomatic characteristics we sketched above, varies: high-modernity, late-modernity, post-modernity, and, simply, modernity. The fact that there are a number of ways to capture the reality of this society by naming it itself tells us a lot about it: the way to observe something is bound to be subject to another observation in this society, and the way that observation is made is also subject to yet another observation. This endless chain of observations of observations, i.e., 'second-order observations', constitutes the ultimate source of the above-mentioned relativisation/loss of the universal/transcendental position, and significantly characterises the society we live in, and in which we are doing archaeology today.

The proliferation of second-order observations and confronting problems resulting from it forces us to face up to the intrinsic nature of *communication*, which makes the proliferation of second-order observations in contemporary society inevitable. Let me explain at length why we have to start by fully grasping the nature of communication, despite the fact that the socio-political and socio-economic factors no doubt contribute to the coming of a world dominated by second-order observations and consequent endless relativisation. The understanding of communication as the most basic social phenomenon, i.e., as the minimum unit of society and the source of the generation of sociality, serves as the background against which this volume's investigation and argumentation are conducted. According to the German sociologist, the late Niklas Luhmann, communication is the unity of three autonomous spheres of choices, information, utterance, and understanding (1995, Chapter 4): (a) what information to utter, (b) how to utter it, and (c) how to understand the difference between the information and the utterance constitute the basic components of communication, the sequential chaining of which constitutes communication. The relationship between information and utterance can be compared to that between *signifier* and *signified*. In communication, a signifier is rarely connected to only one signified; a signifier is usually connected to a number of signifieds. That means that when a signifier is uttered, it opens up a *horizon of choices*: to be more exact, the utterance of a signifier stimulates the person who hears the utterance to differentiate a horizon of choices from which s/he chooses a signified to understand what the signifier signifies. When that happens, neither speaker nor hearer is sure whether the signifier is connected to the *intended* signified. What they can do is to observe the way the other reacts to what each one utters. This means that there is no way to *simultaneously* check if the utterance of information is exactly understood, and this is because one cannot look into the other's head when s/he utters information.

Then, how can we check whether the information we utter is understood by the other in the way we intend? In other words, how can communication occur in the first place? There is no way to check it *directly*; those who are involved in communication have to assume that the information is properly understood if the communication *continues*. A serious problem for the archaeologist, which this finding implies, is that the archaeologist studies the material traces of past human communication and s/he cannot check if s/he properly understands the information which people in the past intended to send, because the latter are long dead. We shall not get into the issue of how to solve this here. What is important for the current argument is that this inevitable/intrinsic *indeterminacy* in communication causes a number of serious problems with profound social implications for the practice of archaeology today.

I have to begin by saying that this indeterminacy is the very source of archaeo-logical imagination: indeterminacy stimulates the generation of new problems, new solutions, and new perspectives in archaeology. In other words, second-order obser-vations are vital for the healthy reproduction of archaeology as a communication system. However, indeterminacy also causes serious problems which haunt archae-ologists the world over today, some examples of which we have already seen in the Yoshinogari discourse and the Catalhoyuk experience.

Before turning to these problems, though, let us imagine how the indeterminacy might be solved. It can be inferred that the accumulation of the experience of the continuation of communication reduces (the sense of) the indeterminacy of commu-nication. In contemporary society, the condition upon which the experience of the successful continuation of communication can be accumulated, i.e., the sharing of the time–space locales of everyday activities, is increasingly difficult to obtain/secure. As a natural reaction to it, an increasing number of micro-discursive spaces come into being, in which a limited number of *like-minded individuals* participate in dense and highly nuanced communication and acquire the somewhat illusory sense of sharing experiences and mutual understanding.[4] In that sense, contemporary soci-ety, regardless of whether it is described as late-, or high-, or post-modern, may be/is characterised by the uncontrollable regeneration of *micro-cosmoses of communication*. The emergence and proliferation of 'post-processual *archaeologies*', it seems, can be understood as a reflection of this wider trend in the general discursive formation of contemporary society (we shall come back to this in Chapter 5).

The post-processual archaeology movement has been understood as an attempt to reconnect archaeology to the reality and concerns of contemporary society, and that has been claimed to stimulate the emergence of many 'archaeologies' each

---

[4] The image of parallel sessions in a TAG (British Theoretical Archaeology Group) conference might spring to the mind of some readers here.

of which is a value-committed reaction to a specific social issue concerning the present as well as the past (e.g. Hodder and Hutson 2003, Chapter 9, esp. 224–233). However, this trend, quite ironically, is accelerating further fragmentation and a further rise in the sense of indeterminacy in archaeological communication. Each of the issues concerning the advocates of the movement is often localised and requires the acquisition of specific local knowledge, which can only be obtained through densely sharing mundane activities. That experience would surely solve the above-mentioned indeterminacy in the form of practically sharing a value system. However, at the same time, that makes the value system, whose validity a practitioner claims, local, parochial and inaccessible to those who do not share the value system. Therefore what often happens is miscommunication and cynicism; the language used in such a discourse tends to be regarded as in-word-laden by those outside, and those inside tend to become hostile to outside criticism because they tend to become self-righteous through their intense, value-laden commitment and the kind of comradeship generated by it.

In addition, there is another source of cynicism and fragmentation, that is, homogenisation through fragmentation. Those who communicate in each of these micro-cosmoses know that there are innumerable other cosmoses out there and that those who communicate in those cosmoses are doing what they are doing, i.e., acquiring a sense of communicability by differentiating what they are doing, i.e., the way they are communicating, from what others are doing. However, as long as they are all trying to communicate differently from others, they end up doing the same, because they all are trying to be different! Hence, a cynical feeling that we are producing an ever-increasing number of 'archaeologies' in order to differentiate self from others becomes widespread. We are living and doing archaeology in a world in which the attempt to be different makes us similar and leads us to further differentiation, which results in further fragmentation. This is an endless process.

One of the serious consequences of this in archaeological communication, which is a desperate attempt at stopping this endless process of fragmentation, is the generation of *narratives of the extreme*, such as the narrative of the largest and the oldest.[5] By ignoring the meaning content of communication, e.g., the nature and character of a site, because it is felt not to be fully understood in any way, but focusing instead solely on enhancing the *quantifiable* content of communication, such as how old/large the site is, one tries to acquire an (actually illusory) mutual understanding of the subject matter. This somewhat desperate attempt to maintain a sense of communicability, however, has a serious side effect: narratives of the extreme tend to be connected to ethno-nationalistic narratives and sentiment (Kohl and Fawcett 1996).

The fragmentation of discursive space, resulting from the above, has led to the fragmentation of the *identity* of the archaeologist as well. Identity here means the

[5] The search for the *origins* of the constitutive elements of contemporary society and being human might be included in the list of such narratives (Gamble 2001, 156–172), but the narratives of the largest and the oldest also have some different implications from that, predominantly to do with the nation-state and modernity (see Chapters 2–5 of this volume).

unity of expectations as to how one has to act in certain contexts, how *others* would act in these contexts, and how others would expect one to act in these contexts. The spatio–temporal extension of the domain within which one's identity is comfortably reproduced becomes increasingly smaller in contemporary society, and in order to cope with the condition one is forced to reformulate one's identity from time to time. It is natural for the fragmented self to seek *transcendental entities* with which to regain the sense of unity/one-ness, and, in modernity, such transcendental entities have been, and still are, fatefully connected to ethno-nationalistic referents. An irony is that such transcendentals, articulated through the generation of narratives of the extreme are, after all, bound to be localised, e.g., the largest in the so-and-so region, and in that sense can easily be relativised. In other words, such narratives are too concrete to be genuinely transcendental. Hence, many competing, 'would-be' transcendental narratives continue to come out, and further accelerate the fragmentation of the discursive space and the consumption of the value and popularity of the sites. Needless to say, this leads to endless relativisation of one's standpoint and *nihilism*.

To seek a way out of this crisis is no simple task. The remedy, apparently, does not lie with a strategy such as referring back to what it was like before the fragmentation began. We can no longer rely on grand, universal/universalising narratives, such as Marxism, which themselves are based upon the existence of a shared communal life–world which no longer exists.

This volume is dedicated to considering the issue by tracing the process through which we have arrived at the present situation and by analysing the constitutive characteristics of the situation. The situation and process can be broadly described as two of the phenomena characterising *modernity*, and the conditions and problems mentioned above are constitutive elements of its current form, which Anthony Giddens describes as radicalised modernity (Giddens 1990), and many other scholars prefer to call post-modernity. The nature and character of each of these conditions and problems, in any case, have been constituted and transformed through the maturation/radicalising process of modernity. By tracing the co-transformation of the constitutive characteristics of modernity and archaeological discursive formation and by analysing the nature and character of their interdependence at each phase of the process, this volume will consider a better way to cope with the difficulties which have been, and continue to be, generated by modernity/modern social formation.

What one has to be explicitly aware of in an exercise of this kind is that the exercise itself is inevitably situated in a condition in which any discursive act is articulated in a vicious circle of interdependence between second-order observations and the fragmentation of communication fields. In that sense, what follows is bound to be a self-reflexive exercise, from an archaeological perspective, in the world of second-order observations/self-reflexion, and so, in that sense, is the process of learning how to carry on re-examining the way we communicate about the conditions in which we communicate. The next chapter begins this undertaking, by looking into the relationship between modernity and archaeology in general terms.

2

Modernity and archaeology

2.1 Archaeology as a modern institution

It has already been recognised that the discipline of archaeology is, by its origin and nature, a fundamentally modern institution. A systematic manipulation of the past, involving kinds of excavations, appears to have taken place in some ancient states (e.g. Trigger 1989, 27–31; Schnapp 1996). The use of the past in the form of the mobilisation of ancestoral images and the place-related memory of past human acts began much earlier (e.g. Bradley 2002). However, the disciplinisation of archaeology, or the beginning of 'scientific archaeology' as Bruce Trigger puts it (1989, Chapter 3), i.e., the articulation of the subject matter, objectives, and methods with which the discursive boundary between what is and is not archaeology can be drawn, took place, as a process rather than as an event, in the formative phase of 'modernity' (Trigger 1989, 73–86).

The concept 'modernity' is defined in various ways and manners. Here, I wish to refer to Malcolm Waters's characterisation as a balanced, and appropriately concrete, definition. According to Waters, modernity is a 'socio-cultural configuration' characterised by the following (Waters 1999, xii–xiii):

(1) production systems are industrial,
(2) an increasing proportion of interpersonal practices are self-interested, rational and calculating,
(3) physical and social objects, including human labour, are defined as commodities, and regarded as exchangeable,
(4) control of the state is specified by social role rather than by personal characteristics and is subject to periodic constituency legitimation,
(5) individuals have citizenship rights that they can claim against the state,
(6) the primary site of legitimacy and responsibility is the individual person,
(7) the value spheres of culture (truth, beauty and morality) are autonomised relative to each other and to other areas of social life,
(8) social units – families, schools, governments, firms, churches, voluntary associations, etc. – are differentiated from one another.

In short, (a) industrialisation, (b) rationalisation, (c) commodification, (d) bureaucratisation, (e) citizenship, (f) deconstruction of kinship/local ties, (g) secularisation, and (h) institutional segmentation and specialisation, are the constitutive elements of modernity. As a historical period, modernity, in that sense, began as all of those attributes came into place, and that took place at about the turn of the nineteenth century (Waters 1999, xiii). They came together and replaced the old, 'pre-modern', system characterised by its hierarchical structures supported by religion and kin/local ties with that characterised by the internal horizontal functional differentiation of the above-mentioned elements. (We shall come back to this structural transformation of the social system later in the volume.) The 'Industrial Revolution' (between c. 1750 and 1820) and the American and French Revolutions (1776 and 1789 respectively), as widely accepted, were two significant episodes in the process toward the establishment of the above-characterised socio-cultural configuration, although, of course, the origin of some of the above-mentioned traits/characteristics predated it.

That the disciplinisation process of archaeology coincided in timing with the emergence and establishment of modernity means that the cause of the disciplinisation can be meaningfully investigated by examining possible causal connections between the character of archaeological practice/activities and the above-mentioned traits of modernity one by one. For instance, parallelism between the elements of modernity and the methodological elements of archaeological excavation established in the late nineteenth century, marking the beginning of 'scientific archaeology' (Trigger 1989, Chapter 3), is quite clear. The excavation, and recording method and technique adopted by the British Lieutenant General Pitt Rivers, excavating, recording and publishing sites in his Cranborne Chase estates during the late nineteenth century, for instance, well exemplifies this point (cf. Lucas 2001). Regarding the connection with *industrialisation*, the 'strip-digging' method he adopted, by which the ground was cleared in a series of successive parallel trenches, the spoil from one being used to backfill the last, was a common method in shallow quarrying in the nineteenth and early twentieth centuries (Lucas 2001, 20). Pitt Rivers saw sufficient search and careful recording as the two crucial tenets of fieldwork: one can see the connection with the spirit of *rationalisation* and *calculation* here. His desire to systematise the procedure of excavation and recording was such that he trained assistants in surveying and draughting (Lucas 2001). His *division/segmentation of labour*, his *specialisation* distinguishing the assistants from the labourers, and his *bureaucratic management* reflect the organisational elements of modernity. His advocation of artefact classification, based upon evolutionary typology (Lucas 2001, 25–26), can be connected to *secularisation* amongst other elements of modernity; things changed, they did not remain the way god created them. In other words, excavation, a definitive element of scientific archaeology, came into existence as an autonomous sphere of social practice embodying and representing the constitutive elements of modernity in its own manner, and it was one of a vast number of such autonomous spheres including other scientific disciplines and their technical sub-disciplines which came into being with the formation and maturation of modernity. As far as its methodological and practical aspects are concerned, in that sense, archaeology was indeed a child of modernity.

However, when it comes to theoretical–discursive characteristics, i.e., how the subject is described and made sense of, the disciplinisation of archaeology can be more meaningfully investigated in terms of its relationship with the emergence of the nation-state and nationalism (e.g. Diaz-Andreu and Champion 1996; Kohl and Fawcett 1996). This is partly due to the fact that the relationship is highly tangible in the form of the manipulation of the archaeological past for various 'nationalist' causes, a well-quoted example of which is the mobilisation of archaeological knowledge for the justification of German borders throughout the late nineteenth century and the early twentieth century: the distribution of a particular artefact/feature or a set of them was equated with the domain inhabited by a particular population, e.g., a 'race', and the archaeological trace of the habitation of a race was considered to validate/legitimise the occupation/annexation by the state, in which the descendant population of that race was believed to constitute the majority, of the area (cf. Wiwjorra 1996). However, it is more important to note for the current argument that nationalism is not only a significant but also an *inevitable* consequence of modernity (cf. Gellner 1983), and typifies its constitutive nature and character. Many of the constitutive elements of modernity, mentioned earlier, are interdependent with the nation-state in terms of their generation and acceleration: it has been well documented that their generation was both cause and consequence of various inter-state competitions over resources and markets that resulted in the establishment of many nation-states in Europe. In that sense, focusing on the connection between archaeology and nationalism/the nation-state in the investigation of the relationship between modernity and archaeology is a natural choice. It has to be stated here, however, that the causality and implications of the connection between archaeology and nationalism/the nation-state can only be fully understood if it is properly situated in the broader landscape of modernity. We will come back to this point repeatedly throughout the volume.

2.2 Archaeology, the nation-state, and the transcendental

The connection between primordialism in ethnic self identification and archaeology as a discourse of the past in the present has been recognised as a constitutive factor behind the connection between nationalism and archaeology (Diaz-Andreu and Champion 1996; Kohl and Fawcett 1996). By primordialism I mean the belief that there are core/innate/determinant elements of an ethnic identity, ranging from biological characteristics through kinship connections to cultural traits such as language, whose origin is believed to go back to the most distant past (cf. Sokolovskii and Tishkov 1996). It has been pointed out that the sense of timelessness and antiquity which derives from this belief gives rise to the illusion of a nation as 'natural' and authentic (Sorensen 1996, 28–29). Most of what has been put forward so far about the mechanism behind this connection, though, takes the so-called 'instrumentalist' stance (Sokolovskii and Tishkov 1996). This emphasises the *otherness* and the manipulability of the past as the basic source and foundation of the connection; the otherness allows the past to be mythologised/mystified. At the same time, this allows that anything, such as the core elements of the identity of an ethnic group, can be found in it that those who look into it would like to see. In other words, primordialist beliefs are articulated as *instruments* for interest-laden claims in the present such as ethnic/nationalist claims for the continuous presence of an ethnic identity. It is vitally important to note, however, that otherness and manipulability are generic attributes of the past, and it remains to be explained why the otherness and manipulability of the past came to be perceived as such in a manner and why that particular manner, called archaeology, in which the otherness was systematically tamed, i.e., made familiar/comprehensible to the masses, became articulated during the formative process of modernity, but not before that.

The constitutive characteristics of modernity, i.e., industrialisation, rationalisation, commodification, bureaucracy, citizenship, and secularisation, though initially emerging at different points in history, came together to form a systemic whole at the turn of the nineteenth century, and that took the form of the *modern* nation-state. By 'nation-state' I mean a political unit consisting of an autonomous state occupied predominantly by a population sharing a common culture, belief in a common ethnic ancestry, and a common language. Prototypes of the modern nation-state are commonly regarded to have emerged earlier (e.g. Britain, France and Spain) but it was not until the mid/late nineteenth century when these traits became fully in place and they began operating, i.e., competing against one another economically, politically, and militarily over resources and markets (e.g. Hobsbawm 1990). The nation-state, like modernity, can be grasped as a configuration, this time a configuration of mechanisms for the integration of the inhabitants of its domain. The word 'integration' here is interchangeable with 'homogenisation'; the inhabitants of the domain had to be made 'citizens', i.e., individuals who were guaranteed their autonomy and rights from the state regardless of their gender, class, and other differences in return for fulfilling their duties to the state, including paying tax and accepting conscription. The relationship between modernity and the nation-state is typified in the concept of *citizenship* in that the traits characterising modernity, i.e., industrialisation, rationalisation, commodification, bureaucracy, and secularisation, all mediate and are all mediated by the existence of the citizen: they are guaranteed the right to sell their own labour and to buy one another's to make maximum profit; their important rites of passage, birth, coming of age/starting a family, death, and so on, have to be witnessed and registered by state bureaucrats, not necessarily by local priests; and everyone is equal on these grounds as long as they fulfil their duty to the state. Coming back to the issue, the mechanisms for integration/homogenisation can be categorised into (1) economic, (2) governing/controlling, (3) ideological, and (4) symbolic mechanisms of integration, and, referring to the French First Republic as an example,

(1) the economic mechanism comprises the expansion and consolidation of transportation/communication networks, the unification of a currency, and the modernisation of taxation systems,
(2) the governing/controlling mechanism is the establishment of a constitution, centralised government, parliament, court of law, police force, prison service, and regular national army of conscripts,
(3) the politico-ideological mechanism involves the establishment of a family register, education systems, museums, political parties, and newspapers,

(4) the symbolic mechanism is the creation of the national flag and anthem, the standardisation of a national language, the promotion of literature and fine arts, the compilation of a national history, and the foundation and organisation of national ritual festivals (Nishikawa 1995).

Those mechanisms and their elements are mutually connected in a systemic, interdependent manner. In considering how the connection between the nation-state and archaeology is situated in this systemic whole, the following fact appears to be of particular importance: the rise of a new nation-state was often associated with the articulation of the narrative of the *ethnic* unity of the state. The implications of this can be examined in terms of the relationship between the perception of ethnicity and nationalistic feelings. Nationalistic feelings are commonly classified into the 'civic' and 'ethnic' types (cf. Smith 2001, 39–42); the former is based upon the idea of the nation as a rational, voluntaristic association of citizens bound by common laws and a shared territory; the latter as an organic whole to which individual members belong because they share an innate national character (Smith 2001). However, they both often converge so that the former, often supported by culture, especially a selected and standardised vernacular language as almost the only *objective* indicator of the unity of a group, is connected to the feeling of ethnic unity. And the rising feeling of ethnic unity, quite often, was supported by the rising popular belief in a continuing ethnic identity from the distant past (Smith 1986, 2001).

Anthony Smith emphasises that the existence of groupings which can be called 'nations' (by nations he means 'felt and lived communities whose members share a homeland and a culture' (2001, 12)) predates the emergence of the nation-state and nation-states were often formed from such nations (Smith 2001). In contrast, Benedict Anderson has pointed out that in many cases it was the emergence of a state, which was a politically integrated unit with clearly drawn boundaries (not 'frontiers', which are fundamentally fluid), that resulted in the articulation of an ethnicity and its underpinning tradition(s) including a national vernacular language and literary tradition (Anderson 1991). Those dichotomous viewpoints epitomise the difference between the 'perennialist' (Smith) and 'modernist' (Anderson) approaches competing in the study of nationalism today (cf. Smith 2001, Chapter 3). According to Ernest Gellner, though, Smith and Anderson are not in such sharp dispute as they might seem (Gellner 1983). Gellner argues that differences which had potential for differentiating groups including what can be called 'nations' were not problematised until the time industrialisation resulted in the uneven distribution of wealth relating to status/positional differentiation in individual political units/states (Gellner 1983). This can be expressed thus: pre-existing 'nations' had rarely been connected to any social division causing advantage/disadvantage to the divided groups until industrialisation. The destruction of agrarian states resulted in the formation of the nation-state and its internal as well as external divisions directly related to competition over wealth, resources and socio-economic advantage.

A particularly important implication of this argument, emphasising the mutual complementarity between the perennialist and modernist stances, is that it

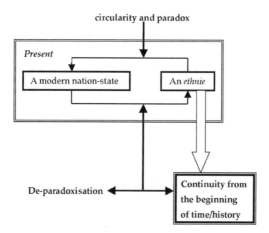

Figure 2.1 Circularity and paradox of the nation-state and the solution (masking and de-paradoxisation).

effectively reveals that the relationship between the *nation*-state and the discourse supporting/legitimising/authenticating its existence is characterised by vicious circularity and paradox: *a nation-state is underpinned by a tradition/ethnic identity as the latter is articulated through the formation of the former.* The search for a language, physical traits, cultural characteristics, and so on, which were supposed to indicate the antiquity of the unity/unified existence of a nation, began either when a modern industrial state was formed or when the formation of a modern state gave rise to the socio-economic/cultural impoverishment of its own internal minority or of one of its neighbouring populations (Gellner 1983), although, it has to be noted, the way those traits were rediscovered/invented and mobilised was different between countries/contexts (Hobsbawm 1990, Chapter 2). It is important to add here, by referring again to Gellner, that the articulation of a socio-economically/culturally impoverished population took place (and is still taking place) when industrialisation put a population with either a minority language or distinct physical/cultural characteristics or both in a disadvantaged position in the labour market (Gellner 1983, Chapter 6). At that point, the articulation of nationalist sentiments is intrinsically connected to industrialisation, a main constitutive element of modernity.

Coming back to our main argument here, the above-mentioned circularity and paradox, it can logically be deduced, need to be dealt with, i.e., masked or de-paradoxised, for the integration of individual nation-states, particularly in their infancy (Figure 2.1). It was the *authenticity* of a cultural group sharing a collective memory of common ancestry, culture, language and so on, i.e., an *ethnie* in Anthony Smith's terminology (1986), that was supposed to be based upon its continuation from a particular point in history, which was often claimed to go back to the deepest past, that was imagined and/or created for the purpose of masking and de-paradoxising circularity and paradox associated with the discursive base of the nation-state (Figure 2.1) (Anderson 1991). By artificially adding time-depth to a synchronic entity, the authenticity of the ethnie is (re)gained and the circularity and paradox 'solved' (or, in actuality, *forgotten*); the invented continuity of an ethnie is made to serve as the cause and reason for the existence of a nation-state at the same time. It has to be added that in this case the word 'invented' is interchangeable with 'articulated' or 'problematised.' As mentioned, quite often a nation-state was built upon a pre-existing cultural unit of some sort as Smith emphasises (1986). In that sense what happened when a nation-state emerged was not necessarily pure invention. However, it is equally often the case that a nation-state was built upon an intentionally chosen shared cultural trait amongst other unshared, often divisive, equivalents distributed within the domain, and the choice was often made for strategic purposes (Hobsbawm 1990, Chapter 2). Besides, such a culture/cultural trait was often only possessed and shared by a particular *class*, most often by the elite (Gellner 1983, Chapter 2): underneath the layer of such a culture/cultural traits were a number of local habits that formed an internally heterogeneous agrarian state bound by an elite culture (Gellner 1983). In order for a culture/cultural trait to be a factor upon which a nation-state was to be built, that trait had to be reinvented as a shareable, unifying, and homogenising factor to a group of people regardless of their class, or religious, and local-group affiliations.

As the notion of continuity, in other words the temporal extension of an *internally homogeneous entity* into the depths of time, helps to hide the fictive element of the nation-state, a modern nation-state as a self-reproducing entity, as already touched upon above, is also made possible by its *internal homogeneity*. Note the circularity which exists between these factors; only something which can be recognised as a unit, internally organically structured/homogeneous, can *continuously exist through time*, as at the same time, in the case we are dealing with, that very continuity serves to show the entity's unity as a unit. As mentioned above, what actually underpins the internal homogeneity of a modern nation-state varies; a currency, a legal system, an ethnicity, a religion, and so on, function to make and keep those who live within the boundary of a modern nation-state homogeneous. To be more precise, these items/media and institutions make those who live within the boundary of a modern nation-state see/observe themselves as homogeneous. To put it differently, in order for a currency, a legal system, and so on to function properly, those who live in the domain within which these media (of social communication) function have to be homogeneous. Note, again, the circularity which exists between these factors; (x) these media of social communication work as such because those whose communication is mediated by them are homogeneous, i.e., they all agree that these are the media of their social communication, and (y) those who use these media of social communication are homogeneous because they use them as the media of their social communication.

In order to properly grasp the nature of this circularity, we have to introduce, again, the concept of citizenship: those who live in the domain of a nation-state have to be *citizens*. By stating this I mean that citizens have to be made to identify themselves not with their concrete, shared experience and local knowledge but with something *abstract*, such as money; money transcends all sorts of barriers (within a nation-state), but most importantly time–space, and signifies value but itself has no use/value.[1] In that sense, a nation-state and its 'homogenising media' mutually mediate their existence.

Here again we encounter circularity and paradox. The internal homogeneity of a modern nation-state is constituted and underpinned by the existence of 'homogenising media' such as above. At the same time, the working of the homogenising media of a modern nation-state relies upon its internal homogeneity. How, then, can the circularity and paradox be logically solved, i.e., de-paradoxised? Let us consider the issue by examining the way homogenising media such as money mediate the communication of citizens.

Homogenising media mediate communication between the citizens in a manner which is totally irrelevant to any group affiliation such as class, religion and local group (cf. Luhmann 1995, 161–163). However, this does not mean that the *selves* of all the citizens are homogeneous; on the contrary, the existence of these homogenising media allows every citizen to be different from one another; they are meant to be relieved from the communal, hence localised, pressure of being the same. All of the constitutive elements of modernity, i.e., industrialisation, rationalisation, commodification, bureaucratisation, citizenship, deconstruction of kinship/local ties, secularisation, and institutional segmentation, come together and mediate/enable/make inevitable the autonomy of the individual/self. This, at the same time, means that the communication systems which used to rely on the sharing of local knowledge/norms are faced with unprecedented difficulty in their reproduction. It means that all the *selves* constituting a nation-state have to be *made* to feel able to communicate with one another, in spite of their mutually predicted differences, and in order for that to be achieved, the citizens have to be made to assume that they all share a set of values, norms, and so on that do not derive from shared and accumulated local knowledge and experiences but come out of something more deep-rooted, abstract, and *de-localised* (within the domain of the nation-state). Sharing such a thing means that they share the ultimate, unified referent for their self identification. By 'ultimate' here I mean, by drawing upon the argument so far, that the referent accommodates two mutually contradictory natures of being delocalised/abstract and being localised/concrete: the referent has to be abstract enough to delocalise the identity of citizens and at the same time be concrete enough to be referred to as the referent for the self identification of the citizens. In other words, a nation-state needs something *transcendental*, such as a god or a god-given value, or something concrete and abstract at the same time, with which its citizens can (re)identify themselves. The transcendental is needed to make citizens feel/believe that they can understand one another anywhere within the domain of the nation-state to a depth which cannot be achieved between citizens belonging to different nation-states. Once the existence of the transcendental is internalised the circularity and paradox become a non-issue. The de-paradoxisation is completed.

---

[1] Except in some highly unusual circumstances, money does not have any use/value, and that which has concrete use/value cannot be used as money (cf. Giddens 1990, 22).

I would argue that archaeology constitutes an *ideal* locus/discursive space where these transcendental entities can reside, underpinning and mediating the working of the homogenising media and internal homogeneity of the modern nation-state. As will be fully illustrated in Chapter 3.8 below, there are structural parallels between the archaeological material and the transcendental. The primary subjects of archaeological investigation are artefacts and features which have been buried. Their identity can be fixed spatio-temporally, and they are meaningless archaeologically unless they are fixed to chrono-cultural positions as far as modern, scientific archaeology (cf. Trigger 1989, Chapter 3) is concerned. At the same time, they cannot be attributed *directly* to anything in the contemporary world. They are archaeological material because they have been left behind, i.e., disconnected with agency, and cannot be linked directly to any concrete human action. They can only be attributed to concrete human actions through mediations (i.e., theoretico-methodological mediations) that take place in the contemporary world. This means that every possible archaeological communication is about what are *temporalised and localised as deposits and are decontextualised through mediation in the contemporary world at one go*. And this combination of *contextualisedness* and *decontextualisedness* in one entity nicely coincides with what is required for the transcendental entities to guarantee the internal homogeneity of nation-states. In that sense, archaeology constitutes an ideal imaginary locus where transcendental entities are imagined to reside.

It was pointed out that it was to make the relationship between the individual and the nation natural and to give it emotional strength that were the concerns of nationalism and they were the needs to which the use of the past/archaeology fits nicely (Sorensen 1996, 28–29). The foregoing explains how such a relationality between the past, the individual, the nation and the related emotions comes about and works particularly well in modernity and in the nation-state, and why; ultimately, the past has, since the inception of modernity and the modern nation-state, always been called up to terminate the vicious circularity and to de-paradoxise the paradox that fundamentally constitutes the modern nation-state.

2.3 The fate and fears of archaeology in modernity: the outline of this volume

If the above were the case, archaeology as a distinct *modern* discursive space would continue to function as a locus where the transcendental, which functions to maintain the internal homogeneity of individual nation-states, resides as long as nation-states exist or, indeed, modernity lasts.

However, the character of both modernity and the modern nation-state has been changed and transformed, and, as illustrated in Chapter 1, the transformation has reached the point at which some scholars have come to characterise the society we live in as something fundamentally different from that of modernity, viz., post-modernity. We should not be bothered too much about the labelling. The consensus is that the social formation of industrialised countries has become what is characterised by such notions and factors as 'reflexivity', 'fragmentation', 'individualisation', and 'liquidisation' (cf. Harvey 1989; Bauman 2000b). They attempt to capture the loss of the stable axes of the structuration of society, stable referents with which to decide how to act in particular contexts, and comprehensive models with which to plan one's life-course, for instance. This phenomenon, quite naturally, has resulted in the generation of a new paradigm of attitudes, which take the form of 'post-processual archaeologies' (e.g. Hodder 1991) in the discipline of archaeology. Saying this might imply that the connection between archaeology as a source of homogenisation and the modern nation-state as an internally homogeneous entity has come to an end because the citizens of a nation-state are now heterogeneous on various levels, temporally as well as spatially. However, the actual situation is not so simple.

Today's world is also characterised by the wave of homogenisation called globalisation. Globalisation means different things to different people, but it can be broadly defined as a group of phenomena relating to the expansion of hyper-capitalistic social formation and (the image and the illusion of) the accompanying lifestyle (e.g. Lechner and Boli 1999). All kinds of *differences* between internally homogeneous/homogenised entities ranging from nation-states through aesthetics are utilised to profit in innumerable ways from hyper-capitalistic social formation (e.g. Harvey 1989). It is not the case that only pre-existing differences, such as those which are based upon nation-states and their boundaries, are utilised. Rather, formerly non-existent/intangible/unconceived boundaries, marked increasingly by symbolic, rather than functional, items and features, are articulated and rearticulated by those who are in possession of the means to create differences and make ever-increasing profits by utilising them (Harvey 1989; Balibar and Wallerstein 1991). For instance, the turnover time of capital, i.e., the time taken for an investment to generate profit, is increasingly shortened by deliberately and chronically abolishing old fashions and advertisements and creating new alternatives in ever-shortening intervals (note the similarity to the ever-shortening of the duration in which public interests in newly reconstructed sites last, mentioned in Chapter 1): the chronic generation of spatio-temporal differences in the circulation of symbols and images, in this case, generates profit (cf. Harvey 1989, Chapter 14). On a macro level, chronologically relocating the place of capital investment, i.e., the place of production, in shorter time intervals than the opponents also gives the investor an edge by utilising the created cost differences (Harvey 1989). New entities have to be articulated all the time, and these new entities, in order to function as units between which differences can be created and engineered, have to be internally homogeneous in one way or another (Harvey 1989). Meanwhile, these created entities often function as the units between which advantages and disadvantages/impoverishment are generated and felt, for instance, in the form of sudden relocation of factories leaving behind mass unemployment and social deprivation in developing countries (Bauman 2000a). This means that archaeology as a source of homogenisation is still in demand, although in a different context and in a different manner from that of classic modernity; an impoverished country/region/group may resort to stirring up nationalistic sentiments in order to resist and counter such selfish moves by international corporations, and archaeology may be mobilised to generate nationalistic primordialist beliefs (many examples in Kohl and Fawcett 1996).

At the same time, the grip of hyper-capitalistic social formation is ever expanding into every part of one's life through various mass media, and it is a natural consequence that its technology influences/is emulated by archaeologists. As well as being a discursive space for the creation of a sense of homogeneity and of an image of the transcendental, archaeology becomes the arena in which the generation of differences becomes the name of the game, as if emulating the shortening of capital turnover time and related socio-cultural phenomena mentioned above. A new theory can be valued solely on its newness, rather than its quality and power to guide one's investigation in the right direction (cf. Hodder 1999, Chapter 1). It can also be added that the individual, the ultimate bearer of, and the minimum unit generating, differences is increasingly given more attention in archaeological interpretation (e.g. Meskell 1999). However, this trend in archaeology is structurally identical to what hyper-capitalism needs/desires. The empowerment of the individual, as the ultimate consumer of differences, is the ultimate strategy of the hyper-capitalist (Bauman 2000b, Chapter 2). The individual, in such perception, is always hungry for change, seeking change for change's sake, because s/he can only find identity through change, and one can only achieve that objective by chronically purchasing new products in order to differentiate oneself from oneself of a moment ago and from all the others. *I am what I buy* (Bauman 2000b). In that sense, the hyper-capitalistic individual is bound to relativise everything: stability, durability, and authenticity are, for him/her, the obstacle to and the enemy of self identification. Ultimate freedom, or nightmare? Can we, or indeed can the innate ability of the human being, bear the burden of chronically changing our identities in order to be ourselves? Should archaeology be used to anchor one's identity or to help transform it? Such a question, which would have been unimaginable thirty years ago, nowadays has to be asked.

Drawing upon the above observations and argument in this chapter, we can now fully outline the structure of this volume. Summarising the arguments, today, we archaeologists are doing archaeology with two fears. One is the fear of being caught up in the constitutive character of the nation-state, i.e., being homogenised internally, and unwittingly supporting the furthering of the control of the state which tends to oppress minority rights and voices. The other is the fear of being caught up in the two forces of radicalising modernity, i.e., fragmentation/individualisation/liquidisation on the one hand and globalisation/homogenisation on the other; and unwittingly contributing to the generation of pathological social phenomena, the destruction of anything local/communal/kin-based, the endless relativisation of everything and apathy ('anything goes'), and the generation and perpetuation of discommunication between groups/individuals. As illustrated, the former is related to 'classical' modern social formation (characterised by 'heavy capitalism'), and the latter to 'radicalised'(/post-)modern social formation (characterised by 'light capitalism').

In this volume, I wish to examine in detail the interconnection/interdependence between these fears and two modern social formations, i.e., classical and radicalised, and consider what remedy we can propose. As briefly illustrated, the interconnection and interdependence between the fears/problems and the characteristics of modernity are multi-layered and have been through a complex trajectory of co-transformation. In order not to lose either the generality or the contextual nuance of the observation and argumentation with such a complex cluster of issues and factors behind them, I will move back and forth between the study of particular cases and wider, general pictures throughout the rest of this volume.

There are innumerable ways to approach modernity and these issues. In Chapter 1, I emphasised the importance of identity and communication in understanding the character of the relationship between modernity and archaeology. Furthering the argument it can be said that there is something unique in the way discourses/discursive spaces are interconnected as well as in the way each of them is constituted and reproduced in modernity. Both of these factors are mediated by communication. The generation and reproduction of communication systems are intrinsically interconnected with the self identification of those who take part in them. If simplified, it can be described thus: in order for a communication to continue, those who take part in it have to mutually predict the next act of the other and decide how to act upon the prediction. In that process what one is, i.e., the identity of an individual, is constituted. What is unique about the process of self identification through communication in modernity is, as illustrated at length later on, that the way one predicts the other's thinking and acts and hence identifies one's position in a communication is *reflexively* monitored, theorised and may alter the way one is involved in the next communication. Such scholars as Anthony Giddens and Ulrich Beck, by grasping this, characterise the radicalised modernity in which we live as *reflexive modernity* in which the institutionalisation of the reflexive monitoring of one's involvement in a field of social communication constantly alters one's identity as well as the way in which the field of communication is constituted (Beck et al. 1994). From this point of view, the theoretical framework we draw upon in this volume has to be one which can grasp this complex relationality between communication and self identification in modernity. This relationality is a *systemic*, and again, *circular*, one in that not one element in it can constitute itself without its connections to the others, whilst constitutive effects/influences from the others are processed and selected by the element in a self-reflexive manner. I found Niklas Luhmann's theory of social systems most useful for this purpose, because his theory deals efficiently with the systemic nature of the relationship between fields of communication and the self-reflexive nature of the reproduction of each of them, which involves dealing with circularity and paradox. (We have already seen its elements in the consideration of the intrinsic nature of communication in Chapter 1.) In Chapter 3 I formulate a theoretical framework for the undertaking by referring to Luhmann's theory.

Chapter 4 consists of three case studies about the interdependence between 'classical' modernity and archaeology and the fears and related problems that the interdependence brings about. Examples will be drawn from the modern nation-state of Japan where I live and work, where I have the necessary familiarity for going into the nuanced detail of the subject. It has to be added that Japan, from its historical background and geopolitical position, went through a unique modernising process in which the constitutive elements of modernity and the modern nation-state were formed in a uniquely intensive, but at the same time somewhat exemplary, manner. For instance, the above-listed constitutive elements of modernity and the modern nation-state gradually came into being over a considerable period in Europe. However, they, particularly the elements of the modern nation-state, came into place very quickly in Japan: many of them were, in fact, hastily and artificially founded as a 'module' by learning directly from advanced nation-states in Europe and the United States in the face of possible colonisation by Western powers (Nishikawa 1995, 25–30). A delegation was sent to these countries in 1871, four years after the so-called Meiji restoration ending the Edo feudal regime. The objective of the delegation was to make formal visits to the premiers of the countries with which Japan had already concluded commercial and diplomatic treaties, but one task entrusted to the delegation was to learn about, and report on the legal, economic, educational, and militaristic systems/institutions of those countries (Nishikawa 1995). This fact implies that not only how those systems/institutions were organised but also how they functioned in the reproduction of the nation-state as a system were brought back and utilised as an epistemic 'package'. This further implies that, in Japan, archaeology, *from the beginning*, was situated in this epistemic mode in which the furthering of knowledge of any type was supposed to be *only* for the sake of the well-being of the state. That makes the interdependence between modern social formation and archaeology constituted in Japan highly intense and tangible. I will try to fully and usefully utilise this advantage to investigate this issue.

Chapter 5 will trace the trajectory of the transformation of modernity from its classical roots to the radicalised/post-modern variant. It is widely recognised that at some time during the 1970s modernity entered a new phase. The universal values upon which modernity was based were thrown into doubt, and the transformation of capitalism, from the mode characterised by large factory labour and heavy industry to the mode characterised by individualised work space/flexible time scheduling and light industry/production of goods whose style is more important than their durability and functionality, led to the collapse of the mental topography and objective institutions which supported the traditional industrial capitalist-based society. The development of electronic communication made the transfer of capital vastly easier and quicker, and the expansion of the labour market made the world an increasingly homogeneous place. At the same time, the exploitation of a cheap labour force in the form of the rapid relocation of factories to seek the cheapest labour is ruining the local economies of third world nations. All of these factors are interconnected and have resulted in the generation of an ultimate social philosophy, namely multiculturalism.

Multiculturalism means many different things to different people. However, by 'multiculturalism' I mean the epistemic attitude which prioritises the maintenance/promotion of differences/diversity over the pursuit of the possibility of reaching mutual understanding and doing common/universal good. This attitude can be characterised by its opposition to essentialism. By 'essentialism' I mean the epistemic stance of taking for granted the existence of the 'essence', or the natural, hence *universally* valid, state in each individual thing, for instance the essence for the family, and the essence for being the individual. This stance implies (a) that cultural differences have to be overcome for the sake of achieving the common/universal good, 'essential' for the betterment of human society and human beings and (b) that cultural media merely *represent/reflect* the essence of things, and do not constitute/transform it. Both points can be easily challenged, but challenging them also leads us to difficulties with diverse philosophical implications. For instance, some advocates of multiculturalism criticise point (a) by saying that the belief in the existence of a 'common good' itself implies the acceptance of the modern western epistemology which functions to sustain the power relations of the contemporary world. However, do we not have to sacrifice, to a degree, cultural differences in order to make the cohabitation of different cultures/groups possible? Some advocates of multiculturalism also claim that cultural media, such as language, do not merely represent the essence of things but constitute the content of things themselves. By that they mean that one's use of language constitutes one's reality and state of existence; and a change in one's language use changes one's reality and state of existence. The so-called 'PC' (political correctness) movement in language use faithfully follows this belief and has tried to create the ultimate value-neutral language in order to eliminate every form of power relation which is mediated by language use. However, does not the elimination of historically value-laden words sometimes conceal the existence of historically generated discriminations and the misdistribution of socio-cultural/symbolic capital? In Chapter 5, it will be argued that multiculturalism ultimately derives from the abandonment of hope for satisfactory mutual understanding and common good in the contemporary world. My contention is that post-processual archaeologies are a form of multiculturalism, and in that sense they face the same problems which multiculturalism faces today. In Chapter 5, so-called 'archaeologies of identities', which have significant resonance with multiculturalism, will be subject to critical scrutiny.

Before moving on, we need to properly situate multiculturalism in the broad topography of contemporary social philosophy. The social philosophy of the twentieth century saw (1) communitarianism, (2) methodological universalism/objectivism, and (3) multiculturalism come and go (Osawa 2002, 11–22). They are interchangeable with (a) traditionalism, (b) modernism, and (c) post-modernism (Osawa 2002). The (1)–(a) problematique presupposes the necessary existence of communally shared experiences/norms in considering the way to make the world a better place. The (2)–(b) problematique presupposes the human ability to agree about the way to communicate with one another and to consider the same issue. The (3)–(c) problematique presupposes the human ability to tolerate each other's differences and live side by side harmoniously *without commenting* on the way others communicate. The credibility of the latter two have been eroded, particularly rapidly and dramatically since the 11 September incident. The human abilities these stances presuppose have been thrown into serious doubt; can the west and the Islamic world, for instance, reach mutual understanding by creating a value-neutral discursive space, or can they tolerate/ignore each other's differences without commenting on them? After 9.11, we have been forced to be pessimistic about the ability of human beings to coexist peacefully. Naturally, the first problematique, i.e., communitarian traditionalism, becomes increasingly appealing. However, clearly, it does not offer us any solution. Resorting to this epistemic stance, which characterises what is happening in the world right now as conflicts between mutually irreconcilable belief/behavioural systems, i.e., 'the clash of civilisations' (cf. Huntington 1998), might be a better stance than painting an illusory picture of expanding hyper-capitalism destroying national/cultural borders as Francis Fukuyama did (Fukuyama 1992). However, what is at issue here is not how to capture the political reality of inter-civilisation relations but how the coexistence of and dialogue between different cultural/interest groups could become possible. Besides, the differences between the civilisations which Huntington talks about have been problematised by contemporary socio-economic changes and radicalised by political events and decisions taken in the 1980s and 1990s (cf. Naito 2004), and what 'clash' are their ways of seeing the world and communicating about it. These are historically constituted tendencies, not innate differences.

However, archaeology, together with other social scientific/humanistic disciplines, was confronted with the above-mentioned difficulty well before the 11 September. Whose interest, if the archaeologist inevitably had to represent an element of the power relations and maldistributed resources, as illustrated at the beginning of Chapter 1, should the archaeologist represent, and how? Can we, amongst archaeologists and between archaeologists and the general public, ever reach/obtain *the* image of the *past*? Is that desirable? Or should we create different pasts for different purposes?

Everything happening on the surface of the earth right now seems contradictory and confusing: homogenisation is accompanied by the reinvention of differences, and the liquidisation/fragmentation of social relations is accompanied by the re-invention and consolidation of 'traditional' customs. One thing for sure is that the number of boundaries dividing human beings is increasing and their existence is felt increasingly strongly by the day. What can we do? What can we do as archaeolgists? Should we make a number of pasts suitable to a number of different needs, or should we defy the trend by insisting on the possibility of reconstructing the *singular past* and promoting the common humanity/value? These issues, again, will be illustrated mainly by Japanese cases in Chapter 5.

Obviously, there is no easy solution and no single answer, because what is at issue here is how to confront the consequences of modernity. However, I am obliged to put forward my own approach to this most serious and fundamental of the issues we confront in the contemporary world.

Chapter 6 will summarise my argument and conclude the volume.

3

Communication, sociality, and the positionality of archaeology

3.1 Introduction

As illustrated, modernity can be understood as a systemic whole constituted by a configuration of industrialisation, rationalisation, commodification, bureaucratisation, citizenship, deconstruction of kinship/local ties, secularisation, and institutional segmentation and specialisation. These factors, although not all coming into being at once but over a period of time, became interconnected and mutually determinant, and their interdependence was mediated by a new form of *sociality*. By 'sociality' I mean the unity of customs and institutions, and a certain mode of sociality which gives rise to a social formation which can be characterised by the kinds of institutions that constitute it and by the way these institutions are interconnected. However, the description of institutions and how they are interconnected does not say much about sociality itself, i.e., how it is generated and reproduced (Giddens 1984). In particular, the sociality we experience in contemporary society is characterised by fluidity and dynamism rather than by static institutional characteristics. What we have to investigate is the dynamic, generative element of sociality, i.e., how sociality itself comes into being and is reproduced.

Scholars such as Anthony Giddens and Ulrich Beck, as mentioned above, characterise contemporary social formation as 'reflexive modernity' (Beck et al. 1994). By that, they mean that virtually every field of social communication is subject to constant reflexive monitoring, the outcome of which is constantly fed back and continually alters the way people are involved in communication, as well as the way communication is structured and reproduced. In such a circumstance, the content and structuring principle of individual social communication fields and the interconnections between them, which were previously stable and constituted what could be described as 'traditions', 'institutions', 'structures', and so on, become fluid and ever-changing.

In other words, if we introduce the concept of *complexity* here (by complexity I mean the state in which there is a horizon of choices to be articulated for human action/communication), the nature of the complexity of society has been transformed from one which can be reduced to a set of 'underlying principles' or institutional axes of social reproduction (i.e., traditions) to one which generates a new state of complexity *each and every time* – the observation and the *observation of the observation* (Luhmann 1995) of the complexity, i.e., 'reflexive monitoring'. Writing this volume is itself an act of observing the complexity of high-/late-/post-modernity through studying the positionality of archaeology. Doing so, i.e., observing the observation of the complexity generated in the present as well as in the past, contributes towards articulating a new horizon of choices, i.e., a new complexity to the society we live in, rather than reducing it. And, of course, this is done in the hope that this deliberate generation of a new complexity and its injection into archaeology opens up a new, positively productive discursive space in contemporary society.

The foregoing suggests that the theoretical framework we draw upon in this volume must not be based upon the premise that the complexity of the world can always be reduced to certain 'fundamentals' which are stable and determine the possible range of deviation for things constituting the world (cf. Parsons 1951). Instead, the framework will be the one which enables us both to accept that recognition of the complexity of the world itself generates a new complexity in the world, and to grasp how human beings coped with this endless reproduction of complexity in the past as well as in the present. If we could grasp the issue that way, the difficulty that contemporary society and archaeology are faced with could be understood to result from the increasing difficulty we have in coping with the ever present/increasing complexity of the world.

In any case, the question we have to begin asking is: how is society/sociality possible despite the complexity inevitably involved in its generation and reproduction?

3.2 How do we live our lives socially?

Let us begin by asking the following: how do we live our lives socially? Or, how can we grasp the nature of sociality?

It is a truism to say that the way in which we grasp the nature of sociality determines the way we study society. Different 'social archaeologies' draw upon different definitions/understandings of the way society works as society. However, we can extract one defining trait almost universally shared by the schools coexisting within the discursive space of contemporary social archaeology; that is, sociality is understood to be all about the *stability* of society or *order* in the working of society.

Since we started to explain, rather than merely describing, the past, we archaeologists have concentrated on how we can explain/understand the causes and mechanisms of the *maintenance* of social stability and order. Even when we claim to be studying social change/transformation, understanding social stability has always been regarded as a prerequisite in that social change is understood as the *disturbance* of social stability and order. Accordingly, we archaeologists are trained to distinguish between what is and what is not relevant to the study of social stability and social order by finding *stable*, that is statistically meaningful, *patterns* (e.g. Clarke 1978). We are trained to choose and process certain types of information which are useful for the observation of the nature and character of the stability and order of a given community (e.g. Renfrew 1984). We are also trained to differentiate/articulate ways in which we describe the causes and mechanisms of social stability and social order and to discuss ways to describe them (Renfrew 1984).

In that regard, systemic, Marxist, and post-processual social archaeologies seem to me not as different from one another as they would like to claim to be. Although their principles of differentiating various archaeologically recognisable phenomena/factors and categorising them into analytical units are different, they are structurally identical

in investigating the causal interconnections between the states of differentiated analytical units, each of which works to maintain social stability or order. The concepts
of negative/positive feedback (systemic approaches, cf. Clarke 1978), the concealment by an ideology of contradictions between analytical units such as infra- and
super-structures (Marxist approaches, cf. Kristiansen 1998), and domination and its
signification and legitimisation in the mode of social relations, i.e., relations between
agents (broad structurationist approaches, cf. Barrett 1994), are all about the production and reproduction of stability and order.

Meanwhile, it has frequently been pointed out that differentiation between stability
and change is futile in understanding the working of society (e.g. Shanks and Tilley
1987, Chapter 6). Instead, the *reproduction* or *continuous reconstitution* of structures
and agents' identities has been proposed as the alternative subject matter for social
archaeology (cf. Barrett 1994). However, it is the *recursive* activation of *internalised*
expectations/values/norms that is often the theme of interpretative narratives put
forward within this framework. Internalised expectations/values/norms inevitably
have to be treated as stable, because internalisation is achieved through *routinisation*, that is the recursive enactment of a certain set of practices. Although the
source of stability here is the 'dynamic' acts of individuals, what is illustrated is the
stable state of the reproduction of identities and structures, and the condition that
makes this possible. Furthermore, this approach tends to reduce diverse implications
of human acts to their recursiveness: unless they are recursively enacted, they are
not routinised/internalised, and hence, insignificant. What cannot be/has not been
explained with this approach is *why* particular types of acts are recursively enacted
and internalised in specific historical contexts and *why* they have to be internalised
in the first place.

It has to be noted that these issues all concern the 'problem of order': why and how
social order emerges and is maintained. This problem is the core subject of modern
social scientific investigations (e.g. Parsons 1951), and most of the theses concerning the issue have either bracketed the 'why' question or presuppose the *pre-existence*
of structural traits (ideology, social norms, etc.) which lead to the emergence and
maintenance of order. It is clear that the latter strategy results in a circular argument:
ideology/social norm mediates the formation and maintenance of an order, and the
maintenance of an order necessitates and leads to the formation of an ideology/social
norm. In short, stability and order are treated as if they are always there if society
works 'normally'. However, is that the case? Contemporary society is characterised
by a widespread sense of the collapse of the distinction between 'normal' and 'abnor-
mal'/'pathological'. Besides, as mentioned, it is the conviction of the pre-existence of
sociality that is currently in serious doubt. I wish to initiate the argument concerning
how to grasp sociality with the following question: how do stability and order emerge
in the first place?

3.3 Order and communication

I wish to build the following argument upon a basic fact: sociality emerges when two
or more individuals are co-present, i.e., share a locale. The first question has to be
how they can initiate their communication because communication is *the* basic unit

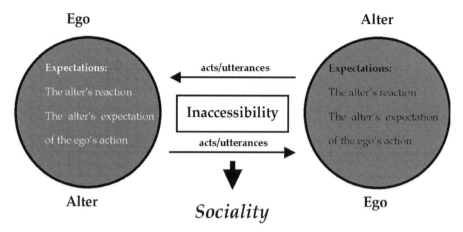

Figure 3.1 Communication and sociality.

of sociality or social order (Luhmann 1995, Chapter 4). It seems that a fundamental difficulty exists in initiating communication in the first place, that is, it is impossible to look inside the other's head: we human beings cannot directly observe what is going on inside others' minds. How on earth can we initiate communication? Here, we are bothered with the fact that we cannot possibly know what others are thinking when we are about to initiate communication. This puts us in a state of indeterminacy: in such a situation what we know is that we do not know what others are thinking and that others also do not know what we are thinking. That means that we cannot anticipate how the others will react to what we do/say, and that the others cannot anticipate how we will react to what they do/say: there is no source by which to decide what to do/say and how (Figure 3.1).

We normally have certain expectations as to how others will react when we act towards them in a certain way in the form of norms, customs, and so on, but without them, i.e., without actually knowing, or feeling we know, how others will react to our act, how can we start communicating?

If we understand the work of individual minds, or 'psychic systems', as *closed self-referential reproduction*, though, this problem, the so-called 'problem of order' in the social sciences in general, becomes a sort of non-issue.[1] An individual psychic system works and reproduces itself by reducing the complexity of its environment, constituted by internal organ systems, other psychic systems (constituting a part

---

[1] The argument which follows draws heavily upon the thoughts of the late German sociologist Niklas Luhmann. He devoted his social-theoretical endeavour to the development of a better way of understanding the relationship between human beings and the world in order to improve the way we reduce the complexity of the world. He left behind an enormous amount of work, which has just begun to be introduced to the Anglophone audience (e.g. Luhmann 1995). I will not attempt to produce an introductory volume to his theory for archaeologists. Instead, I will rethink the way we archaeologists think and write about the past in the present mediated by Luhmann's thought (for a comprehensive summary of his thought in general, see Luhmann 1995), and I will propose alternatives mediated by his theory.

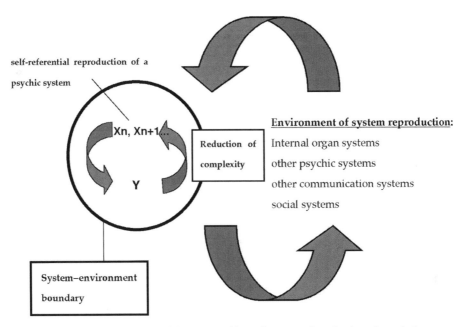

self-referential reproduction of a

psychic system

Xn, Xn+1...

Y

Reduction of
complexity

Environment of system reproduction:

Internal organ systems

other psychic systems

other communication systems

social systems

System–environment
boundary

Figure 3.2 An individual psychic system and its environment: the reduction of complexity.

of other individuals/persons), communication systems, social systems, and so on
(Figure 3.2). By the 'complexity of the environment (or, the world)' I mean that
there always exists in the environment more than two possible choices which can be
differentiated by an individual psychic system, one of which has to be chosen and
acted upon by the system.

The reduction of complexity in the form of making choices is conducted by utilising the boundary, that is by distinguishing between the psychic system itself and its
environment. By utilising the boundary, the psychic system distinguishes and selects
what does and does not matter to it. What is meant by 'closed reproduction' here is
this: by closing and bounding itself, a system opens itself to the environment, i.e., it
connects itself *in its own manner* to the environment by responding to *selected elements*
of the environment (Figure 3.2). The differentiation and selection of these elements
are conducted by drawing upon the psychic system's own internal structure, constituted through its past operations/experiences, and the internal structure of the
system can neither be directly observed from the outside nor can the environment
directly intervene. A system and its environment never merge together. In order for
a person to act socially, in that sense, the person/'ego' has to *guess* what is going on in
the 'alter's' head by observing the alter's act, and act by *predicting* how the alter will
react to it. The alter has to do the same in order to act. In other words, the very fact
that we cannot see what is going on inside the other's mind makes communication
inevitable, and, once initiated, communication has to continue; in order for the prediction to be verified or falsified, the ego has to act/utter something and see how the

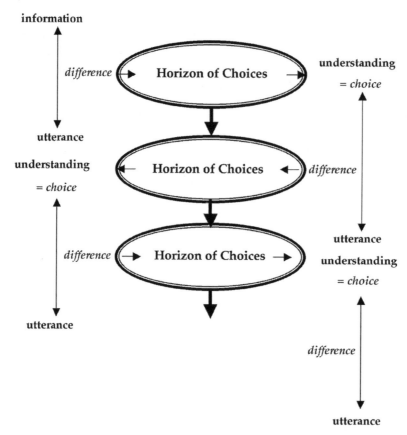

Figure 3.3 Communication as distinction/choice/selection: information, utterance and understanding.

alter reacts to it. Communication goes on in this way, and as long as communication goes on, sociality is generated and exists (Figure 3.1).

3.4 Communication and the subject

Next, we have to consider the nature of communication. We have recognised that without two or more self-referentially reproducing psychic systems there is no communication, hence, no sociality. The psychic systems involved in communication mutually guess what the alter is thinking, and make sense of and predict the alter's acts by way of reducing the complexity of the communication. Communication is constituted by information, utterance and understanding (Luhmann 1995, Chapter 4). The ego, when uttering, has to choose what information to utter and how to utter it. The alter has to choose how to make sense of the *difference between the utterance and the information* in order to understand the meaning of the utterance (Figure 3.3). If the difference between the utterance and the information were not recognised by the alter, communication would not continue; 'Is this a pot?', 'Yes it is', end of story.

The difference between the utterance and the information can be compared to the distinction between the description of the state of matter and the implications which the act of describing the matter can yield. Both of them generate a horizon of choices and necessitate their reduction, the former in the form of the selection of what to describe and how to describe it, and the latter in the form of how to make sense of what is uttered. However, it should be noted that without this distinction there is no complexity generating communication: in that case, the utterance ends up as the mere *description* of something and does not open up a horizon of choices/complexity. Without complexity, communication cannot continue because communication continues as a series of episodes of reducing complexity/making a choice out of a horizon of choices. In that sense, communication is the unity of distinction/choice/selection made by those who are involved in it (Figure 3.3).

It has to be emphasised here, again, that the ego can make sense of the alter's utterance and continue to communicate only in a self-referential manner: whether or not the ego has understood the difference between the information and the utterance can only be *guessed* by the reaction of the alter to the ego's reaction to the alter's utterance. It also has to be noted here that what one is thinking in one's head is often quite different from the way one reports it, and this discrepancy is often the very motivation for communication to continue. Even if the ego is annoyed with what the ego understands the alter to mean, the ego can conceal its annoyance and carry on conversing with the alter with a smile, for instance.

In that sense, importantly, no one involved in communication can control in a straightforward manner the way it continues, nor can one's thinking directly intervene/be connected to/control the way communication goes (Figure 3.3). Rather, communication itself constitutes, as psychic systems do, a closed, self-referentially reproduced system (Figure 3.4).

As mentioned above, communication cannot reproduce itself without the involvement of two or more persons/psychic systems, but the way communication reproduces itself and the way psychic systems reproduce themselves can never be merged. Even if two persons are deep in their own thoughts, they can still utter what they regard as relevant information in the communication, and the communication can continue. This means that communication cannot be reduced or attributed to the work of individual psychic systems. Communication *reproduces itself* in a self-referential manner as though being stimulated by the self-referential reproductions of two or more psychic systems (Figure 3.4).

This recognition questions the validity of treating the individual as the basic unit of social archaeological study (*contra* Meskell 1999, Chapter 1). We do not have to be too much troubled by the issue of whether we can understand the 'subject'/the mind of people in the present as well as in the past; as repeatedly emphasised, the individual subjects are self-referentially reproducing closed systems, and they can never *genuinely understand* each other. (And this is the case in the past as well as in the present.) Rather, it is more accurate to suggest that *they come to feel/come to believe through communication that they understand each other*. (This is the source of uncertainty/indeterminacy in communication. Problems and implications concerning this

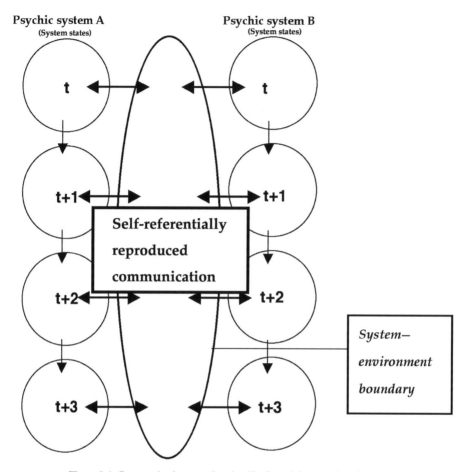

Figure 3.4 Communication as a closed, self-referentially reproduced system.

will be investigated and how to come to terms with them considered throughout this volume, particularly in Chapter 3.6 below and in Chapter 4.) In that sense, how communications reproduce themselves as being 'stimulated' by the acts/utterances of individual persons is more important than how individual subjects/psychic systems work, i.e., think (Figure 3.4).

3.5 Communication, boundary formation and expectations
In order for communication to reproduce itself, its elements have to collapse and be replaced with new ones as long as it continues. One's utterance has to stop in order for others to utter back and make what is going on into communication. Otherwise, what is going on is a *monologue*. In order for communication to reproduce itself, in that sense, it has to differentiate what are its elements from what are not; the new elements replacing the old have to be *selected* on the basis that they enable the communication to continue, otherwise the communication dies out (Figure 3.5).

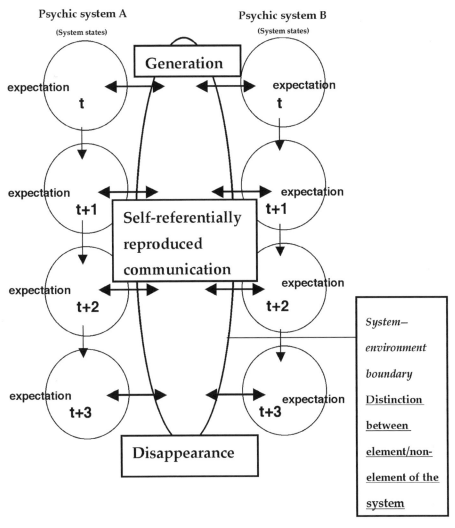

Figure 3.5 The continuation of communication and the reproduction of a system–environment boundary.

How this distinction is made is an important subject of investigation. If we understand communication as a closed, self-referentially reproducing system, this distinction would be grasped as being made by utilising a *system–environment boundary*. The closed self-referential reproduction of a communication system, in that sense, can be grasped as the ongoing process of reproducing the system–environment boundary. A communication system can be metaphorically compared to an island in an ocean of complexity: on the island, guarded by its boundary, the complexity of the ocean is reduced in a self-referentially constituted manner. Those who 'stimulate' the reproduction of a communication system, in return, are provided with reduced complexity in the form of certain expectations (Figure 3.5): anyone who takes part in the reproduction of a communication system comes to feel s/he can predict how the others who take part in the reproduction of that communication system will react to his/her act. This also means that s/he also comes to feel that the others will also predict how s/he will react to their act. This picture can be described thus: a communication system provides those who take part in, or stimulate the reproduction of, the system with the *precondition* for their social action. At the same time, their action provides the communication system with the precondition for the reproduction of the system (Figure 3.5). In that sense, it can be argued, again, that communication is the minimum unit of sociality.

Whether this distinction/system–environment boundary is connected to a certain symbol is also an important point for the generation and reproduction of sociality. In order for sociality to become sociality, it has to be reproduced across a certain time–space extension. In order for this to take place, a communication system has to be similarly reproduced across the same time–space extension. If the system–environment boundary of a communication system could be connected to a certain symbol, this would become possible; the presence of such a symbol as a *symbolic communication medium* would stimulate the communication system to be reinitiated wherever the symbol is present. We shall come back to the issue of how this connection, or generation of *symbolic communication media*, can be made possible later on.

3.6 Solving the uncertainty/indeterminacy of communication

As illustrated, communication can only be reproduced self-referentially. In other words, communication can continue only by drawing upon the *memory* of its past operation of making a distinction between what are and what are not its elements. This means that there is nothing outside a communication that helps those who are involved in the communication to make a distinction between what are and what are not the elements of the communication. In theory, those who are involved in the communication can only guess whether what they do (utter, act, and so on) is recognised by others as elements of the communication by monitoring the way that what they do is responded to by others. If the ego's act/utterance is responded to by the alter in the way the ego expects, the ego can assume that what s/he meant is received by the alter in the way the ego meant it, and can carry on with that communication. If s/he is responded to by the alter in a different way from what the ego expects, the ego has to assume that what the ego meant was not received by the alter in the way the ego meant it, and then has to consider how to act/utter things differently. In other words, it takes time to know whether what one utters enables communication to continue.

If we had to worry all the time about the above happening, the uncertainty/indeterminacy involved in the reproduction of sociality, i.e., the recurrent regeneration of communications, would be far too much. In other words, because the ego has to decide whether what the ego meant was correctly understood by the alter by observing how the alter reacted to the ego's act and made sense of it,

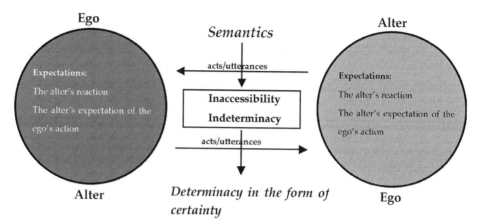

Figure 3.6 Communication, sociality and 'semantics'.

there always exists a *paradox* that it is only the ego that can decide if the communication is going well by referring to anything other than itself. This difficulty, the presence of too high an uncertainty, caused by the intrinsic paradox of communication, is solved/reduced/'de-paradoxised' by what Luhmann describes as 'semantics'. Semantics is a sort of repository of (a) the memories/knowledge of how communications were reproduced in the past and (b) such media as material items, gestures, and so on which are connected to the memories/knowledge that reduce the uncertainty in a certain way and enable those who are about to enter into a communication to anticipate how they are supposed to act (Figure 3.6).

Such a 'semantics' of communication, in other words, is the repository of ways to make distinctions between what are and what are not the elements of a given communication, and solves the uncertainty and indeterminacy of communication. Its nature and character are related to the mode with which communication systems are differentiated and interconnected. Luhmann recognises the following modes that exist in the history of the human being:

(a) In the social formation in which different communication systems are allocated different temporal components and *everyone* belonging to the society is involved in their reproduction, the semantics which ensure the reproduction of those communication systems would take the form of 'traditions'. Luhmann himself describes such a pattern of the differentiation of communication systems as 'segmentary differentiation'. In an archaeo-anthropological evolutionary framework, this can roughly be compared to the Band/Tribal social formation.

(b) In the social formation in which different communication systems are hierarchically organised, the semantics would take the form of 'religion' which verifies the distinction of what are and are not the elements of a communication according to who utters/does what: the hierarchical positionings of people, it was believed, were *predetermined* by god, and the king, the embodiment of the god's will, is regarded as always right in his/her utterances and deeds. In that sense, the god and the king are the ultimate referents for solving the uncertainty and indeterminacy of communication. Luhmann describes such a pattern of the differentiation of communication systems as 'hierarchical differentiation'. In an archaeo-anthropological framework, this can roughly be compared to the Chiefdom/pre-modern state social formation.

(c) In the social formation in which different communication systems are horizontally organised, the semantics would take the form of 'etiquettes', 'tastes', and so on that concern how individuals *ought to act* as individuals regardless of their hierarchical social affiliation. Luhmann describes such a pattern of the differentiation of communication systems as 'functional differentiation'. In an archaeo-anthropological framework, it can roughly be compared to the modern-state social formation and thereafter.

Archaeology, according to this schematic understanding, is the reproduction of a communication system in 'functional differentiation', i.e., the social formation called 'modernity'. This leads us to the inference that the problems and difficulties we archaeologists are confronted with in contemporary society, and that are the subjects of this volume's investigation, are derived from the way we make sense of, or have difficulty making sense of, functionally differentiated communication systems and from the difficulty in reproducing communications, archaeological or otherwise, in functional differentiation.

3.7 Transformation of communication systems and 'semantics'
If we summarise the above argument, social transformation can be grasped as the transformation of

(1) the way individual communication systems are constituted and reproduced,
(2) the way communication systems are differentiated and organised/configured,
(3) the way the reproduction of communication systems is made possible, or their uncertainty and indeterminacy solved, by 'semantics'.

Factor (1) can be observed in the form of a change in the range of the elements of individual communication systems and the way the elements are structured. Factor (2) can be observed in the form of a change in the number of communication systems constituting a society and the way they are related to one another, i.e., either hierarchically or horizontally. Factor (3) can be observed in the form of a transformation in patterns observed in individual communication systems, i.e., recurrent words/phrases, recurrent themes, recurrent gestures/acts, recurrent concepts, and so on.

In actuality, these factors are interconnected, and are experienced as the increasing likelihood of experiencing unfulfilled expectations in the way the communication goes. A change in the range of the elements of a communication system and a change in the way they are connected would make expectations of the way the communication goes, formed through previous experiences, increasingly unfulfilled. That would also be the case when the number of communication systems constituting a society increases and the way they are interconnected/organised spatio-temporally changes. These changes lead to the generation of a new set of semantics, helping the newly-differentiated communication systems reproduce and interconnect smoothly.

The above illustrates the sort of change which Luhmann points out happened during the period between the sixteenth and eighteenth centuries in Europe, and he contends that it marked the transition from hierarchical to functional differentiation. In this case, hierarchical differentiation roughly coincides with pre-modern social formations in which the distinction between what are and what are not the elements of a given communication system is made according to those who utter them. Accordingly, the semantics supporting such a distinction and reproduction of communication systems was related to the hierarchical order of the world and the religious doctrines/beliefs supporting the order. In such a social formation, what the king utters, as the embodiment of the god's will, is always regarded as right, and the uncertainty of communication is and can be solved by referring to the king's words and deeds. In functional differentiation, which roughly coincides with modern social formation, the semantics become non-hierarchical norms such as etiquettes, tastes, morality, and so on which enable individuals to take part and identify their positions/stances in communication systems which are horizontally and functionally differentiated. Hence, the reference to the hierarchical positioning of individuals and the hierarchical world view/order that often took the form of religious doctrines became redundant, and instead how individuals identified themselves in various communication systems became vital for dealing with the uncertainty of communication.

The disciplinisation of archaeology, an example of which we have already seen in the excavation method of General Pitt Rivers in Chapter 2, took place in many parts of the world sometime during the nineteenth century. That means it took place when the transition toward functional differentiation was already well under way. How can this event fit into the above picture? In preparation for investigating the issue, let me briefly illustrate a model of the relationship between functional differentiation and archaeology.

3.8 'Symbolic communication media' of modernity and archaeology

As mentioned, a society based upon functionally differentiated communication systems, i.e., a modern society, is constituted by horizontally differentiated communication systems, each of which reproduces itself in a self-referential manner. In other words, these systems cannot be reproduced by referring to a single, unifying structuring principle and allied factors such as social hierarchy and the religion/cosmology supporting it. Instead, they reproduce themselves by referring only to themselves, i.e., how they were reproduced before. Through such self-referential reproduction, individual communication systems develop distinct *binary codes of distinction* by which what are and are not the elements of a given system are distinguished.

For instance, the economic communication system reproduces itself by the distinction between payment and non-payment; the political communication system by the distinction between being in power and not being in power; the scientific communication system by the distinction between truth and fallacy; the religious communication system by the distinction between moral and immoral; and the education communication system by the distinction between what is good or bad for one's development/career. Each of these binary codes is connected to a symbolic communication medium, for instance the economic code may be connected to money: when money is present, the communication to be articulated is bound to be about payment or non-payment.

How does archaeology fit into the picture? In considering the position of archaeology in functional differentiation, referring to the foregoing, one thing seems to me of particular importance: that is, a parallelism between the nature of the symbolic communication media of functional differentiation/modernity and that of the archaeological material. Saying this might be confusing initially, but it seems there is something *homologous* between, for instance, the way money as a symbolic communication medium functions as money and the way archaeological material functions as archaeological material. In order to fully understand the homology between money and archaeological material, we have to embark on a rather lengthy process of exploring the function and its mechanism of symbolic communication media.

Working as the medium of a communication means that it is perceived to signify something, a 'distinction' in our framework, in the communication. Signification, in that sense, as illustrated in Chapter 3.4, characteristically opens up two *horizons of choice*: the signification of something by a medium leads one to two domains of choices: (1) choosing one referent from a range of equivalents; and (2) choosing how to react to the signification, i.e., how to act upon the choice which he or she has made about it. Communication goes on as a process consisting of the recurrent sequence of the emergence/articulation of such horizons and certain choices made about them.

The symbolic communication media of functional differentiation direct people to making certain choices and enable communication systems to reproduce smoothly across time and space. In other words, in order for money to function that way, those who live in the domain within which it functions, i.e., is circulated as a currency, have to be *homogeneous*. Let me explain. Those who are mediated in their social communication, in this case, transaction by a currency, have to be directed to a certain horizon of choices, the horizon of choices consisting of the payment and the non-payment. In other words, they have to be able to believe that they share a certain horizon of choices and a tendency to make a certain choice in it, i.e., payment. Homogeneity here means that people are homogeneous in sharing/believing they share a set of expectations concerning the communication reproduced through the mediation of a currency: they are homogeneous in that they can predict the ways in which the others sharing the domain react to them in the transaction mediated by the currency regardless of their backgrounds, i.e., group affiliations (including 'class affiliation'), the regions they live in, the religion they practise, and so on. It can be deduced from this that the people whose communication is mediated by a currency are made to identify themselves not with their directly shared, hence concrete and localised, experience but with something *abstract* and *universal*. By 'universal' in this case I mean that *something* is perceived, within a certain spatio-temporal domain, to

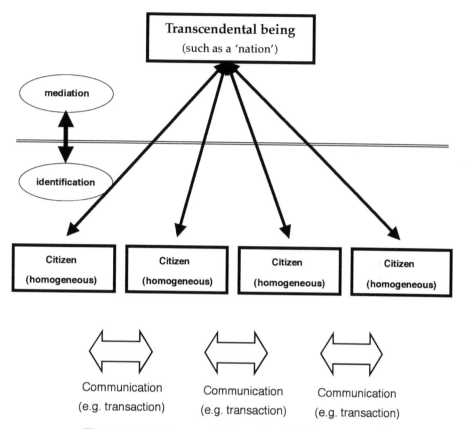

Figure 3.7 Symbolic communication media and the 'transcendental'.

guarantee that a system of signifiers signifies a system of referents. In this contemporary world, i.e., modernity/functional differentiation, a nation-state constitutes the basic unit which functions as such a domain, and a conceptual construct with the potential to gravitate all sorts of meanings and memories called a 'nation' functions as that 'something', something abstract and universal, i.e., the *transcendental* (Figure 3.7).

Within the domain of a nation-state, people are disembedded from their localised existential base and are made into homogeneous and abstract entities called 'citizens', as mentioned in Chapter 2 above. In that sense, what makes money work as money is the coupling of the disembedding of the individual person from the localised existential base and the re-embedding of the individual person in abstract constructs such as the nation, and it has been pointed out that this took place in the formation process of modern nation-states, as illustrated in Chapter 2.2 (cf. Anderson 1991). In other words, the mutual, i.e., circular, mediation between symbolic communication media and the homogenisation of the people constituting a society was mediated by the existence of the nation-state.

The nation-state and its symbolic communication media such as money mutually mediate their own existence. The latter mediate the communication between citizens in a manner which is totally irrelevant to their localised base of self identification. What is particularly important here is that this does not mean that the *selves* of all the citizens are made homogeneous; on the contrary, the existence of these symbolic communication media allows every citizen to be different from one another; they are relieved from communal constraints to be the same. That means that all the *selves* constituting a nation-state have to be *made* to feel able to communicate with one another in spite of their mutually predicted differences, and in order for that to be achieved the citizens have to be made to assume/imagine that they all share a set of values, norms, and so on that do not derive from shared and accumulated, hence concrete, *local* knowledge and experiences but come out of something felt to be more deep-rooted, abstract, and, most important of all, *delocalised* within the domain of the nation-state. In other words, a nation-state needs a *transcendental* entity with which its citizens can *identify* themselves. A transcendental entity is needed to make the citizens, despite their predictable differences rather than similarities, believe that they can understand one another anytime anywhere within the domain of the nation-state to a degree which cannot be achieved with citizens belonging to other nation-states.

Now we can start looking into the homologous parallelism and interdependence between the nation-state, symbolic communication media, and archaeological material. Let me begin by reiterating the following: in order for the transcendental to be genuinely transcendental, it has to be abstract, i.e., it has to be *delocalized* and *detemporalised*. It has to be stable and remain unchanged in any circumstances in order for it to fulfil the functional requirement illustrated above. The ultimate form of such transcendental entities, in that sense, is 'nothingness': only the non-existent entity, itself a contradiction of the concept, is totally and completely free from any contextuality/value commitment. However, no such entity exists, nor can it exist; transcendental entities can function as communication media because of their *existence* as media, i.e., their existence as something to mediate something, which inevitably makes them localised and temporalised to a degree.

There are two strategies to overcome the trouble. One is to bring such entities ever closer to 'nothingness' (Figure 3.8). Another is to make them appear *unfixable* to any spatio-temporal position. A good example of such strategies at work would be the Japanese imperial family.[2] (This analogy will later come to have concrete implications for the argument of this volume.) It exists, but it does not fulfil any explicitly meaningful function, nor is the meaning of the existence explicitly explained. It is formally defined in the constitution as the 'symbol of the integration of the nation', and its members engage in various public ceremonies. However, it does not do, and avoids being engaged in, or avoids being publicly seen/perceived to be engaged in, anything which is directly linked to the life and interests of the citizens of Japan (e.g. Ruoff 2001). Its members do not have a family register, i.e., they are legally *no*

---

[2] Cf. the home page of the imperial household agency www.kunaicho.go.jp/eindex.html.

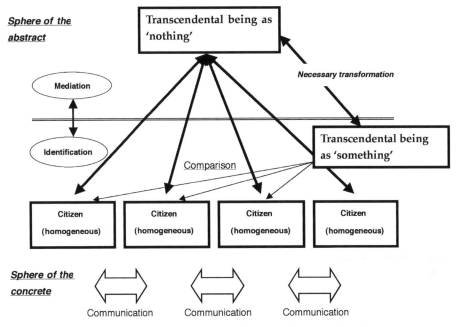

Figure 3.8 The nation-state, the citizen and the transcendental.

one. Their genealogy is believed to go back to the beginning of *history*, shrouded in the mists of time (Ruoff 2001). They are there to be known to be there, but no one knows nor can describe who exactly they are or what they are for. They, like a vacuum which has to be filled by 'floating signifiers', accumulate meanings and memories of every possible sort. It has to be hastily added, however, that the imperial family's functioning as a symbolic vacuum does not mean that their existence is unrelated to the generation/execution of power and dominance in Japan as a nation-state. On the contrary, their existence and their ontological status in the Japanese psyche generated and is still generating power in the form of structuring the psyche, and hence disposition, of the Japanese and their behaviour (e.g. Sakai 1996, Chapter 5). We shall come back to this point in the next chapter.

There are certain structural parallels between archaeological material and such transcendental entities, and that makes archaeological discourse an ideal locus where such transcendental entities reside. The primary subjects of archaeological investigation are artefacts and features which have been buried. They fix their identity spatio-temporally in the form of being attributed to certain strata, and they are meaningless archaeologically unless they are fixed to certain chrono-cultural positions. At the same time, they cannot be linked directly to anything in the contemporary world. They are archaeological material because they have been left behind, i.e., disconnected with agency, and cannot be attributed to any concrete, directly observable, human action. They can only be attributed to concrete human actions through mediation, i.e., theoretico-methodological mediation, which takes place in the contemporary world. Besides, the identification of the chrono-cultural positions of archaeological material itself inevitably has to be through a theory/method-laden mediation process in the present, because it is well recognised that the identification of the boundaries of a stratum, for instance, is influenced by the way the observer make sense of the stratum's position in a wider context and that understanding is constituted by the observer's theoretico-methodological position taking in the contemporary topography of archaeological method and theory (Hodder 1999, Chapter 5). This means that every possible archaeological communication is about that which is temporalised and localised as deposits and at the same time about that which is decontextualised through mediation in the contemporary world. And this coupling of *contextualisedness and decontextualisedness in one entity* nicely coincides with what is required for the transcendental guarantee of the internal homogeneity of nation-states.

In that sense, archaeology constitutes an ideal imaginary locus where the transcendental is imagined to reside. And, in that sense, for instance, it is natural that the coupling of archaeology and the Japanese imperial family, embodied by the study of reconstructing the genealogy of the ancient paramount chiefs, the supposed predecessors of the present emperor, by studying the gigantic keyhole-shaped tumuli, one of the most intensely studied topics in Japanese archaeology, tacitly but significantly contributes to the maintenance of the sense of the internal homogeneity of the nation-state of Japan, as will be fully illustrated in Chapter 4.4. To put it differently, the archaeological communication system of the Japanese emperor system and its roots provides other communication systems with the feeling that their reproduction, going on in a self-referential manner in actuality and in that sense having nothing outside to guarantee their truth/existence, is guarded and guaranteed by a shared, homogeneous set of values, norms, and so on: i.e., a shared identity, which is most often described as a 'nation'. In that sense, archaeological material functions as a symbolic communication medium, like money, in the form of distinguishing between what is and what is not relevant to the identification of the Japanese and, hence, distinguishing what is and what is not good for the identification of the Japanese.

A considerable portion of this volume's investigation and argumentation is to be devoted to the analytical, 'thick' description of the working of this fateful coupling of modernity, the nation-state and archaeology, and the functioning of archaeological material as a symbolic communication medium, by looking into the case of Japan.

Before concluding this chapter, though, we have to pose a question: what can we do about this fateful coupling?

3.9 Communication, modernity, and the positionality of archaeology
Can we ever overcome the fateful coupling of modernity, the nation-state and archaeology, which constitutes the *positionality* of archaeology, and which has continued to generate hostility and division between what are imagined or desired to be internally homogeneous, such as 'nations', 'ethnic groups', 'cultural groups', or whatever? The answer would have to be 'no' as long as we continue to live in the social formation which is described as functional differentiation/modern, which is based upon a drive

to homogenise people and things within a domain of shared interests and a drive to differentiate those who do not or are perceived not to share them. Both endless homogenisation and endless differentiation need the transcendental as the ultimate guarantors of their continuation. It is very difficult, in actuality, to detach archaeology from the desire to seek the transcendental, because it is the positionality of archaeology, which is identical to that of the symbolic communication media of functional differentiation/modernity, which enables archaeology to exist as such.

Furthermore, the tendency that this positionality implies, i.e., its functioning as a generator of a symbolic communication medium, mediating communication and homogenising those who are involved in it, is being enhanced as functional differentiation is reaching the point where imagining the transcendental, which ultimately mediates the reproduction of horizontally juxtaposed communication systems, is increasingly difficult. In systemic response to this, dangerously exaggerated views enhancing the transcendental quality of the archaeological narrative, as well as that of other narrative fields, are increasingly common. (We will come back to this issue in Chapter 5.)

However, despite the difficulties, and despite recognising them, we have to start somewhere. We can at least seek a better way to understand the positionality of archaeology, i.e., the nature and underlying logic of the coupling between modernity, the nation-state and archaeology. If we were able to do anything about it, we would have to start there, and, seeking a better way to understand it, by drawing upon the above-illustrated theoretical framework, is the ultimate theme of this volume.

4

Nation-state, circularity and paradox

4.1 Introduction

As mentioned above, the connection between nationalism and archaeology is now well recognised (e.g. Hodder, ed. 1991, Diaz-Andreu and Champion 1996, Kohl and Fawcett 1996). Innumerable papers have been written describing the ways in which particular elements of nationalism and archaeology are connected. It has also been pointed out that individual nation-states functioned, and still function, as the boundary-markers of the contexts in which specific connections between modern institutions and archaeology were, and are, constituted and reproduced. However, the *mechanism* and *process* at work behind the seemingly organic interdependence between nationalism, modernity and archaeology do not appear to be fully investigated. For instance, why was archaeology mobilised particularly intensively in the constitution of national identity? The question has often been answered by referring to the artificiality, or constructedness, of the modern nation-state and its necessary masking/naturalisation, and it has been claimed that archaeology and archaeological narratives have been mobilised to naturalise/mask it (e.g. Sorensen 1996). However, the question still remains: why archaeology? Why has archaeology been mobilised to fulfil that function in such an intensive manner?

I proposed a tentative answer to this question in Chapter 3 by arguing that archaeological material suits the function of a *symbolic communication medium* which, being connected to *transcendental* concepts and beings such as primordial ethno-national identities and, in the case of Japan, the emperor and his genealogical longevity (cf. Smith 1986, 2001, 51–57), helps to reproduce communication systems necessary for the maintenance of a modern nation-state across time and space within the boundary of that nation-state. What follows will examine the validity of that thesis and also investigate the actual processes through which archaeological material comes to function as a symbolic communication medium. This work, meanwhile, will also be a process of investigating the *positionality* of archaeology as a communication system in *classical* modernity/functional differentiation.[1] By 'the positionality of archaeology' I mean which communication system(s) constituting modern society is/are coupled with (mutually influence) the archaeological communication system particularly deeply and in what manner?

I will conduct the work by using the history of Japanese archaeology and Japan as a modern nation-state as the subject of three case studies. Modernisation and the

---

[1] See the definition of this concept and its difference from late-/high-/post-modernity in Chapter 2.3.

formation of the modern nation-state, as touched upon in Chapter 2 above, took place as a highly integrated process in Japan (Nishikawa 1995), and archaeology played a significant role (cf. Teshigawara 1995, 33–120; Oguma 1995, 73–86). The process was accelerated by pressure from the outside, mainly from western colonial powers, and led Japan to become the only country in the region of East Asia not only spared colonisation but also to colonise neighbouring countries/areas, namely Korea and Taiwan (Oguma 1995). In all, Japan experienced not only modernisation and the formation of a nation-state but also colonialism almost as a single, unified process. As a result, the inevitable artificiality surrounding the nation-state, which was illustrated in Chapter 2, was exposed in a highly tangible manner and yet concealed in a sophisticated way at the same time. That makes Japan a particularly intriguing and suitable arena in which to investigate and interpret, by fully utilising the theoretical package illustrated in Chapter 3, the nature and character of the interdependence between *classical* modernity and archaeology.

The history of Japanese archaeology also offers us an interesting case of the connection between modernity, various fields of self identification and archaeology. As illustrated below, the national identity of Japan and the *boundary* of the Japanese, i.e., how the Japanese should be defined, or who was and who was not Japanese, were constituted in two semi-autonomous but mutually influencing spheres (e.g. Oguma 1995, Komori 2001). One was reproduced through colonial expansion to neighbouring countries and the other was reproduced through the negotiation of the position of Japan as a newly founded nation-state with the west (e.g. Oguma 1995; Kan 2001; Komori 2001). The coexistence of these two spheres in the discourse of the national identity of Japan and the boundary of the Japanese had a significant effect upon the way Japanese pre-Second World War archaeology operated and upon the way it functioned as a communication system tightly interconnected with the constitution of the identity of the Japanese.

After Japan's catastrophic defeat in the Second World War in 1945, the former sphere virtually disappeared, and the arena of the reproduction of national identity and the identity of the Japanese became pretty much confined to the sphere of the negotiation of identity with the west, in which the United States played a crucial role not only as the most influential politico-economic force in the western block but also as the axis along which the dividing line in the *shared* realm of perception between right and left, progressive and conservative, and so on, was drawn. In other words, Japan and its psyche were firmly and strategically embedded in the Cold War equilibrium.

This unique socio-political/economic landscape of self identification basically continued to exist until the end of the Cold War era, when the relatively stable structure of the post-Second World War socio-political/economic landscape in which Japan had been firmly situated since 1945 collapsed and not only national self identification but also the self identification of individual citizens came to face increasing difficulty (cf. Osawa 1998). This last change, which we will investigate in Chapter 5, is also deeply related to the intensification of the constitutive characteristics of modernity/functional differentiation, which is commonly described as the coming of the high- or late- or post-modern (Osawa 1998).

The above-mentioned events and factors also make Japan particularly suitable to investigate the issue, 'why archaeology?'; the situation surrounding Japan as a nation-state has been through drastic changes over a relatively short period of time, and the changes went hand-in-hand with changes in the way archaeological narratives are articulated and mobilised. However, it will be suggested that there exists an unchanged 'core', in other words 'structuring principles', which function to differentiate what is *suitable/appropriate* from what is *unsuitable/inappropriate* for the reproduction of archaeological discourse.[2] By revealing the unchanged structuring principles underpinning changing archaeological narratives (it will be suggested that they are deeply related to the emperor system), it is hoped that we can reveal what makes archaeology particularly relevant to the formation of modernity and the nation-state.

What follows, consisting of three case studies, will tackle the above-mentioned issues from three different angles. We shall begin by tracing the history of Japanese archaeology from the foundation of the modern Japanese nation-state (AD 1868) to the 1970s by focusing on the *co-transformation* of the basic structure of the archaeological discourse/communication system and the way that national identity and the identity of the Japanese are constituted. How the *paradox* and *artificiality* (see Chapters 2 and 3, 3 in particular) of the nation-state of Japan were de-paradoxised through the mediation of the archaeological past, by way of 'finding' unique 'ethnic characters' in the past, will be given particular attention; and the shadow cast by, and the crucial function fulfilled by, the emperor system will be examined. As briefly touched upon in Chapter 3.8, the emperor is an example of the 'transcendental', universally mobilised in the process of the foundation of the nation-state.

The second case study concerns the visual representation of the past: an analysis of a textbook drawing. Representation, here, does not simply mean the depiction of a scene which might have been seen in the past. Rather, it means the creation of a *space* where a specific horizon of choices is visually differentiated, and different, competing ways to make certain choices are articulated. In other words, representation opens up a space in which the hegemony is fought over the way a symbolic communication medium functions. By referring to or being helped by a symbolic communication medium, as mentioned, people make distinctions in a certain manner between what are and are not the elements of a communication system, whereby the communication system is reproduced smoothly and with a certain directionality across time/space barriers. Hegemony, in this case, is sought over the control of the *expectations* which people have when they enter the communication system. This means that representation is also about hegemony over the way people identify themselves, because what expectation one has of others when initiating communication

---

[2] The existence of such stable structuring principles is itself a symptomatic characteristic of *classical* modernity (see Chapter 2).

is his or her identity itself. School textbook drawings, in that sense, are spaces for struggle over the hegemony of the identity of children, or, to be more specific, the identity of the (future) citizens of a nation.

The study will reveal that the ideal model of a nation-state adopted in the construction process of the modern nation-state of Japan, in which the emperor system played a key role, constitutes the axis of dispute/distinction in the drawing and officially ordered redrawing of the picture, despite the fact that the model is supposed to have been denounced and discarded as the fundamental source of the catastrophe which Japan experienced in the process toward and during the Second World War. It will be argued that symbolic images of the ethnie are repeatedly evoked whenever the legitimacy and continuation of the nation-state becomes an issue, and the images tend to copy the image of the ideal society which was constructed at the time of the foundation of the nation-state, at the time of the Meiji restoration.

The third case study concerns the dominant trend in the approach to the beginning of the Kofun (mounded tomb) period (c. third to sixth century AD), which is characterised by gigantic keyhole-shaped tumuli, a number of which are designated as 'imperial mausolea' (Figure 4.1) (cf. Mizoguchi 2002, Chapter 2, esp. 40–42). One of the dominant approaches to the study of the period is to trace the sequential order of the keyhole-shaped tumuli of a regional unit in order to reconstruct the regional chiefly genealogy. The approach presupposes a number of things, one of which, of importance for the argument in this volume, is that the system of unilinear male-line descent was already established at the beginning of the Kofun period, when keyhole-shaped tumuli sequences began to be formed in many regional units of the western half and parts of the eastern half of the archipelago (e.g. Kobayashi 1961, Chapter 4). However, the outcomes of recent osteoarchaeological analyses and related reanalyses of the mortuary practices of the period prior to the beginning of the Kofun period, i.e., the Late Yayoi period, have revealed that neither the system of unilinear male-line inheritance had been established nor had the position of the chiefly household of a given regional unit been consolidated. This strongly suggests that the status of the predecessor of the imperial household had not been established/consolidated when the formation of the sequential construction of large keyhole-shaped tumuli began in the present-day Nara prefecture, central Honshu island.

Other types of archaeological information also suggest that the centralisation of power and authority had not yet been achieved at the beginning of the period and remained thus until the beginning of the later part of the period. However, the main trend of the study of the Kofun period appears to take it for granted that the beginning of the period marked the establishment of the system of unilinear male-line descent/inheritance and the centralisation of power and authority possessed by those who were buried in the earlier examples of the largest keyhole-shaped tumuli of the present-day Nara prefecture. It tries to interpret the available data, which quite often do not fit the above-mentioned presumptions, in the illustrated way. My contention will be that here again is the shadow of the emperor system and its positionality in contemporary Japan: the presence of the emperor and the imperial family as

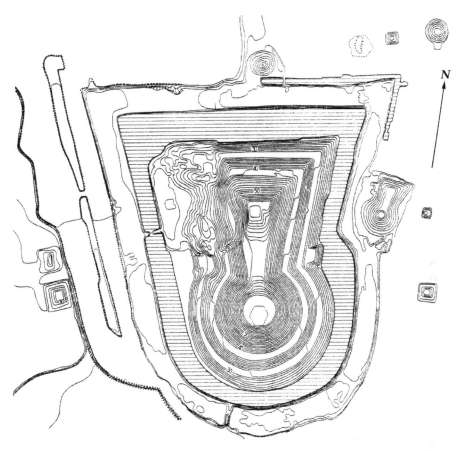

Figure 4.1 The 'mausoleum' of Emperor Ojin (length: c. 415 metres, diameter of the round part: c. 256 metres. Width of the end of the rectangular part: c. 330 metres. The second largest tumulus in the archipelago in length. Modified from Fuji et al. 1964).

the 'symbol of the integration of the nation', and, more importantly, the symbol and embodiment of the continuous existence of the Japanese ethnie (Smith 1986; Okubo, et al. 2005, 5–6), has constituted the axis along which archaeologists' approaches to the period are determined, regardless of whether consciously or unconsciously and regardless of whether archaeologists are for or against the emperor system. In that sense, the emperor system functions as a symbolic medium which helps to initiate and reproduce communication concerning the Kofun period, and one of the determinant traits of this symbolic medium is the mythology of the continuation of the imperial household, the mythology of the uninterrupted, unilineal genealogy since the beginning of its history, *the* history, the history of Japan. At the same time, archaeology functions to reproduce communication concerning the emperor system and its uninterrupted unilinear genealogy since the beginning of the Kofun period. This is a typical example of the circularity surrounding the nation-state and the ethnie.

The Japanese experience up to the end of the Cold War era, examined through the three case studies, mirrors the difficulties which the individual, stimulating the reproduction of the function-differentiated communication systems of modernity, was faced with. The case studies will illustrate the particular semantics and symbolic communication media generated to solve the problem of indeterminacy in function-differentiated communication systems and that of the artificiality and paradox of the modern nation-state as a spatio-temporal unit mediating their reproduction as theoretically deduced in Chapter 3.

4.2 Unbearable artificiality of being: the state and the emperor system

Archaeology and the self-imagining of a nation

Edward Sylvester Morse, an American zoologist who taught biology at the Faculty of Science, University of Tokyo between 1877 and 1879, is widely regarded as the founding father of modern Japanese archaeology (parts of the following arguments in this section are from Mizoguchi 2005a). His excavation of the Omori shell-middens on the outskirts of Tokyo and the publication of the findings in the form of a volume entitled Shell Mounds of Omori (*Memoirs of the Science Department, Vol. 1, Part 1*) are highly praised today as the work of a Darwinian evolutionary theory influenced, and hence at the time a most progressive, modern scientific mind (Kondo and Sahara 1983, 185–188; Teshigawara 1995, 33–35).

Meanwhile, it has been pointed out that Morse's academic legacy was not properly inherited (Kondo and Sahara 1983, 211–214). The seeming abruptness and deliberateness of the 'cut-off' are often emphasised. For instance, Shogoro Tsuboi, the first professor of the Department of Anthropology in the Faculty of Science of the University of Tokyo (founded in 1893), and a founding father of Japanese modern archaeology, is recorded to have actively denied not only influence from but also contact with Morse on numerous occasions, despite the fact that Tsuboi himself recorded that he contacted Morse for the identification of pot sherds he had collected (Teshigawara 1995, 39–40). It has been speculated that resentment of the outside influence, in this case one from a colonial power, was the cause (e.g. Oguma 1995, 30). In fact, though, a very particular part of his legacy was inherited; that is, his interest in the first inhabitants of the archipelago (Kondo and Sahara 1983, 136–153). The issue of the origin(s) of the 'Japanese' was the subject of a heated debate which characterised the early history of Japanese archaeology.

The issue of the origin of a nation, or a race which constitutes the foundation of the nation, surfaces and comes to be pursued as an issue of self identification almost whenever the condition surrounding a nation-state is problematised, and the background against which it takes place has already been explicated theoretically in Chapter 3. The history of Japan from the Meiji restoration (AD 1868) up to the end of the Second World War can be written as the continuous reproblematisation of the national identity and the boundary of the Japanese as a category of people. The two above-mentioned spheres of self identification: (a) self identification through colonial expansion and (b) self identification through negotiation with the west, coexisted as their proportional significance continuously changed in relation to one another, and those spheres were integrated in the realm of perception through the mediation of a conceptual construct, viz. the notion of *Koku* (nation/state)-*tai* (body), the 'national body'.

As illustrated in Chapter 1, the formation of a 'nation' is an important condition for a nation-state to establish the institutions which inevitably 'disembed' people and transform/reorganise them into *citizens*. Anthony Giddens defines the concept of disembedding thus: the 'lifting out' of social relations from local contexts of inter-action and their restructuring across indefinite spans of time–space (1990, 21). With the purpose of adjusting it to the argument which follows, by 'disembedding' I mean the uprooting of a behavioural norm and set of expectations for everyday life that were formerly embedded in the local knowledge which was formed and reproduced through the *direct, recurrent sharing* of experiences. In order to enable those who are uprooted to live in a proper way, or *function*, in a systemic whole called a nation-state, whose domain far exceeds that of immediate, day-to-day experience, an imag-inary communal unit such as a nation, based upon an imagined/articulated 'ethnie' (Smith 1986), whose spatial extension is perceived to coincide with the domain of a nation-state, has to be created in order to re-embed them in an imaginary sphere of shared/for sharing everyday experiences, and to enable them to imagine and believe that they are organically connected to one another despite the distance lying between them, and to make them 'feel secure' again, i.e., feel they know how to behave in virtually any kind of context as long as it is either situated in the domain of the nation-state or occupied by those who belong to that nation.

The 'national body' of the nation-state of Japan was a unique variant of the con-cept of the nation. Citizenship, a prerequisite for the establishment of a nation-state, had to be established very quickly in Japan as the new nation-state had to be hastily created to counter pressure from western colonial powers, which had already colonised China (in the 1840s) and India (in the 1850s). However, it was a daunting task. In the case of the European nation-states, the establishment of citizenship had been a long, slow-moving process which began during the era of absolute monar-chy. The precursors of modern institutions, such as a standing army and taxation, gradually disembedded people from the conceptual as well as the physical land-scape formed through their local, everyday, and predominantly agrarian experiences (e.g. Foucault 1977). The working of these institutions also prepared people for their re-embedment in the artificial conceptual landscape of the nation-state. In the case of Japan, however, the feudal system had to be transformed to a nation-state in a very short period. As touched upon above, the process was engineered to be short by introducing the constitutive elements of modernity as a *module* from the then advanced modern nation-states of Europe and the United States (Nishikawa 1995, 25–30). However, the transformation of the way the people perceived their life–world and lived in and constituted it was a tough undertaking. The necessary institutional/material base upon which the people were transformed into citizens could be founded in a relatively short period of time as long as sufficient invest-ment was possible. In fact, the improvement of the means of transportation in the form of the foundation of the railway (from 1872 on, only four years after the Meiji restoration), the introduction of the Gregorian calendar (1873) and the foundation of national holidays, the foundation of compulsory education/schooling (1873) and so on, were quickly accomplished, and they contributed to the homogenisation of space, time, and the body within the domain of the state of Japan (Nishikawa 1995, 31–38). However, they had to be complemented by the technology of systematically and rapidly homogenising the mentality/psyche of the people inhabiting the domain. The concept of the 'national body' was invented for this purpose.

Let us begin by distinguishing the distinct characteristics of the 'national body' from other variants of the 'nation'. As a conceptual unit, the 'national body' was embodied by the emperor. The status of the emperor in the newly founded constitution (the so-called 'Meiji constitution') was defined and constrained by the constitution, but in fact it was that of an absolute sovereign: the emperor had the right and obligation to make the final decision on every matter concerning the running of the country. The executive, the parliament, the judiciary, and the military were entrusted not to the people but to the emperor.[3] The people were assured by the emperor of the proper running of the country and in return had to be ever thankful, to respect, and obey the emperor. Here, again, we can recognise the working of the *paradox* and *circularity* characterising modernity in general and the nation-state in particular, mentioned in Chapter 1: the embodiment of state power embodied power based upon respect and voluntary obedience by the nation; and the nation respected and voluntarily obeyed this embodiment of state power because without him no one could embody state power and run the nation. The paradox had to be *de-paradoxised*, and a device for the de-paradoxisation had to be invented.

Those who were incorporated in the 'national body' were made to perceive themselves as directly related/connected to the emperor. The relationship was often portrayed as that of father and child. The disembedding of people from the localised values/norms and the de-paradoxisation of the paradox of the relationship between the emperor and the subject were achieved in one go by the creation of this imaginary *personal* relationship/fictive kinship: the people became disembedded, hence independent individuals *voluntarily* fulfilled their responsibility to the country through becoming individual 'children' of the emperor, rather than through becoming autonomous citizens. At the same time, situating the emperor in the position of father of the nation made the circular, symmetrical relationship between the emperor and the nation asymmetrical and solved the problem of circularity and paradox. In other words, the individual was re-embedded in this imagined community, portrayed as functioning as a *body*, in which they were *organically united* as children of the great father. This was indeed a smart conceptual machine which disembedded people from the conceptual landscape of small local agrarian communities and at the same

---

[3] There is an ongoing debate concerning the character of the power and authority provided by the Meiji constitution to the emperor and that actually executed by the emperor. A significant issue is the relationship between the emperor and the executive, the emperor and his ministers to be exact. Whether it was his ministers who executed absolute power by posing to help the emperor to execute his will or whether it was the emperor who executed absolute power and overturned the decisions made by the ministers at will is the most significant consideration. However, it is generally agreed that the emperor was *regarded* as having the 'final say' in every matter concerning the running of the state (e.g. Yasuda 1998).

time re-embedded them in a state and integrated them as a nation without going through the process of making them citizens.

At the same time, the 'national body' had to be an entity with a certain spatio-temporal extension and boundary, and for that it needed be defined and visualised/materialised by the differentiation and articulation of what could and could not be incorporated into the 'national *body*'. The image and the positionality of the emperor and imperial family, and the spatio-temporal boundaries of the 'national body'; i.e., the national boundary and the origin of the imperial genealogy became the basic conceptual constructs which functioned as the main constitutive elements of the 'national body', as the perfectly preserved, pure ethnie from the beginning of its origin.

As mentioned, a significant characteristic of this concept is that it was a purely conceptual construct. The concept of the nation has elements of artificiality. However, as Anthony Smith suggests (1986), nations were commonly constructed through the mobilisation of pre-existing, actualistic similarities and differences, and Anderson suggests that these similarities and differences needed to be differentiated, or made tangible, in one way or another, and articulated into 'ethnies' or 'traditions'. In contrast, the discourse of the 'national body', perhaps ironically, could not totally rely on the traditional 'Japanese' way of life, because *westernisation* was the policy of the then government. Accordingly, the introduction of the items of 'Western Civilisation' was regarded as more important than the articulation of uniquely Japanese traditions (Komori 2001). Because of that, the 'national body' was articulated by relying heavily upon image and the historical positionality of the emperor and the imperial family rather than upon the traditional way of life and other traits of the ethnie. Accordingly, the basis/foundation of the concept, inevitably, could only be found in artificial discursive formation, not in the realm of concrete experiences by the nation, and the intrinsic artificiality of the concept of the national body, deriving from this fact, necessitated the invention of a range of devices for the concealment of its artificiality: academic discourses were heavily mobilised for that purpose, and at the same time they were strictly regulated so as not to cast doubt on its authenticity.

Archaeology was mobilised particularly intensely to support the above-mentioned two main constitutive elements of the 'national body': (a) the image and the positionality of the emperor, and (b) the spatio-temporal boundaries of the 'national body'.

The image and the positionality of the emperor
These were the most important and most vulnerable of the constitutive elements of the 'national body'; the imperial household under the Edo feudal regime was an obscure entity to commoners: it has been revealed that the image of the emperor was often connected to deities of local folkloric religions and was not at all perceived as representative of the nation (cf. Fujitani 1994). Social formation under the Edo feudal regime comprised a typical hierarchical differentiation (Fujitani 1994, 9–11). Society was vertically divided into clearly marked hierarchical status-classes and horizontally divided into feudal domains. Rather than homogeneity throughout

Edward Morse

the domain under the control of the Tokugawa feudal clan, differences and controlled discommunication between the status-classes and between feudal domains were mobilised for the maintenance of the stability of society. Political authority and capital were monopolised by the feudal clans and warrior class, and the integration of the systems of the society did not rely upon the acceptance by the majority of a symbolic norm and order (Fujitani 1994, 10–11). In all, the social formation of the Edo feudal regime was one which was not easily transformed to that of a modern nation-state; it was not only hierarchically differentiated but also lacked a symbolic entity which could be mobilised for the construction of a sense of unity and homogeneity. Hence, the image of the emperor and his positionality as the representative/embodiment of the nation and the centre of its integration had to be hastily formulated from scratch over a relatively short period of time around the Meiji restoration and the consolidation period of the nation-state (Fujitani 1994). A range of media were mobilised for the purpose, and the imperial mythology featured in such imperial chronicles as Kojiki and Nihon-shoki, compiled in the late seventh and early eighth centuries to legitimise the then newly established ancient state of Japan and the imperial household (e.g. Isomae 1998), was utilised in a particularly intense manner. The mythology described how the ancestors of the imperial family descended from heaven, created the land and, somewhat contradictorily, conquered and assimilated *aboriginal populations*. The story implied that traces of the migration of the ancestors of the imperial family and, effectively, the Japanese, were identifiable in archaeological evidence if the story reflected what actually happened. Interestingly, it was foreign scholars who first took an interest in the origin of the Japanese, including Edward Morse who initially argued that the heaven mentioned in the chronicles was somewhere outside the archipelago and that the ancestors of the imperial family were a migrant population (Oguma 1995, 19–24), and this view was inherited by Japanese scholars. This further implied that the archaeological evidence of the period before the migration of the ancestors of the imperial family was a trace of the life of the aboriginal populations, and in that sense was from the *prehistory* of Japan. The true history of the Japanese, from that point of view, started with the ancestors of the imperial family coming from outside the archipelago.

This also meant that the study of the *true* history of the imperial family and the Japanese, the archaeology of the periods *after* the supposed migration, had to be strictly regulated because, naturally, the study of the material evidence of the periods after the migration could throw doubt on the validity of the mythology-based contents of the image and the positionality of the emperor and his family. In the 'officially' accepted view, a consensus existed that the Jomon 'culture' of hunter-gatherers was the culture of aboriginal populations (*senjyu*(indigenous)-*minzoku*(race)) which were conquered and assimilated by the ancestors of the imperial family[4] (e.g. Tsuboi 1887, 95; Hashiba 1889, 236–237; Yagi and Shimomura 1893, 388–389; Teshigawara 1995, 46–47). So, the study of Jomon 'culture' (its position in the relative

---

[4] *Ten*(heaven)*son*(descendant)-*zoku*, meaning the group descended from heaven, from which the entire Japanese population at that time was claimed to have descended.

Table 4.1 *The 'safe' and 'dangerous' domains in Japanese pre-Second World War archaeology*

'Safe' archaeology	'Dangerous' archaeology
The Stone Age/Jomon = The *aboriginal* population of the Japanese archipelago = *Before* the descent of the imperial ancestors (Tanson-zoku) from 'Takamagahara' (heaven)	*The Yayoi* = Beginning of the 'rice cultivating Japan' = History of the population (Tenson-zoku) decended from 'Takamagahara' (heaven) *The Kofun* = The origin of the *imperial* ancestors = History of the population descended from 'Takamagahara' (heaven)
Nothing to do with the imperial history and its genealogical continuation	Might cast doubt on the authenticity and the genealogical continuity of the Imperial family

[handwritten margin note: mentioned in histories]

chronology of Japanese prehistory, particularly its transition to the Yayoi period, was not fully established until the 1920s/30s) and the period before this was a 'safer' domain for the state authority and, hence, archaeologists, because it had nothing to do with imperial history, the history of the *tenson-zoku* group and, hence, nothing to do with Japanese history. However, the cultures coming afterwards showed, from the above-illustrated (fictional) framework, evidence of the history of the imperial family and the 'national body' which it embodied. Hence, the study of these latter cultures and periods was regarded as 'dangerous', i.e., potentially casting doubt on the authenticity of the narrative of the national body (Table 4.1).

[handwritten margin note: Chronology of Japanese prehistory]

This division of archaeology into two domains, i.e, the 'safe' and the 'dangerous', rather than the 'true' and the 'false', constituted an important binary code for the structuration of the archaeological communication system of the pre-Second World War period of Japan, and the binary code was used to make a distinction between *appropriate* and *inappropriate* archaeological commentaries: appropriate being the commentaries supporting/not casting doubt upon the authenticity of the narrative of the national body, and inappropriate being the commentaries potentially endangering the public perception of the authenticity of the narrative of the national body (Table 4.1).

The spatio-temporal boundaries of the 'national body' This section will illustrate particularly vividly how the notion of the 'national body' played a constitutive role in the reproduction of the archaeological communication system of the period. (a) Who were the first inhabitants of the territorial domain of Japan and (b) how the make-up of the people occupying it have changed since then were issues which were investigated, speculated upon, and vigorously debated not only by anthropologists/archaeologists but also by scholars of various other disciplines, politicians and social activists (cf. Oguma 1995, 1998), i.e., intellectuals and the elite. This was partly because the study fell into the category of 'safe' archaeology (see

Table 4.1). This also exemplifies the significant role commonly played by intellectuals in the invention of tradition/ethnie underpinning a new nation-state (Kan 2001, Chapter 2). However, there appears to have been another, overtly political, reason.

The theses put forward can be classified into the following: (1) The Japanese are racially singular and their content has not changed much since the beginning of the habitation of Japan; and (2) the Japanese are racially mixed and plural, and their racial mix has changed as a number of foreign populations invaded/joined through time. The latter is further subdivided by differences on such points as to who was the *first* inhabitant of Japan and how many migrant populations came to the archipelago and conquered and assimilated the aboriginal population. These two statements functioned as two axes of discursive formation and were articulated in specific political issues and agendas.

The theses which fell into category (1) were articulated in the discourse of the necessary *consolidation* of the 'national body', and were vigorously promoted and debated from the Meiji restoration to the end of the nineteenth century (cf. Oguma 1995, 50–55). After that, the theses gradually ceased to be issues of public debate as Japan completed the initial phase of nation-building through westernisation and began colonising neighbouring countries.

The theses which fell into category (2) were articulated in the discourse for the legitimation of the colonization of neighbouring countries (Oguma 1995, 242–249). The necessity of legitimising the territorial expansion, i.e., colonisation, which inevitably involved the incorporation of peoples of colonised regions/countries into the 'national body' in one way or another, rose, and the discourse of the plural *origins*, not the singular *origin*, of the Japanese became the main axis of the discursive formation underpinning and legitimising this unfolding reality; the claim that Japan had been through a history of *incorporation* and the *assimilation* of a number of racial groups was actively mobilised for the legitimation of ongoing colonisation and the policy of assimilation, and adopted in a particularly drastic manner in the case of the colonisation of Korea (Oguma 1998, Chapter 8).

Let us examine in detail the debate about the 'first inhabitants' of the archipelago, because this typically shows how the boundaries of the 'national body' were drawn and redrawn as the socio-political context in which Japan as a newly founded nation-state was situated changed, and how archaeology was involved in the boundary drawing/redrawing.

The point of dispute was whether the Ainu were the first inhabitants of the archipelago or not. The Ainu (issues concerning their ethno-genesis are far too diverse to be covered here, cf. Hudson 1999) inhabited Hokkaido and the smaller islands in the vicinity, and their population was so small that it was not regarded as relevant to the security of the Edo feudal regime (cf. Oguma 1998, Chapter 3, from which the factual information for the following is derived). However, due to pressure from Russia towards the end of the Edo period, when the fear materialised in the form of territorial threats, the Ainu were put under the direct rule of the feudal domain entrusted to control Hokkaido Island, called the Matsumae feudal domain. Once the Meiji government came to recognise Hokkaido Island as a subject of 'internal colonisation' and started sending a large number of people there, the importance of controlling the Ainu and claiming them as Japanese in order to make a territorial claim against Russia ceased.

However, as the living conditions of the Ainu rapidly degenerated as a result of the colonisation, and Christian missionaries began conducting various aid and educational activities, the national government was forced to take notice of the Ainu again. The Ainu issue now, from the national government's point of view, became a sort of issue of aboriginal minority. The intellectuals' reaction to this change of situation varied, but Tsuboi Shogoro, the above-mentioned founder of anthropology in Japan, for instance, actively intervened in the debate about governmental policy concerning the Ainu by comparing them with the native American population and by quoting an example of the attempt to assimilate them to the western way of life by Christianising them (Oguma 1995, 81–83).

Regardless of inferring the Ainu as the first inhabitants or not, it was argued that the early inhabitants of Japan were, without exception, conquered by a group coming from outside the archipelago, most often inferred to have come from mainland Asia, to which, it was further argued, the genealogy of the imperial family and the Japanese nation could be traced back (see Table 4.1) (cf. Teshigawara 1995, 91–99). The redifferentiation and rearticulation of the Ainu as an *aboriginal* minority in the newly established domain of the nation-state of Japan and their assimilation to it would have been compared to the pseudo-historical narrative of the foundation of the roots of the 'national body' in which the ancestors of the imperial family conquered and assimilated aboriginal populations comparable to the Ainu, and would have been mobilised to support this imaginary creation, i.e., the narrative of the roots of the national body, by providing it with a pseudo 'direct historical parallel'. In other words, the Ainu and the 'first inhabitants issue' functioned to allow those who were concerned to re-enact and relive the origin of the nation and national body. This might partly explain why the issue attracted such intense interest and debate. And, because the historical narrative of the foundation of the 'national body' was the narrative of the coming of new groups from outside and the assimilation by them of the aboriginal populations, the methods employed in the relevant studies were those which enabled the archaeologist to trace the *diffusion* of the incoming populations and the cultures they brought and to find the *traces of the habitation of the old aboriginal groups* (see Table 4.1).

In that sense, only the methodological tools and theoretical premises with which to trace the migration of people and their assimilation of pre-existing, aboriginal populations were necessary, and other archaeological concepts and methods which would potentially systematise inferences about the past were not only unnecessary but (categorised in the perception of the people as) dangerous (Table 4.1). After all, the public appears, quite naturally, to have been aware of the mythical, thus imaginary, nature of the narrative of the foundation of the national body (Teshigawara 1995, 78–79), and the executive appears to have been well aware of its fragile foundation. Hence, any development in archaeology, methodological or otherwise, which had the slightest possibility of endangering the foundation of the notion of the national body and its antiquity, e.g., the authenticity of the imperial mythology and the genealogical continuity of the imperial family from the beginning of history, was regarded as dangerous and subject to censorship and persecution.

Elsewhere, the development of diffusionism as a conceptual/explanatory framework for archaeological practice and that of typo-chronology went hand in hand (Trigger 1989, Chapter 5). However, in Japan, the development of the latter was significantly delayed. Archaeology had not been taught as an academic discipline until the establishment of the first Department of Archaeology in the Faculty of Literature of Kyoto University in 1916, and the most basic methodological tools of archaeology, such as stratigraphic excavations and typo-chronology, were not systematically introduced and adopted until the first quarter of the twentieth century (Teshigawara 1995, 108–115). Until that time, the field of archaeological knowledge production/discourse had not had any means or markers with which to differentiate itself from anthropology and history (cf. Teshigawara 1995, 109–110), and that made the field a most suitable arena (and the easiest to manipulate) where the discourse of the formation of the national body was reproduced by not excluding but involving a wider community of intellectuals who consciously and unconsciously played a role in supporting the maintenance and re-enforcement of the foundation of the 'national body' (Kan 2001, Chapter 2). However, the delay in the disciplinisation of archaeology, I would argue, was also to do with the fact that the disciplinisation in the form of methodologisation would have undermined the authenticity of the intrinsically diffusionist narrative of the invasion of the imperial ancestors and their assimilation of the aboriginal populations of the archipelago (Table 4.1).

The systematisation of archaeological studies progressed from the first quarter of the twentieth century, and speculative diffusionist accounts, such as the Jomon 'culture' as the culture of the aboriginal population, continued to be practised in the periphery of the expanding horizons of new, higher 'cultures' coming from the outside, such as the Yayoi and the Kofun (mounded tomb) (Figure 4.2) (Teshigawara 1995, 139–143), gradually vanished. These 'cultures', instead, were gradually reorganised into intra- and inter-regional chronological stages, and the progression of the construction of a nation-wide chronological network (Figure 4.2) effectively threw doubt on the validity of the mythology-based diffusionist narratives. They nicely fit into the narrative of the foundation of the roots of the national body, illustrated in Figure 4.2.

However, importantly for the current argument, these doubts were carefully concealed by archaeologists themselves or modified so as not to contradict the doctrine of the national body. And interestingly, the Kofun (mounded tomb) period, characterised by gigantic keyhole-shaped tumuli, the largest examples of which were designated as the mausolea of ancient emperors, was the period about which the construction of a chronological system was slowest (cf. Teshigawara 1995, 69–72); the systematisation of the archaeology of the Kofun period would have almost certainly contradicted the mythology-based early imperial history; and the investigation of the period, especially from the viewpoint of the emergence and development of social stratification, was carefully and intentionally avoided. Instead, the study of the

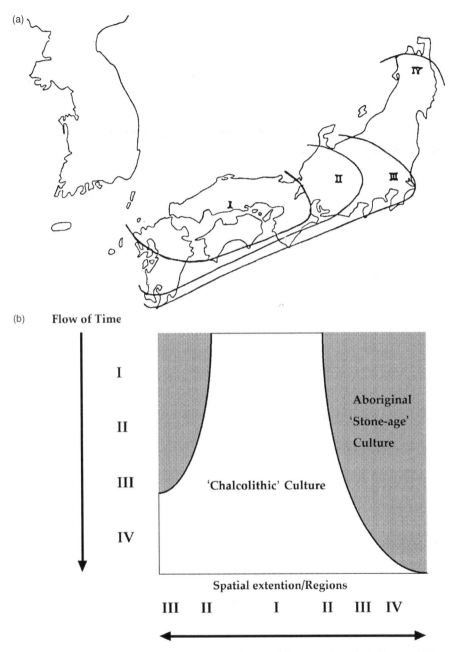

Figure 4.2 From the 'coexistence and assimilation of cultures' image to chronological charts (a) from Nakaya 1934, (b) by the present author. (a) and (b) show the image commonly shared that the 'Chalcolithic' Yoyoi culture coming in from the Korean peninsula gradually replaced the aboriginal 'Stone-Age' Jomon culture over a number of centuries, during which time different 'cultures' coexisted in different parts of the archipelago. This view was replaced by modern typo-chronological charts such as 4.2 (c) which is a modern typo-chronological chart, created by Sugao Yamanouchi (1937).

'Stages and sub-phases in the classification of the Jomon pottery' created by Sugao Yamanouchi (1937)

(c)

	渡 島	陸 奥	陸 前	関 東	信 濃	東 海	畿 内	吉 備	九 州
早 期	住吉	(+)	槻木 1 〃 2	三戸・田戸下 子母口・田戸上 茅山	曾根？× (+)	ひじ山 柏畑		黒 島×	戦場ケ谷×
前 期	石川野× (+)	円筒土器 下層式 (4型式以上)	室浜 大木 1 〃 2a, b 〃 3—5 〃 6	蓮田式 {花積下 / 関山 / 黒浜} 諸磯 a, b 十三坊台	(+) (+) (+) 踊場	鉾ノ木×	国府北白川 1 大歳山	磯ノ森 里木 1	轟？
中 期	(+) (+)	円筒上 a 〃 b (+) (+)	大木 7a 〃 7b 〃 8a, b 〃 9, 10	五領台 阿玉台・勝坂 加曾利E 〃 (新)	(+) (+) (+) (+)			里 木 2	曾畑 / 阿高 / 出水 } ?
後 期	青柳町× (+) (+)	(+) (+) (+)	(+) (+) (+)	堀之内 加曾利B 〃 安行 1, 2	(+) (+) (+) (+)	西尾×	北白川 2 ×	津雲上層	御手洗 西 平
晩 期	(+)	亀ケ岡式 {(+) / (+) / (+) / (+)}	大洞B 〃 B—C 〃 C1, 2 〃 A, A'	安行 2—3 〃 3	(+) (+) (+) 佐野×	吉胡× 〃 × 保美×	宮滝× 日下×竹ノ内× 宮滝×	津雲下層	御 領

The original caption (in Japanese) says: (1) This chart is tentative and shall be revised. (2) (+) indicates a temporal type not yet named. (3) (×) indicates the name of the site where pots originally from other regions which are relative-dated have been excavated. The rows indicate the Earliest, Early, Middle, Late and Final stages, and columns indicate regional units of the archipelago.

Figure 4.2 *(Cont.)*

period was confined mainly to cultural reconstruction such as that of the usage and function of funerary features and artefacts by comparing the data to the contents of such ancient imperial chronicles as Kojiki and Nihon-shoki in an uncritical manner (e.g. Takahashi 1914). Meanwhile, touching upon anything social appears to have been carefully avoided. In contrast, the construction of a nation-wide chronological system progressed most rapidly in the study of the Jomon 'culture'. The *prehistory* of the imperial family and the Japanese hence fell into the category of *safe* archaeology (Table 4.1).

Ironically, the domain of organising archaeological evidence into nation-wide chronological systems, aided by the notion of stratigraphic excavation/observation and typology introduced[5] in the second decade of the twentieth century, almost half a century after Morse's Omori shell-middens excavation, came to function as a kind of 'refuge' for archaeologists who were forced to conceal their political consciences and scientific observations and instead immersed themselves in the mechanistic, descriptive practice of constructing pottery typo-chronologies.

Archaeology, under such circumstances, on the one hand had to organise its discourse to fit the discursive formation directly regulated by state power and on the other had to confine itself to practices irrelevant to the dominant discursive formation

[5] By Seiryo Hamada, who studied under the tutorage of Flinders Petrie in London and was appointed the first professor of the Department of Archaeology of Kyoto University, the first ever archaeology department founded in Japan. cf. Hamada 1918.

concerning the past. The concept of the body of the 'nation', which was a variant of the technology of integrating the nation-state by creating a transcendental conceptual construct with which disembedded individuals reidentify themselves (see Chapters 1 and 3.8), occupied such a dominant position in discursive formation that individual communication fields were, regardless of being for or against the concept, condemned to be structured by it.

Japanese post-Second World War discursive formation and archaeology

Post-Second World War archaeology here means the period between the end of the war and the late 1970s. It constituted its discursive formation by the continuing existence of the basic structure of the pre-war discursive space. As illustrated later, this was necessitated and helped by the rapidly crystallizing Cold War equilibrium of global socio-economic/political systems, which also made the general discursive formation of the time highly stable. Bearing this in mind, let us begin by examining the cause and effect of the continuation of the basic structure of the pre-war discourse into the post-war period. The concept of the 'national body' again played a pivotal role (parts of the following arguments in this section are from Mizoguchi 2005a).

Japan's catastrophic defeat in the Second World War seemingly changed the situation completely. The old systems, embodied by the 'Meiji constitution', were abolished or replaced by the new, and the 'national body' ceased to be mentioned in public. However, the structuring principles of general discursive formation and archaeological discourse as one of its fields remained almost unchanged (Kan 2001, Chapter 5). This was partly because Japan had to be quickly resituated in a new, rapidly crystallized structure of politico-economic powers which was later to become the foundation of the Cold War equilibrium; Japan, in that structure, was designated to function as a front-line nation with the US and its allies against the USSR (Kan 2001). In order for that to be achieved, the conceptual machinery proven to be most effective in integrating the Japanese, i.e., the 'national body' and its principal features, the emperor and his historical positionality, had to be preserved.

The emperor, whose previous status had been absolute sovereign of the nation, became the 'symbol of the integration of the nation': he became, constitutionally, detached from the realm of the running of the country, but he remained officially the embodiment of the *voluntary unity* of individuals constituting the nation. This meant that the 'national body' as a multi-functional conceptual entity remained intact although it was rarely overtly mentioned: as long as what was perceived to embody this entity, the emperor system, remained intact, the entity itself was naturally perceived as intact. Besides, the very nature of the entity as a conceptual, artificial, and hence extremely flexible construct, worked as its strength; Japan had lost its colonies and the territories it had gained during the war, but that was conceived by the intellectual class (who had formerly produced narratives supporting and legitimising the changing/expanding spatial extension of the national body) as the *purification* of the content of the 'national body' (Oguma 1995, Chapter 17). They claimed that the national body was now constituted by a single, hence pure, race. They claimed that this was the original form of the national body, and the national body and the authentic nature of the Japanese had become polluted through an irresponsible misadventure conducted by a hyper-ambitious bunch of individuals in the military and the executive during the years up to the end of the war. The narratives of the multiple origins of the Japanese, which were mobilised for the legitimation of the colonisation and occupation, were conveniently forgotten or abandoned, and the loss of the colonies and occupied areas was tacitly portrayed as a returning-back to the genuine, authentic state/shape of the Japanese as a single-race, hence 'pure', nation.

Quite ironically, the rise of the single origin/race theory was also convenient for those who were trying to form a counter discourse against the 'national body' discourse, the advocates of a Marxist history and archaeology. They were under varying degrees of influence from USSR-led communism/Marxism; and a unifying element of their not-so-unified discourses was the doctrine of 'racial self-determination' as a slogan against US-led 'imperialism', i.e., the forceful expansion of the/a capitalist economy and of the 'Western block'. The slogan increasingly gained reality as it became apparent that the US was utilising the emperor system and the continuation of the concept of the 'national body' to reconstruct Japan as a successful capitalist state by preserving the old institutions, both economic and political, which were regarded by many as the sources of the ills of pre-war Japan. For Marxist historians/archaeologists, the critical investigation of the origin of the imperial household as an original source of the ills of pre-war Japan had to be conducted hand-in-hand with a historical investigation of the (singular, not plural) origin of the Japanese race because the study of the origin of the Japanese nation had to seek not only the origin of the ills of Japan as a *state* but also the source of pride to be Japanese as a *nation* (e.g. Toma 1951a). Seita Toma, a Marxist historian, portrayed the Japanese state-formation and that of the polities on the periphery of the Chinese empire, by drawing heavily upon archaeological evidence, as a process of continuous struggle for laying the foundation of the nation under the shadow of the powerful Chinese dynasties (cf. Toma 1951b). It can easily be inferred from this that China was metaphorically compared to the US; and the struggle against US-led imperialism, which was preventing the total reform and democratisation of Japan, was compared to the Japanese ancient state formation as a process of struggle in the sphere of strong Chinese influence. We can see a kind of seed of a core–periphery/world-systems perspective here, although it was never systematically compared to Wallerstein's version (Wallerstein 1974) or those archaeological works influenced by it.

These factors constituted the post-Second World War structure of archaeological discourse until the 1970s. The ghost of the notion of the 'national body' continued to play a pivotal role in discursive formation, and one's position in the discursive space continued to be determined, even if tacitly/unconsciously, by one's attitude to the very notion: although the notion itself gradually became unrecognisable as an explicitly articulated concept, it continued to legitimise the continuation of reactionary discourses and institutions continuing from the pre-war period, and that effectively preserved the pre-war division of archaeology into safe/apolitical and dangerous/political/anti-imperial domains. The former was embodied by Jomon archaeology and the latter by Marxist archaeology.

Marxist archaeology

Let us begin by examining Marxist archaeology. The foundation of the discourse dates back to the 1920s/30s. Deepening economic difficulty and influence from communist Russia encouraged a group of historians to initiate a project analytically revealing the roots of the nature of the historical trajectory leading to the formation of a Japanese version of an imperialist capitalist state (Watabe 1936, 1937). From the Marxist perspective, they regarded the investigation of the origin of social inequality as an absolutely vital component of the project. To understand this historical event by situating it in the universal theory of the *developmental stages* (which claimed that every human society evolved from a stage of primitive communism through ancient slavery and feudalism to the stage of capitalism) was of particular importance for deciding what strategy should be taken to lead a socialist revolution in Japan (Yoshida 1972) because, according to the communist doctrine of the time, the strategy of the socialist revolution of a given country had to be decided according to the historical trajectory the country had taken (Yoshida 1972).

The large tumuli of the Kofun (mounded tomb) period, including the designated 'imperial mausolea', were thought to be an indication of the establishment of the rulers of a despotic character and of the power which enabled them to mobilise a large number of people like slaves. Their study and the study of the preceding histor-ical process was conducted aiming at 'scientifically' (i.e., from the Marxist point of view) revealing the origin of social inequality not only as the root of the problems of a capitalist society but also of the ills of the Japanese nation-state, i.e., the emperor system, a vital constitutive element of the 'national body', and the machineries of the imperialistic capitalism ideologically based upon the emperor system (Toma 1951a). As mentioned in the previous section, basic archaeological tools, concepts and sys-tems were underdeveloped at the time, and the involvement of archaeologists in the project was minimal (cf. Hara 1972): many of the practitioners were politically active historians. The outcome of the study, retrospectively, inevitably included many shortcomings. However, this pre-war development constituted the backbone of the Japanese Marxist approach and was equipped with a strong political self-awareness.

Any Marxist approach, as a holistic interpretative framework, sorts a concerned body of evidence into interconnected/interdependent units and investigates in which connections/ties 'contradictions' reside; contradictions, for the Marxist, are *the* source of social change, and change is the intrinsic nature of society. In the case of Japanese Marxist archaeology, the contradictions leading to the formation and estab-lishment of a class-difference based stratification, the differentiation based upon the possession and non-possession of the *means of production*, were the ultimate subject of study, and the Yayoi period (between c. the sixth century BC and the late third century AD) and the Kofun (mounded tomb) period (between c. the late third cen-tury AD and the sixth century AD) were grasped as the decisive phases in the process (Figure 4.3).

The introduction of rice paddy-field agriculture at the beginning of the Yayoi period, c. sixth century BC, ignited the process of widening contradiction between tribal social organisation, based upon communal labour and communal ownership, i.e., communal storage and consumption of products, and smaller semi-autonomous units, functioning as the basic unit of daily corporate labour and accumulating

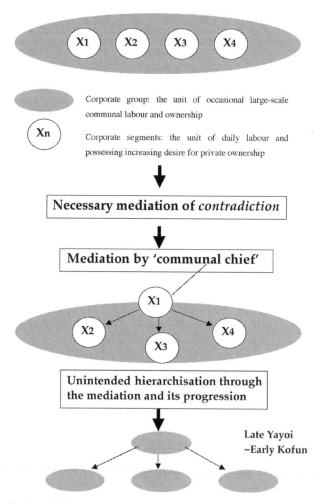

Figure 4.3 The Yoyoi and Kofun periods as the decisive phase in the process toward the establishment of a class-difference-based stratification, i.e., an ancient state: a model. The intensification of the mediation of *contradiction* and the consequent rise in the status of communal chiefs are widely thought to be reflected in the increasing size of bronze ritual implements (see Figure 4.4).

privately owned wealth. The process was interpreted as having led to the generation and enhancement of communal chieftainship which was entrusted by the rest of the community to mediate the contradiction between the principle of communal ownership and the accumulating desire of the smaller, actual unit of daily labour of private ownership. Through the mediation of the contradiction and inter-communal negotiations and tension, the authority and power of the chief was increasingly enhanced through the Yayoi period, and the process reached a kind of threshold in the transitional phase between the Yayoi and Kofun periods when an alliance of local chieftains covering most of the western portion and parts of the eastern portion of the archipelago was formed from the increasing necessity of the organisation of inter-regional exchange and collaboration. In this thesis, the formation of the distributional horizon of the earliest keyhole-shaped tumuli and a homogeneous set of grave goods was interpreted as having reflected the formation of fictive kinship ties between the local chieftains in which the chieftains of the Nara basin and the Kawachi plain in the present-day Kinki region became dominant (e.g. Kondo 1983). This assembly of the chieftains of the Kinai region became the ancestoral foundation of the imperial household, around which the ancient Japanese state was established in the seventh century AD.

In order to investigate this long-term process from the Marxist perspective, the body of evidence was classified into such analytical units as infrastructural elements and superstructure/ideology, units of social integration of various scales, and so on, and their interrelations and co-transformations were studied as the indicators of a deepening contradiction. For instance, the dominant trend in the stylistic development of Yayoi bronze implements such as bronze weapon-shaped implements and bronze bells, the enhancement of their visual impressiveness by enlarging their size and visually distinct traits (Figure 4.4), was explained as the reflection of the developmental process of an ideological device concealing this deepening contradiction between communal interest and private ownership. As illustrated above, principles indispensable for the maintenance of communal egalitarianism such as communal ownership were undermined by the increasing autonomy of smaller units of actual daily agricultural labour. However, the mobilisation of the labour force from a larger corporate group scale, consisting of a number of smaller units of actual daily labour, was of absolute necessity in the case of the construction and mending of irrigation systems for the opening and maintenance of paddy fields: the maintenance of a small number of paddies was possible for a smaller unit, but in the case of the sudden destruction of an irrigation system due to a natural disaster such as a typhoon, for instance, the coordination of a larger corporate group scale was necessary (cf. Kondo 1983). Therefore, the larger corporate group based upon and sustained by communal egalitarianism needed to be preserved. The thesis contended that the communal ritual in which the bronze implements were mobilised functioned to conceal this ever-deepening crisis, and the importance of the ritual increased as the contradiction between the necessity of maintaining communal order and the increasing autonomy of the unit of daily labour deepened. Accordingly, those who were entrusted by the community to be in charge of the ritual accumulated authority and power, and, quite ironically, the deepening crisis consolidated the status of those who were in charge of the ritual. However, they needed to disguise themselves as representative of communal interests, and, accordingly, the meaning content and appearance of the ritual they conducted increasingly inclined to an emphasis on communal togetherness. The thesis contended that the enlargement in size and exaggeration in the visual characteristic traits of the bronze implements reflected this process of the co-transformation of social domains (Figures 4.3 and 4.4).

As illustrated, the study of the process of social stratification and the emergence of the ancient state deriving from Marxist perspectives resulted in the methodological

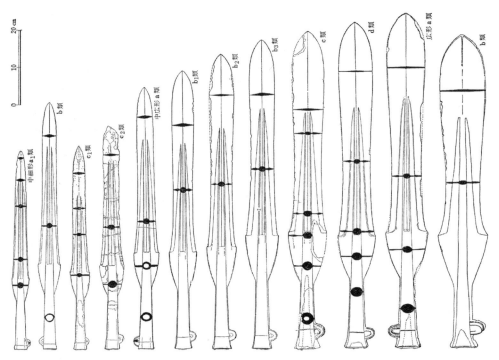

Figure 4.4 The development of Dohoko bronze spearheads (from Iwanaga 1986). Each of the specimens shown represents a typo-chronological stage of the temporal sequence of changes progressing from left to right.

systematisation of the practice of Japanese archaeology, which had formerly been somewhat undisciplined, and led to the formation of a unique tradition of social archaeological theorisation and praxis, to which we shall return later.

However, it has to be noted here that what was behind the formation of this social archaeological theorisation and the systematisation of archaeology was the shadow of the 'national body'. Since the 1950s, the revival of the symbols of the ills of pre-war Japan, such as the redesignation of the 'anniversary' of the founding of the nation as a national holiday, using a date taken from imperial mythology (cf. Aston 1972), was gathering pace, and the danger of going down the same road to the catastrophe of another war was acutely felt. The theorisation and systematisation, in that sense, were firmly based upon a sense of reality, the reality of doing something good for society, and this feeling provided practitioners with a stable self identity: they felt they knew who they were in terms of the expected effect of what they were doing for society. Both the systematising tendency of Marxist theorisation and the sense of connectedness to social reality provided by the historical background and political objective of Marxist discourse functioned as a source of stability in the archaeological discursive formation of the period.

Jomon archaeology, meanwhile, shows a stark contrast. The study of Jomon culture during the pre-Second World War period constituted a 'safe' domain, i.e., a domain which was regarded as harmless and irrelevant to the validity/legitimacy of the position of the emperor and the imperial household. Jomon 'culture' was regarded as the culture of *aboriginal populations* conquered and assimilated by the ancestors of the imperial family and the Japanese people (Table 4.1). That would have been a reason why the attempt at reconstructing certain elements of the social organisation of the culture (e.g. Kono 1935) could be made, even if sporadically, unchecked by state power during the pre-Second World War period. This positionality of the study of Jomon culture, despite its recognition as a temporal entity, a 'period', after the establishment of the nation-wide chronological system around the 1920s/30s (Figure 4.2; cf. Yamanouchi 1937), remained intact after the Second World War: innumerable, seemingly endless attempts at refining the intra- and inter-regional chronological systems were made, but the period was predominantly the subject of culture-historical *reconstructions*. The functional reconstruction of individual material items was a major topic of study, and the investigation of individual settlements and their interrelations/interactions was conducted for the reconstruction of the social organisation of the phase to which the settlements concerned belonged (e.g. Mizuno 1969). The study of the Jomon period remained as the reconstruction of the contents of a *synchronic* 'slice' extracted from the trajectory of the reproduction and transformation of society, except for a few attempts at incorporating the Jomon period and its internal phases into the narrative of Marxist developmental stages. This 'synchronism' constituted a distinct characteristic of the discourse of Jomon studies and reinforced its tacitly perceived character as *pre*-history, i.e. *changeless*, hence *historyless* period of Japanese prehistory.

The coexistence of these two discourses in the discursive space of the period had some significant implications. The contrast between Yayoi–Kofun archaeology and Jomon archaeology in terms of their structuring principles influenced the ways in which western archaeological theories and methodologies were introduced to Japan (Table 4.1).

The Yayoi–Kofun discourse was Marxist and political, and produced some remarkable case studies conducted with a strong critical awareness of their political implications on both micro/local and macro/national scales. A good example is the excavation of the Tsukinowa tumulus in Okayama Prefecture. The residents of a small mining town in the Chugoku mountain range became interested in local history through the encouragement of a group of archaeologists, and learnt the way to connect the condition in which they lived to the past as a sequence of episodes forming a trajectory leading to the present, which had many problems yet to be overcome (Tsukinowa kofun kanko kai 1960; Teshigawara 1995, 214–218). The Marxist thesis of developmental stages, and the notion of contradictions taking place between the infra- and superstructures of a social whole that moved society upward in those stages, helped the residents connect their living conditions and the contradictions they faced there to a point/stage in the historical trajectory and make sense of the causal connections between them. This discursive characteristic of Marxist theory, which explained *the present in terms of the past*, made those who advocated it feel that the ills of the present had their roots in certain points in the past, and in that characteristic converged two aims of post-Second World War critical archaeology, one a critique of the concept of the 'national body' and the other the critique of the ills of the present continuing from the past, together. The critique of the past became the critique of the present in the discursive space of Japanese Marxist archaeology, which might deserve to be described as a precursor of the critical social archaeology which emerged in the west in the 1980s. However, in actuality this constituted the condition in which neither the processual nor post-processual developments in the west were enthusiastically accepted in Japan, because on the one hand the processual theoretico-methodological package looked, to the practitioners of the Japanese Marxist tradition, anti-historical, and, hence, apolitical and reactionary, and on the other hand the significant characteristic of the post-processual approach, i.e., its critical political self-awareness, looked very familiar. At this point, though, it has to be added that an effort to articulate and synthesise ways to bridge/mediate the gap between abstract Marxist theory and archaeological reality in the past and in the present, in other words an effort at opening up the domain of bridging argumentation of various scales and degrees of abstraction, was rarely made (although in actuality it was tacitly made in each individual case study in a rather undisciplined manner by classifying the evidence into analytical units and by explaining the reason why particular units were given deeper, more careful treatment than others). This anti-theorisation tendency in Japan was deep-rooted and its cause was complicated (Ikawa-Smith 1982). However, in the case of Japanese Marxist archaeology, a mixture of these factors significantly contributed towards indifference to theoretical developments abroad.

At the same time, the discourse of pre-Yayoi–Kofun archaeology, i.e., Jomon archaeology, was, as illustrated above, dominated by the reconstruction of the static, synchronic slice of social reproduction and transformation; and some constitutive elements of processual archaeology such as the application of 'middle-range' research strategy and systemic thinking fitted nicely into the range of its analytical requirements. This formed the background against which both the autonomous development and the introduction of the processual methods and perspectives took place relatively easily in the Jomon discourse. The application of site-catchment analysis (cf. Hayashi 1979, 114; Akazawa 1983) and the reconstruction of the subsistence scheduling of the Jomon period (Akazawa 1983) are two notable examples.

This discursive division was also supported and in a way embodied by the differential distribution of the Jomon and Yayoi–Kofun sites between the eastern and western portions of the archipelago. The distribution of the former is denser in the east than in the west, and that of the latter is vice versa (cf. Nihon Daiyonki gakkai et al. 1992, 82–85, 128–131). This naturally resulted in different daily archaeological experiences such as what one saw in the museums, what one dug up at the sites, and what one talked about, and these all added a strong spatial dimension to the discursive division (Mizoguchi 2002, 31–38).

In all, what characterised the discursive space of the post-Second World War period in the history of Japanese archaeology was its *stability*. The two discourses, the Jomon discourse and the Yayoi–Kofun discourse, that coexisted in the discursive space of

been conducted: there was once a body of people whose mutual ties were so tight that they effectively laid the foundation upon which a nation was to be built. The circularity (between a nation-state and an ethnie) was transformed to a directional, causal sequence of events in this de-paradoxisation strategy in which the (invented) pre-existence of an ethnie was the cause, and hence guaranteed the legitimacy, of the formation and sovereignty of a nation-state.

What makes the Japanese case unique is twofold: the existence of the emperor and the underdevelopment of the disembedding mechanisms such as the national currency, taxation, and conscription when the foundation of the modern nation-state of Japan began. Instead, the emperor became the principal de-paradoxisation device. The emperor was made to be the embodiment of *Japaneseness*, and many of the traditions and mental characteristics which were supposed to characterise the Japanese nation were invented in relation to the mythology, again, invented to shroud the emperor system. However, in order for the emperor to be the embodiment of the Japanese people, which would have been the prerequisite for this de-paradoxising device to work, a narrative directly connecting the emperor and the people was necessary. For that purpose, a metaphorical kinship between the emperor and the people was also invented, in the form of the myth that the descent from heaven of the founder(s) of the imperial genealogy also marked the beginning of the Japanese people (cf. Isomae 1998). These fictitious factors, because of their fictitiousness, emphasised their organic interrelations and were put together to form the conceptual construct of the 'national body' in which each Japanese person was situated in a way in which neither the individual nor the national body could survive without one another.

However, this tight relationship of mutual mediation/support was a mere elaboration in the realm of perception, and because of that it had to be further shrouded with layers of supporting narratives and material symbols. Archaeology was mobilised to create/support them.

Education was a discursive space where such narratives and material symbols were invested in the most intensive manner because education is one of the most effective/efficient ways for engineering the masses, engineering the nation to make it take the mutual mediation of the nation-state and the emperor system for granted. Chapter 4.3 examines how this circularity and interdependence between the nation-state and the emperor system are dealt with in the domain of education.

4.3 The illusion of enlightenment and social engineering: archaeological knowledge and education

Two versions of a textbook drawing
Figure 4.6 shows two drawings. They are two versions of a drawing for a school textbook, depicting a scene which, the title claims, would have been seen somewhere in the western part of the Japanese archipelago back in the third century AD, the era of the 'Yamatai-koku' polity recorded in a Chinese official document, the imperial chronicle of 'Weizhi' of the Wei dynasty.

We have already observed in Chapter 1 the unique position which the Yamatai and Queen Himiko discourse occupies in Japanese archaeology and the Japanese perception of the past in general. As we saw, Weizhi was used as the ultimate source of reference when the reconstruction of the unreconstructable was attempted at the Yoshinogari, designated the first national historical park, and the discourse functioned to mediate the conflicting and contradictory interests of the stakeholders involved. In other words, the Yamatai and Queen Himiko discourse was mobilised during the uncertainty which might have disturbed the continuation of the discourse concerning the reconstruction at the site. Concerning the fact that the stakeholders involved include not only the archaeologist but also the general public, the media and the state, it can be inferred that the discourse has a sphere of influence cutting across the borders of various sectors constituting society.

The textbook featuring the drawing was published in 1989 for sixth-grade primary school students aged eleven to twelve. One is the original and the other amended following instructions from a committee appointed by the then Ministry of Education (since then reorganised and renamed the Ministry of Education, Culture, Sports, Science and Technology, which abbreviates itself as 'MEXT'). The supposed function of the committee is to check and authorise the 'appropriateness' of the contents of textbooks for the primary, secondary and high schools in Japan (www.mext.go.jp/a_menu/shotou/kyoukasho/).

Both the original and the amended versions are meant to be accurate, or at least based upon factual evidence, archaeological as well as historical, even if some 'inference' is involved for the purpose of making the drawing effective in helping the student understand what the society of the period was like. In that sense, the original drawing would not have needed any significant amendment except for unlikely factual errors. However, as illustrated below, amendments which were not necessarily to do with obvious factual errors were recommended and implemented, whilst some obvious factual errors were left untouched.[6] It is striking to see how minute and subtle many of the amendments are. Some of the alterations are so subtle and small in size that one cannot see the point of making them at all in terms of 'correcting' the content of the textbook; schoolchildren would not even notice them even if they were shown the original and the amended side by side. In other words, it is quite unlikely that the act of 'correcting' recommended by the education-ministry appointed committee had any pragmatic effect upon the way in which the drawing was understood.

Then, why did the committee do, or feel obliged to do, such a 'fine job'? The set of criteria set up for the school textbook screening (sometimes described as 'censorship') requires the textbooks submitted to be authorised by the ministry to be fit for the purpose of observing the objectives and guidelines provided by the

---

[6] Akira Teshigawara not only noticed some of the amendments made, which will be examined later in this section, but also put forward a thesis inferring the intention behind them (1991). The following is much inspired by his pioneering work, though the current author's interpretation differs considerably from Teshigawara's and tries to go further into the character of the discourse, i.e., the communication system of those who are involved in the production and amendment of the picture and its positionality in contemporary Japanese society.

Fundamental Law of Education and the School Education Law, and detailed criteria are set up to examine appropriateness in coverage, level, selection of topics and their structure and quantity, accuracy, manner of description, and expression.

The criteria specifically include that a given textbook's contents need to be politically and religiously neutral, impartial in the selection of topics and in expression, accurate, and properly observing what are provided by the two above-mentioned laws.[7] This means that even the most minute of amendments has to be done if required, regardless of what could or could not be accomplished by making the alterations. However, as mentioned above, some alterations appear to have nothing to do with accuracy or other considerations such as impartiality, as we will see later in detail. It might rather be the case that the members of the committee simply *could not stand* what were depicted as the 'facts' of the life of the people in the third century AD. It might be the case that they made such subtle and minute 'corrections' being fully aware that schoolchildren might not care at all. In other words, it might only be whether or not a depiction is fit for the continuation/disturbance of communication amongst the appointed committee members rather than what to amend and what not to amend that matters.

In any case, no definite answer is obtainable, firstly because the school textbook screening exercise, often dubbed 'censorship', has long been such a hotly debated topic among intellectuals, politicians, teachers and activists of both left and right that no one involved in the work would, if tracked down and interviewed, give their account or 'genuine' feeling about what they did and why. It also has to be noted that the amendment of this particular drawing is now 'history', a materialised segment of a discourse in the past, and history can only mediate communication in the present; i.e., it can only be interpreted and can never have its 'truth' revealed, even by those who were directly involved in it. In other words, any interpretation of and communication about history can only open up a continuously rearticulated horizon of choices (see Chapter 3.4). Then, what can one expect to achieve by examining this drawing and its two versions? Is there any significance in doing this?

Communicating about the drawing

Let us begin by considering the purpose of drawing and amending the picture. For the moment, let us bracket out the officially stated purpose emphasising its universality and impartiality as we saw above. This drawing and its two versions were supposed, or intended, to be appreciated by children. Children grow up to become adults, like those who drew and those who amended the drawing in 1989. By drawing or amending the drawing, they would have hoped that the children who saw it would become adults like them: adults who would imagine what the past was like from the way in which the drawing was drawn or amended. Their acts, if this were the case, were, ultimately, acts of projecting 'their' versions of the past onto the future through the mediation of children, acts attempting to make their version

---

[7] See the Ministry of Education, Culture, Sports, Science and Technology (MEXT) webpage: www.mext.go.jp/english/org/f_formal_16.htm, 'Elementary and Secondary Education', Section 3 'Textbooks'.

of the future 'everyone's future'. In that sense, what we see as a drawing of the past was actually a space where different hopes and desires for the future, in the form of different opinions over how a particular period of the past would have looked, were competing for dominance and hegemony.

Despite the different hopes and desires which those who drew and those who amended the drawing appear to have had, they seem to have shared a deep-rooted feeling: they had an utter commitment to doing what they were supposed to do, despite the likelihood, as mentioned above, that the implications and messages of their works would never be fully appreciated. Where did this commitment come from? How could one maintain one's enthusiasm when one knew that what one was doing was destined to be almost in vain? Could one be so serious and enthusiastic, had one not believed that what one created/amended would have some impact upon the way readers of the textbook, i.e., primary school children, would see the world and do things in future? Almost certainly, they did know that what they did would not bear any substantial and visible fruit within the short term.

To believe that the consequence of socially organised mass supervision, including education, could be rigidly controlled and engineered for the common and universal good was an important element of modernity, classical modernity to be precise (cf. Bauman 1988, 9–27). To eliminate the uncontrollable elements of society by making the mass look, behave and think like one another was the ultimate objective of education. The project of modernity, in other words, was the act, by those who occupied a privileged position in the expanding topography of the uneven distribution of reason, knowledge, wealth and power, of differentiating the educated/civilized self from the uneducated/uncivilised others.[8] In order to change society, those who were to educate the uneducated first had to articulate the latter as a unified and internally homogeneous category by imposing the classificatory scheme which moulded the created/discovered 'other' into the 'savage'/'barbaric' (cf. Trigger 1989, Chapter 4), and the desire of 'discovering' and 'articulating' the *unenlightened* (i.e., thinking and behaving differently from the modern self), for the self identification of the educated/*enlightened*, was not only projected onto the realm of the 'other', i.e., the periphery of the colonial/imperial expansion and beyond; it was also projected onto the inside of the habitat of the enlightened itself. In Japan during the early years of the Meiji period, for instance, folkloric beliefs and shamanistic religions were persecuted as backward-looking superstitions, and various folk customs such as gambling were legally prohibited (Fujitani 1994, 26–27): those who practised them were stigmatised as unenlightened and obstacles to the construction of a modern nation and subject to various projects of enlightenment including school education.

---

[8] Here, we have to be reminded that the beginning of the colonial era, i.e., the late fifteenth century and the early sixteenth centuries, also witnessed the emergence/articulation of vernacular/national languages to be the subject of grammatical systematisation, hence, to be *taught* to the unenlightened (the publication of the first book of the grammar of Castilian by Antonio de Nebrija was 1492, the same year that Christopher Columbus reached the Americas), and the enlightenment and modernisation were inseparably associated with the articulation of the child as a distinct human category/agency (Aries 1965).

Discovering, creating and educating the other is the operation of a self-referential system, which can only reproduce itself by creating a boundary between itself and its environment, and by reducing the complexity of the environment by controlling incoming information from the environment and outgoing reaction to it by utilising the boundary as a filter (see Chapter 3.5). Without the boundary, the system could not exist and reproduce itself. The 'discovery' of the child and childhood, in that sense, can be understood as a consequence of unfolding functional differentiation and the emergence of allied semantics (cf. Aries 1965, see Chapter 2). By utilising the boundary between themselves and children, they, the adults, resecured their identity, which was previously situated in social hierarchy and hierarchically organised communication systems. Such concepts to do with the character of the individual as 'self discipline', 'diligence', 'industriousness' and so on, together with various 'etiquettes', came to constitute the semantics for the articulation of functionally differentiated, hence horizontally organised, communication systems, the reproduction of which could no longer rely on social hierarchy and allied religious cosmology (e.g. Luhmann 1995, 426–430 and see Chapter 3.6, 45–46). Instead, these types of semantics, themselves being fragmentary, were connected to such non-hierarchical, universal factors as 'reason', and were made to help articulate the horizontally organised, fragmentary communication systems (Luhmann 1995, 340–344).

In other words, those concepts, i.e., self discipline, diligence, and so on, which were to do with the way the self itself regulated the way the self was constituted (a self-referential operation), enabled communication systems to de-paradoxise themselves and to continue across time and space without referring to such hierarchical notions as the god and the king, and because of that they fitted the reproduction of functionally differentiated social formation. The rise of functional differentiation and the 'modern self', was, in that sense, destined to be accompanied by the semantics of an *educational* character, and that move was also associated with the rise/ differentiation of the uneducated/uncivilised, consisting of the child and the barbarian. In that sense, the differentiation of the child as a social category and of education as an autonomous communication system was an essential condition for, and a consequence of, the articulation of functionally differentiated communication systems. In addition, it has to be emphasised that firmly programmed in the semantics of the reproduction of functionally differentiated communication systems and modernity was the notion that the intrinsic character of society and social being was chaos, or constant renewal of everything, and that both society and social being had to be disciplined and structured, i.e., educated, constantly and recurrently.

To see it from a different perspective, adults who are given the honourable duty of educating and enlightening the child were once children themselves. In that sense, children are the unenlightened within, and they are so in two ways: the child inhabits the same life–world as the adult, and the child inhabits the adult in the form of memory. The feeling that the child has to be educated, disciplined and structured is naturally acute because educating, disciplining and structuring the child, as far as the above is concerned, is educating, disciplining and structuring the adult him/herself through the mediation of the memory of his or her having been a child. The child was, in that sense, the closest 'other', from which one differentiates oneself to *identify* oneself.

Those who were involved in the creation and amendment of an image of the past in the form of a textbook drawing, as far as the above argument is concerned, were likely to have acquired, constituted and maintained their self identities by involving themselves in the project of educating the child as the unenlightened. The author(s) of the textbook and those who amended it were in dispute over the way the past should be imagined and projected onto the future, but they were united about one point: *they were what they taught*. Their seriousness and enthusiasm can be inferred to have been derived from it. Once this type of attitude and the technology of self identification had crystallised, it would not matter much whether what they did bore fruit or not; it was to discover/differentiate such 'others' as the child, the poor, the religious fundamentalist or whatever and to educate/enlighten them that mattered most because in modernity education has constituted an ontological base of human existence, or an essential semantics for the articulation of communication. In that sense, the discourse about/the communication system generated through the drawing and amendment of this particular drawing (including this writing itself), depicting a scene in the *past*, is about the *present*, and, as a communication system, the discourse continues by reducing the complexity created by various other communication systems such as the socio-economic, socio-political and socio-historical in a self-referential manner, and hence by articulating various desires and hopes for the future.

Examining the drawing

As mentioned above, this textbook drawing has two versions, the original and the amended. The drawing is entitled 'people of (the era of) the Yamatai-koku polity' (Figure 4.6).

Let us begin by comparing the two and picking out one by one the 'amendments', i.e., alterations ordered by the committee, and then proceed to examine historical and archaeological evidence and analyses for and against the original and the amended versions.

No doubt the most striking and visually significant alteration made is the facial expression of the three persons walking down the road at the centre of the drawing (Figure 4.6). In the original, their faces look arrogant and aloof with their eyebrows raised and mouths stiff. In the amended version, the facial expression is softened by altering the way the eyebrows and the mouths are depicted. This point was made by Teshigawara (1991, 7). Besides, it is noticeable that the head of the person leading the party is made to slightly lean forward compared with the original, as if looking with affection at the kneeling person who looks up at him. If we look into the detail further, it can be pointed out that the line of the shoulder and the upper sleeve of the garments worn by this person leading the party is also softened. This last point is so subtle that one can imagine how thorough and far reaching not only the instructions and requests of the committee were but also the way the recipient of the instructions reacted to them. It is as if the amendment were intended not only

Figure 4.6 Two versions of a textbook drawing. Left: original, right: amended (originally in Teikoku Shoin 1991, featured in Teshigawara 1991, by kind permission from Teikoku Shoin, June 2005). Note amended parts marked by circles, and the relocation of the mother and child marked by arrows.

to reduce the hierarchical gap between those who walked down the road and those who knelt down in the roadside bush but also to transform the relationship between them from a hostile one to one of *mutual affection* and *respect*.

There is another series of significant amendments, that were not noted by Teshigawara (1991). That is the alteration of the positions of the three persons kneeling on the roadside (Figure 4.6). In the original, all three persons are out of the bush, and two of them are depicted bowing deeply as one of them looks up at the person who leads the party walking down the road. In the amended version, the position of the person who looks up is left unchanged, but the other two are, interestingly, moved into the roadside bush.

The person who looks up is bearded and can safely be inferred to be depicted as male. Given that, the individual next to him can be assumed to be male as well, because their clothes are similar. Concerning the fact that this bowing man is depicted to be smaller and skinnier, he can safely be assumed to be a juvenile. The person who is on the opposite side of the road wears different garments, something which looks like a 'poncho', and the hair is styled differently. From the size of the body, this person is depicted as adult. From these differences, this person can be inferred to be depicted as an adult female. The person who remains in the same position after the alteration is the adult male, and the two who are moved into the roadside bush turn out to be the juvenile male and the adult female. It is as if these persons are depicted as a family, a nuclear family-like component to be more specific, and it seems that the amendment has widened the depiction of the status gap/difference between the husband/father, the wife/mother and the son.

We have two mutually contradictory sets of alterations here in terms of the way social positional differences are depicted. The first, which includes the softening of the facial expression of the individuals who are walking down the road (noted by Teshigawara), reduces the gap between those who appear to be higher-ranked individuals and those who appear to be members of a lower rank. The second widens the gap between the sexes and age groups within the lower-ranked individuals. What sort of hopes and desires are behind this mutually contradictory series of alterations? In order to obtain some clues, let us firstly examine what sort of information is chosen in creating and amending the drawing and how.

First let us examine the clothes the individuals wear. As far as the description of the Chinese imperial chronicle Weizhi goes, the clothes worn by those who kneel at the roadside are more or less 'accurately' depicted. Weizhi records in detail the different garments worn by the male and female of the people of 'Wa', the name given to the population occupying the domain roughly coinciding with present-day western Japan (Yamao 1986).

However, the clothes which those who are walking down the road wear are quite problematic: these individuals, who appear to be male, are depicted wearing different clothes from those kneeling. The description of clothes in Weizhi does not say anything about the existence of rank-related differences in the clothing. In this regard, both the original and the amended make a serious 'error', or a misleading over-inference, on factual grounds. To be precise, the original had an error, and the committee failed to ask for its amendment/elimination.

As far as the comparison between what Weizhi says and the depiction of the clothing goes, the following are clear: (1) both the original and the amended contradict Weizhi by depicting those who kneel and those who walk down the road as differently attired; and (2) the clothes worn by those who kneel more or less conform to the description of Weizhi in both the original and the amended versions.

Those who were involved in the making of the original seem to have felt it necessary to make explicit the existence of a fairly rigid social stratification by putting different clothes on those who knelt at the roadside and those who walked down the road. In contrast, relationships among those who knelt were depicted as 'egalitarian' in the original, agreeing with the description in Weizhi. In the amended version, though, relationships among those who knelt were made 'non-egalitarian' by relocating the juvenile male and the adult female to different positions.

In order to make sense of this emerging complex picture of following and defying the descriptions in Weizhi in both the original and the amended versions, let us now turn to the problem of whether a rigid system of stratification/ranking existed in the period depicted in the drawing. Weizhi describes how the population was divided into two ranked strata (e.g. Yamao 1986, 169–177; Yoshida 1995, 82–96). The division, Weizhi says, was marked with such etiquette as the lower-ranked kneeling when meeting the upper-ranked. The upper-ranked male is also described as marrying four or five females while a few of the lower-ranked males married two or three.

Let us turn to archaeological evidence. The period of the Yamatai-koku polity is widely thought to date from the transitional phase between the Yayoi and the Kofun (mounded tomb) periods, around AD 250/275 (e.g. Tsude 1998). The preceding Late Yayoi period, dating between c. AD 1 and AD 250/275, saw the beginning throughout western Japan of the custom of burying three or four adults of both sexes

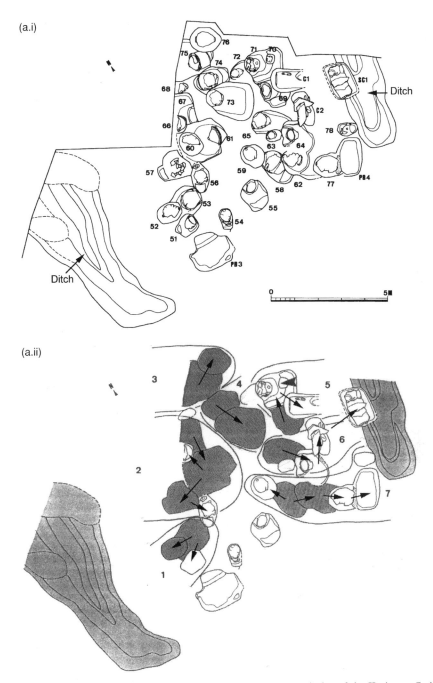

Figure 4.7 Middle and Late Yayoi mortuary compounds: (a.i) general plan of the Kuriyama C site (from Mizoguchi 2005b). (a.ii) Burial sequences at the Kuriyama C site inferred to have represented distinct lineages/clans (from Mizoguchi 2005b). Key: 1–7: Burial sequences; Arrows: formation process of individual sequences.

(b)

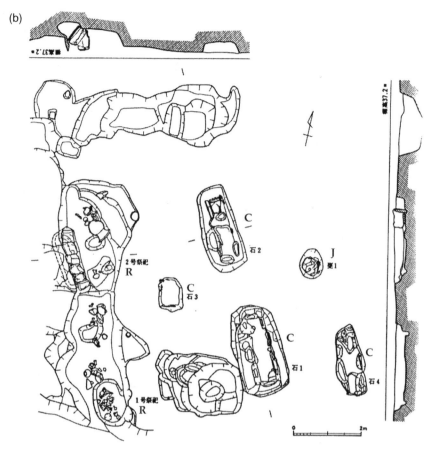

Figure 4.7 (*Cont.*) (b) The Mikumo-Teraguchi site (Fukuoka PBE 1983).
Key: C: cist, J: jar burial, R: ritual feature.

and a small number of infants or children in a mortuary compound, often either covered with an earthen mound or encircled by a ditch (Figure 4.7 (b)) (Mizoguchi 2002, 190–193).

In the preceding late Middle Yayoi period, between c. 100 BC and AD1, the custom of burying a limited number of the dead in a mortuary compound was practised (Figure 4.7 (a.i)). However, those who were buried in the mortuary compounds appear to have been the individuals chosen from wider corporate units such as clans (Mizoguchi 1995, 2002, 149–183). Those who were buried at each of the mortuary compounds do not appear to have been members of a household/lineage. A large majority of those who were buried in the compounds were male, and they were buried as if forming burial sequences; a newly dead person was quite intentionally buried right next to a pre-existing burial, and that practice was often repeated to form a spatio-temporal sequence of burials (Figure 4.7 (a.ii); Mizoguchi 1995, 2002, 2005b). Each of the compounds has a number of such burial sequences (Figure 4.7

(a.ii)). Besides, those mortuary compounds with burial sequences tend to have existed only at large-scale settlements of a central-place-like character (Mizoguchi 2005b). These facts lead to the inference that those who were buried in the mortuary compounds of the late Middle Yayoi period were members of clans constituting a regional community such as a tribe and were chosen to be buried there as representatives of individual clans (Figure 4.7 (a)) (Mizoguchi 2005b). If this were the case, the social organisation would have been the one which is commonly described as 'tribal', the social stratification of the period would have been minimal and higher status would have been *achieved* rather than *ascribed*. In that sense, the emergence during the Late Yayoi period of the custom of burying individuals, likely to have been members of a group on a household scale, together in a segregated mortuary compound can be understood to have marked the beginning of social stratification and ascribed status differences based upon inter-household differentiation. As shown below, a household, at this period, can be inferred to have been a lineage-scale or sub lineage-scale grouping (for a more detailed description of the matter, see Mizoguchi 2001, 153–155; 2002, 190–193). That the dead buried in the mortuary compounds of the Late Yayoi period included infants, buried in the same manner as adults, e.g., buried in cists (Figure 4.7 (b)), supports the thesis that the status of infants would have been determined by their group affiliation rather than by their achievements.

Concurrently, a significant change took place in the settlements. A segregated ditch-encircled cluster of around five pit dwellings and raised floor buildings, inferred to be granaries, emerged in settlements (Figure 4.8) (e.g. Takesue 2002, 68–74). In the preceding Middle Yayoi period, individual settlement sites consisted of some clusters of pit dwellings. Occasionally, such settlements were encircled by a ditch, but none of the clusters constituting such a settlement was ever individually ditch-enclosed. In that regard, the emergence of the segregated, ditch-enclosed, single residential compound amongst the clusters of pit dwellings constituting a settlement site is important. Concerning the fact that around five pit dwellings constituted a cluster and each dwelling can be inferred from its size (c. 40 square metres) to have been occupied by a nuclear family-scale group, those who lived in such a cluster, around twenty or thirty in number, would have formed a lineage-scale group (Mizoguchi 2001, 153–155). Considering that granaries were exclusively located in a segregated, ditch-encircled compound, the phenomenon suggests that stratification between lineage-scale groups, relating to the control of the storage of agricultural products, emerged during the Late Yayoi period.

The mortuary and settlement evidence of the period suggests that the society, as the textbook drawings depict, was divided into two strata, the upper one being occupied by the lineage-scale groups, living in segregated, ditch-encircled residential compounds, buried in segregated mortuary compounds, and being in charge of the control of agricultural products (Mizoguchi 2002, 190–193).

The existence of a social stratification consisting of two strata, as far as the descriptions of Weizhi and the related archaeological evidence go, appears to be certain. The next problem is whether rank difference was as 'severe' as that depicted in the drawing, particularly in the 'original' version. There is another description in Weizhi of

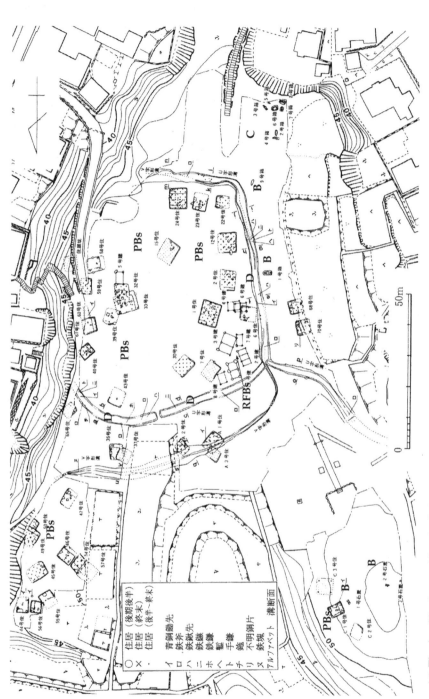

Figure 4.8 The site of Sendoyama. Note the ditch-enclosed compound in the right-hand of the plan with pit dwellings and raised-floor buildings (probably granaries) (from: Kiyama-machi Iseki hakkutsu chosa-dan 1983).

Key: PBs: pit buildings (probably pit dwellings), RFBs: raised-floor buildings (probably granaries), B: burials, C: mortuary compound, D: ditch.

✻ Rank, Yayoi / Koguryo

the stratification in the society. This was about the way in which communal meetings were carried out (cf. Yamao 1986, 173). It says that there was no difference between male and female in their code of conduct/etiquette at the meeting. It is also mentioned that the lower-ranked just clapped hands rather than kneeling down when meeting those of higher-rank on such occasions. In contrast, the existence of a strict rank-related code of conduct at such meetings is depicted for the polity called 'Koguryo', located in the northern part of the Korean peninsula and the southern part of north-eastern China. Here, the commoners were not able to mingle with such upper-ranking people as the messenger of the 'king'. Compared with this, the rank division and rank-based code of conduct depicted to have been played out in communal gatherings in the archipelago appears minimal.[9]

In addition, it has been claimed from an osteoarchaeological reconstruction of the kin organisation of the Late Yayoi and Early Kofun periods that the unilinear male-line descent of the chieftainship had not yet been established. According to Yoshiyuki Tanaka, the male and female individuals buried together in a mortuary compound of the Late Yayoi (see Figure 4.11) are, concerning genetically inherited traits such as affinities in tooth-crown measurements and non-metric characteristics of the skull, brothers and sisters or cousins rather than husbands and wives (Tanaka 1995, 140–145). This suggests that spouses were sent back to their original corporate groups, such as their home lineages, and buried there (Tanaka 1995). If this were the case, it would further suggest that kin affiliation remained important, and that the basic function of the lineage and the clan as the unit of communal ownership and the inheritance of wealth and right was preserved to a significant degree. In other words, *communal egalitarianism* still remained in place.

Let us now turn to sex/gender relations. Weizhi records that there was no difference between male and female etiquette at communal meetings. This suggests that the relationship between male and female was not as strictly stratified as the original version of the textbook drawing depicted, and which the amendment, intriguingly, further exaggerated. Weizhi recorded that the upper-ranked males tended to have four or five wives and some lower-ranked males also had two or three wives. This might be taken to suggest that polygamy, a trait of the patriarchal family-based social organisation, was practised. However, again, the above-mentioned osteoarchaeological research suggests that the post-marital residential rule of the period was bilocal (Tanaka 1995), and in some cases a mode in which a man visited a number of women in a loose relation of marriage would have been practised (Obayashi 1977, Chapter 5). This rather points away from the polygamy thesis. It is rather more likely to have been the case that those who gathered the information for the compilation of Weizhi tried to make sense of what was going on in the domain of Wa, which no doubt appeared to them a primitive place compared to an equivalent-looking practice in

[9] Akira Yoshida emphasises the severity of the rank differentiation by interpreting the act of clapping to show respect to the upper-ranked as a unique indigenous custom as courteous as kneeling (Yoshida 1995, 83–85). However, if his interpretation were indeed the case, it still is undeniable that the Koguryo custom did not allow the commoners to be co-present with the messenger of the king and hence it must have depicted a much severer rank-based code than that of the Yamatai-koku polity.

[handwritten annotation: ✷ Women in Mounds of early Kofun]

contemporary China, one of the empires of the ancient world, where patriarchal authority and polygamy were already well established.

The archaeological mortuary evidence of the phase does not support the strict stratification of the relationship between male and female either. Females and infants/children were buried in the same manner as males in the mortuary compounds of the Late Yayoi, and a female was sometimes buried in the central cist on top of the round part of the keyhole-shaped tumulus in the Early Kofun period, partially overlapping the time of the Yamatai-koku polity (cf. Tanaka 1995).

The above have further complicated the picture. As far as the depiction of ranking is concerned, the softening of the expression required by the committee is 'relatively' closer to what Weizhi and the archaeological evidence suggest. However, concerning the depiction of the age–gender-based relationship, i.e., the relationship between male, female and juvenile, what the committee required strongly contradicts what the document recorded and what the archaeological evidence suggests.

In all, both the original and the amended versions contain elements which clearly contradict both the contemporary document, i.e., Weizhi, which is regarded as the most valuable source for the investigation of societies in the archipelago in the third century AD and also the contemporary archaeological evidence. Why?

Competing desires

The complex picture emerging from the above suggests that desires driven by the zeal to educate, a significant constitutive element of the technology of self identification in classical modernity, forced the scholars involved in writing and amending the textbook to articulate an image of the past which contains elements contradicting the available evidence. Both those who created and those who amended the drawing can safely be inferred to have been operating according to different agendas, can be assumed to have been equally motivated by a sense of 'duty' to make the pupils *proper citizens*, which, again, is a constitutive element of the technology of modern self identification, and *knowingly* and selectively ignored parts of the available evidence, as revealed above. Then, what are the agendas behind the creation and the actual amendments of the drawing?

The investigation in Chapter 4.2 has revealed the decisive role played by the notion of a 'national body' in the structuration of both the archaeological and the general discursive space of Japan since its foundation as a modern nation-state. This leads to the inference that differences dividing those who produced the original drawing and those who demanded its amendment are in some way related to differences in their attitudes toward this notion. Bearing in mind that the notion of a national body is constituted by a network of metaphorical inter-references between basically somatic/kinship-related units and concepts (see the previous section), it can be further inferred that the points of dispute are related to differences in the way such units as a family and its constitutive elements are *properly*, or *desirably*, depicted. On this basis, let us interpret the differences between the drawings.

Drawing upon the above, let me begin by holistically formulating a hypothesis: for those who amended the drawing, promoting a patriarchy as the ideal organisational

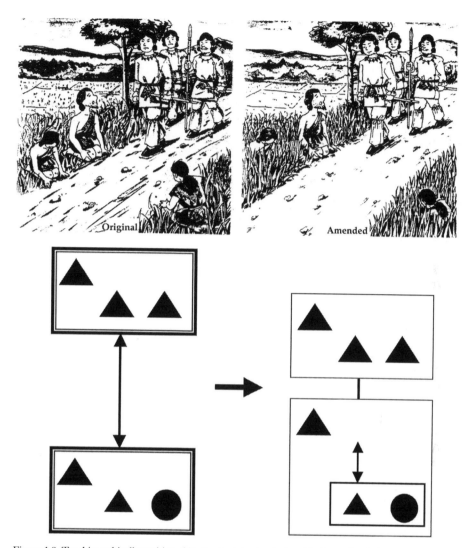

Figure 4.9 Two hierarchically positioned levels of patriarchy depicted in the textbook drawing. Note that the relationship between those who walk down the road and those who kneel is made significantly less severe and that the difference in status between the father and the mother and the son who are kneeling is made more obvious (see schematised diagrams below the drawings).

model for society as well as for the desirable family unit was the agendum with which to operate. In relation to the notion of the national body, the patriarchy depicted here appears to consist of two hierarchically positioned levels (Figure 4.9).

As shown in Figure 4.9, a probable 'family', kneeling at the roadside, looking rather like a modern nuclear family which would not have existed as a basic unit of social organisation back in the third century AD (as fully illustrated in Chapter 4.4 below, the basic unit of social organisation at the time was a lineage-like grouping), was depicted in the original as fairly 'egalitarian' in its internal structure in comparison with the amended version (Figures 4.6 and 4.9). In the amended version, in contrast, the 'father' not only looked up at the face of the person leading the party of higher-ranked individuals walking down the road but was also positioned differently from the 'mother' and the 'child': the father remained kneeling *out of* the roadside bush, while the 'mother' and 'child' were relocated to kneel down in the bush with their torsos almost hidden by the grass (Figure 4.9). The status of the father, in terms of his relational distance from those who walked down the road, was made higher than the original: he was allowed to be out of the roadside bush and to look up while the mother and the child were not allowed to be out of the roadside bush nor to look up at the faces of those who walked down the road, i.e., the higher-ranked.

Another hierachical relation depicted here lay between those who knelt in the roadside bush and those who walked down the road. The latter, the superior, can be inferred to be depicted as male from their hairstyle, attire and accessories, and in that sense they are situated in the position of patriarchal figures relative to those kneeling (Figure 4.9).

The amendments made to these two hierarchically positioned patriarchal relationships includes another very suggestive clue to the character of the patriarchal organisation which those who amended the drawing considered desirable/ideal. In the amended version, the person leading the party was made to smile gently at the kneeling father. This amendment was carried out with such a degree of care as to add some wrinkles to the shoulder part of his cloth (Figure 4.6). Those who followed him were made to smile too. The contrast with the stern faces in the original is significant. What is this gentleness and air of sympathy, coexisting with authority and dominance?

Here we have two seemingly mutually contradictory axes of alterations coexisting in the drawing: one exaggerating hierarchical relations, the other softening the relation of dominance and authority (Figure 4.9). I would contend that they draw upon a unified intention. In other words, a social model has to be sought which can accommodate two axes of the alterations, i.e., (a) the alteration concerning those kneeling, and (b) the alteration concerning those who walk down the road, if we wish to make sense of this hidden intention (Figure 4.9).

Let us begin by confirming a simple fact: (a) and (b) are both to do with authority, domination and subordination. In (a), the relation of dominance exists between a male (father), a female (mother) and a child (son), and in (b) it exists between those who walk down the road and those who kneel. What we can do next is to look for a dominant–subordinate relation which can accommodate them as two different expressions of a *single cause/character* (Figure 4.9).

Let me put forward a model: as suggested, the relationship between those who kneel and those who walk down the road depicted in the amended version can be transformed to that between the father as the dominant figure and the other family members as the subordinates as a community (Figure 4.9). If this were accepted, it would not be too far fetched to infer that the relationship between the dominant and the subordinate was amended by the committee appointed by the education ministry to be depicted as one of *mutual respect* and *affection*. If the two dominant–subordinate relationships, (a) and (b), were in the relationship of mutual mediation/transformation, and if one of them depicted the relationship as one of mutual respect and affection, the other would also be understood to imply the same, or at least be designed to draw one's understanding in that direction (Figure 4.9). In other words, the whole scene is transformed from the depiction of the *stricture of dominance* to that of *gentleness and mutual affection*.

I put forward an inference at the beginning of the above argument that the disputes between the original and the amended versions of the drawing were over the notion of the national body. The inference appears to have turned out to be feasible, to say the least. The national body, as illustrated in the previous section, is conceptually constituted by the *fictive kinship* between the emperor and the subject, the former the father and the latter his children, and by the organic ties imagined to exist between them. The amendment, as far as the outcome of the above investigation is concerned, tried to strengthen the authority and power of the patriarchal figure in the depiction of the commoner family and to ease the air of domination, subordination and tension in the depiction of the social hierarchy of the society. We have already revealed that both the original and the amended versions include contradictions to the available written and archaeological evidence. Let us now look into the implications of these findings. In order to undertake the task, we have to begin with the positionality of the 'Yamatai-koku discourse' in the general discursive formation of Japanese classical modernity.

The emperor and the subject
The period of the 'Yamatai-koku' polity is treated in archaeology as well as in lay knowledge as the period beginning with the formation of the polity later to become the 'Yamato court' polity which ruled the archipelago except for the Ryukyu islands, Hokkaido island and the northernmost part of Honshu island (e.g. Fukunaga 2002). The 'Yamato court' was ruled by successive 'Okimi' (O (great)-kimi (leader)) paramount chiefs, to whom the genealogy of the current emperor is 'believed' to be traced back. This understanding is actually quite problematic archaeologically as well as historically, and this will be fully illustrated in the next section in this chapter. However, the belief, as illustrated in the next section as well, has a strong hold within the discourse of the origin and identity of the Japanese. Bearing this information in mind, i.e., the widespread association between this specific period and the origin of the emperor system, our attention is naturally drawn to the contrast between the current status of the emperor (and imperial family) and that before the end of the Second World War.

The amended drawing seems to depict the idealised relationship between the emperor and his subjects: the emperor as the *authoritative* but *affectionate* father-figure of the subject and the nation before the end of the Second World War, in contrast with the emperor as 'the symbol of the unity of the nation' as stated in the new constitution founded just after the end of the Second World War. It is quite striking, as illustrated in Chapter 4.2, that the image and function of the emperor and his family, the existence of which was blamed as the deepest cause of the devastation of the Second World War, remained structurally almost intact long after the war. However, what is more striking is that it seems to be the case that the system of images and role models for all categories of the subject, originally created in the formative period of the Japanese modern nation-state in organic association with the creation of the aforementioned image of the emperor, symbolised by the metaphorical unity between the emperor and the national-body ('Koku-tai'), appears to be still alive and kicking in the mind of the committee which ordered the amendment and, hence, the legislator.

In the Meiji constitution, which was replaced with the current one just after the Second World War, the exclusive right of control over family properties and other matters concerning the life-course of family members was legally guaranteed to belong to the head of the house (*Ka*(house)-*cho*(chief)), i.e., the father, who was commonly the eldest son of the family of the previous generation. This was accompanied by the quite artificial formation of specific role norms/models for other members of the family: the wife as faithful and obedient, the daughter to strive to be like her mother, and the son to be like his father and a good soldier willing to sacrifice his life for the emperor and the nation. One aim of the projects was to transform the feudal state into a nation-state with the ability to compete against colonial powers, having already colonised regions surrounding the archipelago (see Chapters 2 and 4.2). To make the family unit stable and clearly defined in order to secure a constant supply of soldiers as well as tax revenue was one of the most important tasks the first modern government of Japan (the Meiji administration which replaced the Tokugawa feudal government) had to accomplish. An image of the patriarchal family consisting of the affectionate but strong and strict father, the obedient and supportive wife/mother and healthy and obedient children was promoted in order to create the 'modern' Japanese family for the 'modern' nation-state by using as wide-ranging media as possible, including school textbooks. And, above all, the image of the emperor Meiji, the first emperor, hence the most significant symbolic capital available to the legislator, of the modern Japanese nation state, was promoted as the father of the nation: the family was made the mirror image of the state, and the state was made the mirror image of the family (Taki 1988).

It has turned out that the whole picture symbolised by the amended version of the picture is as if we are still haunted by the ghost of the political ideology of the pre-Second World War era. What is interesting here, though, is that we feel we no longer live in conditions in which the promotion of an image like this has any pragmatic effect upon the way we live our lives. As briefly mentioned in Chapter 2.3 and fully elucidated in the next chapter, we live in late-/mature modernity, i.e., a society characterised by functionally differentiated social systems, in which the indeterminacy and paradox of communication can no longer be solved/de-paradoxised by referring to the *transcendental* such as the emperor. In such conditions, it is quite unlikely that the desire of the committee and the legislator can be fulfilled: their desire is not only detached from the reality of contemporary society, a society lacking the transcendental, but may also be exposed to harsher relativisation and cynicism because of its relying on the old strategy for reintegrating fragmented communication fields, which looks not only outdated but even ridiculous. Then what is the point of sticking to the image?

Exactly the same problem can be pointed out in the original drawing. The intentions behind the original version of the drawing, which can be assumed to be found where the drawing contradicts the available evidence just as in the case of the amended version, can be relatively easily detected by referring to what has been revealed above: why did those who walk down the road have to look arrogant and attired differently from those who kneel down at the roadside, contradicting the description of Weizhi?

It appears that the relationship between those who walk down the road and those who kneel at the roadside, i.e., the relationship between the dominant and the subordinate, had to be depicted as *antagonistic* rather than affectionate and respectful. Why should it be depicted this way? The reason appears to lie in the discursive space in which the mind-set of those who were involved in the act of amendment were caught up.

Immediately after the end of the Second World War, one of the most important objectives set up by historians (including archaeologists) deriving from the experience of the devastation of the war was to deconstruct the firmly embedded mind-set which unconditionally accepted the transcendental status of the notion of the national body and the emperor system as its embodiment (see Chapter 4.2). When the Meiji state was founded back in the late nineteenth century, what was formulated as the ideal model for the newborn nation was what can be described as a modified Asiatic-despotic model; the paramount chief (=the emperor) is the paramount patriarch of the patriarchal communities constituting an Asiatic state. The paramount chief is, in that sense, perceived as the father of the nation, and his will unconsciously represents the will of the nation. The notion of the individual as the independent, active and creative 'self' does not exist. The destiny of the state symbolised and embodied by the destiny of the paramount chief is the destiny of everyone, and their hope can only be accomplished through the mediation of the chief. In this *organic* relationship between the dominant and the subordinate, which is suitably captured by the notion of the *Koku*(nation)-*tai*(body)=national body (see Chapter 3), the conceptual boundary which divides individual bodies and minds is blurred: it is an extreme form of *mutual affection*.

The blurring of individuality and the effective denial of the individual as the active agent were exactly what were felt by intellectuals to be the cause of the devastation of the Second World War. Unless this iron cage of the episteme of ultimate dominance over the mind and body of the nation was deconstructed, 'progressive', socialist-Marxist historians (including some archaeologists, see Chapter 4.2) believed that Japan as a nation-state would never be fully modernised and would go down the path to yet another devastating war. In the domain of historical and archaeological studies, this belief took shape in the debate about the emergence and transformation of despotism in general and the timing and mechanism of the emergence of an *antagonistic* relationship between the dominant and subordinate 'classes' in particular (eg. Rekishi-gaku kenkyu-kai 1951, 11–28).

The debate was motivated to deconstruct the belief that the relationship between the emperor and the subject, since the moment the emperor emerged, had always been one of affection and voluntary respect. Regardless of whether the ancient Japanese state was defined as an Asiatic-despotic state or otherwise, as far as Marxist doctrine was concerned, the social relations characterising any state were antagonistic between the dominant and the subordinate classes. In that sense, the relationship between the emperor and his subject, since the foundation of the Japanese ancient state, had never been what could be characterised as organic mutual affection and respect but had always been what could be characterised as *disguised antagonism*. And this appears to be exactly what the original tried to depict, as far as our investigation so far is concerned.

Interestingly enough, however, and contrary to what the original drawing appears to be trying to depict, the transitional phase between the Yayoi and the Kofun (mounded tomb) periods, the time of the Yamatai-koku polity, commonly and even by 'Marxist' historians and archaeologists, was not interpreted as the phase which witnessed the rise of this antagonism. Rather, the thesis that the relationship between the chief and the subordinate had been stratified but remained tied through kin-based corporate bondage was put forward and became subject to a lively scholastic debate during the late 1940s and 1950s (cf. Hara 1972, 396–408). This thesis argued that the chief behaved as the *heroic* leader of the corporate group throughout the early part of the Kofun period (Hara 1972). What motivated the debate was an interest in the process and mechanism of transformation from a truly organic, affectionate relationship between the chief and his subject based upon kin ties, to an antagonistic, oppressive one under the disguise of continuing mutual affection and kin-based bondage. Since then, the timing of the establishment of the ancient Japanese state has been constantly debated, but the dominant trend in the study of Japanese history has consistently designated it as after the end of the Kofun period (cf. Hara 1972). (In that regard, it is intriguing that the thesis designating the establishment of the ancient Japanese state as at the beginning of the Kofun period enjoys a certain support in archaeology. We shall investigate what is behind this phenomenon in the next section.)

Despite that, the scholars involved in the creation of the original apparently tried to depict the Yayoi–Kofun transitional phase as the time when the relationship between the chief and *his* subjects had already become highly hierarchised and antagonistic by ignoring the general trend. This is revealed in a much bolder manner in another textbook drawing (Figure 4.10). Here, we can recognise an amendment intending exactly the same thing as we saw in the previous drawing: the bow which the subordinate standing off the road made to the dominant walking down the road is made shallower in the amended version. We can infer from this that the dispute over the reconstruction of the society of the time is identical to what we investigated. However, there is another amendment which is, at first glance, difficult to make sense of. In the original, there is a figure walking away from the scene behind those walking down the road (Figure 4.10). In the amended version, however, this figure is erased (Figure 4.10). This figure is so obscure that it is unlikely that a student could spot

Figure 4.10 Mysterious elimination of a figure from a textbook drawing (originally in Osaka Shoseki 1991, featured in Teshigawara 1991, by kind permission of Osaka Shoseki, June 2005).

its erasure without instruction even if the original and the amended were put side by side. This suggests that the amendment was related to matter deeply connected to the mentality and identity of those who were involved in the amendment.

If we situate this rather mysterious amendment in the dispute over the relationship between the dominant and the subordinate, interpreted to metaphorically represent that between the emperor and the subject, we can make sense of what is behind it. The figure erased in the amended version is walking away from the scene where the relation of either domination and subordination or affection and respect is being played out. This field of the reproduction of a particular mode of social relations is made possible by the gaze of those who are walking down the road; regardless of whether they are affectionate leader figures or not, their gaze makes those who happen to be on the roadside stop doing what they were doing and bow to them. If the nature of the relationship is that of mutual affection and respect, even if it were ignited by the gaze of the beloved leader figures, the respect would always be in the mind of the subordinate. However, if the relationship were one of *antagonistic* domination and subordination, as soon as the gaze was withdrawn, the subordinates would immediately stop showing false respect and go back to what they were doing.

This, I would argue, is what those who were involved in the amendment feared: they can be inferred to have feared to have the drawing interpreted that way. And, considering that the meaning of why this figure has to be here in the original is also very difficult to make sense of, the intention of the producers of the original to put this figure here can be inferred to have made the relationship between those who were walking down the road and those who bowed on the roadside appear to be antagonistic; the affection from the subordinate to the dominant was so artificial that the former walked off as soon as they escaped the gaze of the latter.

✳ way of depiction

Enduring dichotomies

To sum up, both those who were involved in the creation of the drawing and those who were involved in its amendment attempted to *invent* rather than *reconstruct* the image of the past, in a way which reflected their desire for the future in a rather complex manner. Their motive in doing this, I would argue by referring to some characteristics of classical modernity illustrated earlier in this section, derived from the belief that society could be engineered in a certain direction, and that the engineering could be conducted through the disciplining of the unenlightened within the society. Education was obviously the most effective means with which to accomplish this. Through education, the nation would be transformed from the unenlightened, a mere object controlled by the elite, to the enlightened, subject to voluntarily fulfil their duty to the state (cf. Fujitani 1994, Chapter 1).

The belief that creating an image of the past which reflects one's desire for the future can do something to engineer the present always and inevitably implies that the moment in the past which is depicted in the image was the moment when something which one wants to *praise/accuse* either emerged from, or was already in action. Besides, in order to enlighten the unenlightened, it is desirable that the past appears the 'same', i.e., something which can be made sense of, because otherwise the unenlightened cannot understand what the past means to them by comparing what the past was like with their own experience in the present. Against such backgrounds, the past was depicted by those who were involved in the amendment as the ideal image for the present and the future, and by those who were involved in the production of the original as the time when the evil which led to the devastation of the Second World War had emerged.

This dichotomy, being for or against the emperor system, as illustrated in the previous section, originated in the aftermath of the Second World War. Defeat in the Second World War and the devastation which it brought resulted in a crisis in the reproduction of self identity for most Japanese. What they had believed to be right and identified themselves with collapsed overnight. This 'spiritual vacuum' had to be filled quickly by something else, and the US-led allied forces occupying the land, as well as the Japanese elite and intellectuals, knew it (Kan 2001, Chapter 5). That constituted the background against which the emperor system and allied structuring principles of the general discursive space of Japan were carefully protected with a minor, almost cosmetic change in the vocabulary used to describe them (Kan 2001). Mixed feelings towards this necessary compromise have been the backbone of the enduring dichotomy along which the dichotomies structuring the reproduction of various communication systems, such as right versus left in the political communication system and conservative versus progressive in the educational communication system, are formed (see Figure 4.5).

This 'fundamental dichotomy' of post-Second World War Japan has, until recently, been functioning as an iron cage in which virtually every discursive formation is locked up. Chapter 4.4 will explore the interior of that iron cage by examining the way the archaeological study of the Yayoi–Kofun transitional phase, the time period of the Yamatai-koku polity, has been studied.

4.4 The invisible iron cage: Kofun (mounded tomb) archaeology and the narrative of continuity and homogeneity

The positionality of Kofun archaeology

The study of the Kofun (mounded tomb) period, between circa the late third century and the sixth century AD, occupies a unique position in the discursive space of Japanese archaeology. The keyhole-shaped tumuli, the feature by which the period is defined (cf. Kondo 1983), are often monumental in their scale and dominate the sphere of the visual representation of not only the archaeology of the period but also of Japanese archaeology in general, often in the form of bird's eye view plans of its largest examples (Figure 4.1). Many of them are designated as 'imperial mausolea', i.e., the resting places of the supposed direct ancestors of the present imperial family, and taken care of by the imperial household agency ('*ku*(palace)*nai*(interior)-*cho*(ministry)').

As a category of archaeological material, the keyhole-shaped tumulus has a distinct characteristic: each tumulus can be treated as a sort of a *macro-context*, and the finds and the features can be treated as forming an assemblage. (Although, of course, a tumulus was sometimes reused for further burials and other activities and might yield artefacts from more than one archaeo-chronological stage.) Accordingly, individual finds and features have been subject to intensive typo-chronological and stylistic investigations, and their chronological positions and techno-cultural provenances have been investigated to an ever-increasing extent (e.g. Kondo 1991).

The combination of those traits/characteristics of the main material of the Kofun archaeology, the keyhole-shaped tumulus, constitutes a significant structuring principle of the discourse of the Kofun period. A strong emphasis on typological sequencing and the construction and elaboration of the chronological system of various items ranging from portable artefacts to the earthen mounds makes the main objective of the study of the period the uncovering of *continuity*, i.e., *gradual* change in the techno-stylistic traits of such individual items, as a necessary prerequisite to classifying the items into chronological types and temporal units (Kondo 1991).

The pursuit of continuity, however, is not confined to the sphere of chronology building. That many of the largest examples of the keyhole-shaped tumulus are designated by the imperial household agency as 'imperial mausolea' and are regarded by archaeologists as the tombs of the paramount chieftains, i.e., the ancient emperors (described as *Okimi* or *Daio*, the latter being the customary way archaeologists describe them), means that the reconstruction of the sequential order of the largest keyhole-shaped tumuli of the present-day Kinki region of central Japan, particularly of the Nara basin and the Kawachi plain (described as the 'Kinki core region' hereafter), is the reconstruction of their materialised *genealogy*. Here, again, *continuity*, i.e., the continuous line of the *unilinear descent*[10] of the paramount chieftainship, is the presupposition of the study. In summary, both the methodological requirement and the inevitable connection to the study of the ancient emperors make the pursuit

---

[10] Whether the system of unilinear descent was practised at the time remains the subject of dispute (see Chapter 4.3), and we shall come back to the issue later.

of continuity a norm/structuring principle of Kofun archaeology as a communication system.

We have to remind ourselves that the above-mentioned structuring principle of the Kofun archaeology, namely the pursuit of *continuity*, is firmly connected to the main theme of post-Second World War Japanese archaeology, to *trace* the *origin* of the source of the ills of pre-Second World War Japan which brought devastation and suffering to the nation, i.e., tracing the origin of the imperial family, as illustrated in Chapter 4.2. In that sense, Kofun archaeology has functioned as a critical discourse of Japan as a modern nation-state. Meanwhile, as the following will illustrate, Kofun archaeology as a communication system has been, and still is, locked up in the *paradox*: Kofun archaeology as a critique of the emperor system contributes, though negatively, to the constitution and maintenance of the binary code with which the discourse of the emperor system itself is reproduced, and upon which the discourse survives, the binary code being genealogical continuity from the beginning of history versus genealogical discontinuity.

What follows will try to illustrate the fateful *paradox* of the self-referential repro-duction of a communication system in modernity. In contrast to the communication systems of hierarchical differentiation (i.e., pre-modern social formations, see Chap-ter 3.6), which can de-paradoxise themselves by referring to hierarchically organised values and norms such as religious doctrines, class-based virtue/codes of conduct, and so on, the communication systems of functionally differentiated society can only de-paradoxise themselves by randomly referring to other communication systems (i.e., what one utters is recognised as right when referring to what is going on in one particular domain of society, but recognised as wrong when referring to another). In other words, once the relation of mutual de-paradoxisation was formed between two communication systems, they would not be able to be genuinely critical of one another because *a critical discourse can only be made possible by the existence of what it criticises*. The relationship between Kofun archaeology and the emperor system is an example of this paradox. What follows is an attempt to reveal the relation of mutual mediation/de-paradoxisation between the discourse of the emperor system and that of Kofun archaeology.

The origin of the keyhole-shaped tumulus, the origin of the imperial genealogy?
The study of the origin of the keyhole-shaped tumulus, which is defined as marking the beginning of the Kofun period, typically shows the characteristics of the discourse of Kofun archaeology described above: the pursuit of origin and continuity.

If the origin of the keyhole-shaped tumulus and the beginning of the Kofun period marked the beginning of the continuity, i.e., the continuity of the line of the unilin-ear descent of the paramount and regional chieftainship, both (a) the domination of the paramount chieftainship over the regional chieftainship and (b) the system of the unilinear descent of the chiefly status, would have had to have been established at or before that 'point of origin' (Mizoguchi 2000a). Accordingly, these factors, i.e., fac-tors (a) and (b) above, have been treated not as *hypotheses* to be verified/falsified but as *prerequisites* for study (Mizoguchi 2000a). In other words, materials are recognised as the constitutive elements of the communication system of Kofun archaeology, i.e., recognised as relevant to the discourse of Kofun archaeology, should they fit into the picture deriving from these prerequisites. Those materials which cannot be fitted into the picture tend to be ignored. Let us begin by examining the way the process towards the beginning of the Kofun period has been studied.

Mortuary studies have not only played a crucial role in the study but also well exemplify the trend. In order to illustrate the case, we have to begin by examining the way the period before the beginning of the Kofun period, i.e., the Yayoi period, has been studied. The study of the mortuary practices of the Yayoi period (c. 400/500 BC to AD 250/275), which witnessed the systematic introduction of rice paddy-field agriculture from the Korean peninsula and the subsequent increase of social complexity, has been conducted to reveal the process of social hierarchisation, on both intra- and inter-regional polity levels, towards its *completion*, which is regarded as having been marked by the emergence of the keyhole-shaped tumulus, its allied mortuary ritual package, and their spread throughout western Japan and parts of eastern Japan (e.g. Kondo 1983, Chapter 7). The emergence of the keyhole-shaped tumulus is regarded as having marked both the establishment of the unilinear male-line descent of chieftainship and the establishment of the domination of the polity of the Kinki core region over the regional polities throughout eastern and some parts of western Japan (Kobayashi 1961, Chapter 4, esp. p. 145). Let me illustrate these points by looking into two exemplary case studies.

Hiroaki Takakura studied the temporal changes in the cemetery spatial structure of the northern Kyushu region, regarded as one of the core regions of Yayoi social evolution, with the assumption that they reflect changes in social organisation towards the establishment of social hierarchy at the intra-regional polity level (1973).

Takakura recognised the following trends in the temporal changes in intra-cemetery spatial structure and inter-cemetery relations.

(1) Both the number of burial groups (clusters of graves) constituting a cemetery and the number of graves constituting individual burial groups decreased through time.

(2) The gap between the burial groups constituting a cemetery and that between the burials constituting a burial group in terms of the quality and quantity of the grave goods and the size and structural sophistication of the mortuary facilities widened through time.

(3) The gap between the cemeteries in a regional unit in terms of the quality and quantity of grave goods and the size and structural sophistication of mortuary facilities widened through time.

Takakura suggests that these trends were associated with the following changes in social organisation.

(a) A number of extended family-scale groups (lineages/clan-segment scale groups: the reading of the present author) would have been integrated to form a corporate unit undertaking the cultivation of a unit of rice paddies. Through the undertaking of communal labour organised by such a corporate unit, the leadership necessary for the coordination of work would have emerged. The necessity for negotiations with neighbouring corporate units concerning a range of matters, including occasional collaboration over the maintenance of irrigation facilities for paddy fields and the exchange of goods and people, would also have necessitated the establishment of such leadership, and the relationship between the extended-family scale groups constituting a corporate unit would also have become hierarchised as the group to which the leader belonged became dominant over other groups.

(b) Various factors concerning rice agriculture, such as accessibility to a water source, soil conditions, and so on, together with other factors such as accessibility to exchange networks and degree of success in accumulating wealth through manipulating exchange systems, would have generated and widened the gap between these corporate units.

(c) Stimulated by factors (a) and (b), the individual extended-family scale groups(/lineages, although Takakura himself does not use the term and concept) constituting a corporate unit became internally divided (disintegrated) into smaller units and their relationship hierarchised.

The trends observable in the transformation of the cemetery spatial structure (1)–(3), Takakura inferred, reflect the progression of trends (a)–(c), which led to the gradual erosion and eventual destruction of communal egalitarianism and the mode of social integration based upon it: mediatorship, necessitated by an increasing social complexity resulting from the maturation of rice paddy-field agriculture-based social organisation, initially took the form of communal, first-amongst-equal type, leaders. However, their status was gradually consolidated and led to the stratification of social relations in the form of intra- and inter-communal social stratification and the associated destruction of the corporate ties internally binding such communal units as lineages and clans. This multilayered process, Takakura contended, finally reached the point around the end of the Yayoi period/the beginning of the Kofun period when both the chieftainship of a regional polity of floodplain scale and the chieftainship presiding over a number of such floodplain-scale polities were established and the chieftainship also became monopolised by a particular lineage/household and inherited by its members. In all, Takakura's work traced the process toward the establishment/*origin* of the unilinear descent of the chieftainship on a regional (floodplain-scale) polity scale.

Hideji Harunari, by assuming that the spatial structure of a cemetery reflects the organisation of a corporate group as Takakura did, tried to reconstruct the post-marital residential patterns of the Yayoi period by analysing intra-cemetery spatial structure in terms of who was buried where (1984, 1985). His work exemplifies the tradition which presupposes that the establishment of unilinear male-line descent coincided with the establishment of centralised power and that of authority covering western Japan and parts of eastern Japan, i.e., the beginning of the Kofun period (cf. Kobayashi 1961, Chapter 4), and attempts to detect where the process towards

✱ Gender during the
Kofun period ↙

it progressed most *smoothly* and *rapidly* by studying the transformation of the spatial structure of the Yayoi cemetery.

The assumption is that the area where the system of unilinear male-line descent had been established *first* coincided with the centre of the spatial extension of the social integration reflected by the distributional horizon of the earliest keyhole-shaped tumuli, i.e., the present-day Kansai region (See Yukio Kobayashi's articles for the earliest examples of work based upon the above-mentioned assumption, collected in Kobayashi 1961).

Harunari examined the sex and age of the deceased and where and how they were buried in individual rectangular mortuary compounds (*hokei-shuko-bo*). He described the Kansai region, where the keyhole-shaped tumulus is thought to have emerged and where, hence, it is widely regarded to have been the centre of a newly established system of integration of a wide area including the northern Kyushu, the Inland Sea, the San'in (Japan Sea coast) and Kinki regions. He pointed out that the custom of burying an adult male and an adult female side-by-side in a square-compounded burial group was widespread in the Middle Yayoi period and inferred that they were the wife and husband of individual household units (Harunari 1985). From the fact that hierarchical differences appeared to exist between the square-compounded burial groups and flat graves without markers of spatial segregation, often coexisting together in a cemetery, he contended that those who were buried in the former were members of higher-ranked *patriarchal* households and the others were members of lower-ranked households. By referring to the fact that mortuary square compounds with single burials situated at their centre in the Late Yayoi period emerged in the same region, he argued that the system of unilinear male-line descent had been established by the Late Yayoi period in the Kansai region: the male who was buried at the centre of a square mortuary compound of the Late Yayoi, Harunari infers, was the patriarch of the dominant patriarchal household of an internally disintegrating corporate group.

In contrast, he argued, the social organisation of the northern Kyushu region as a core region of the Yayoi social evolution, as far as the kin organisation inferred from the cemetery spatial structure is concerned, remained based upon the system of bilinear/bilateral descent. This system would have prevented a hierarchical social structure from consolidating because the inheritance/line of descent of a social status and property would have been unstable and would have prevented the accumulation of wealth by a particular household. (I do not examine the validity of this inference itself here.)

From these factors and inferences, Harunari concluded that the Kansai region, where the system of unilinear male-line descent had been established earlier than other core regions of the Yayoi period, had achieved integration and internal hierarchisation of the polity first, and gained a dominant position over other polities across western Japan and parts of eastern Japan.

Despite their superficial differences, these studies, exemplifying the two dominant approaches to Yayoi mortuary practices and social organisation, share a fundamental trait, which is to presuppose that the beginning of the Kofun period and the emergence of the keyhole-shaped tumulus marked the *goal* of an evolutionary process.

This process is regarded as having been constituted by two interdependent spheres: (a) the process of increasing social complexity and hierarchisation (investigated by Takakura); and (b) the process towards the establishment of the system of unilinear male-line descent (investigated by Harunari).

However, some evidence which contradicts the above-illustrated findings and inferences can easily be found. (We shall come back to the implication of the issue of this 'easiness', i.e., why such obvious faults have been overlooked, later on.) Let us begin by examining Harunari's model.

The core contention of Harunari's thesis is that the system of unilinear male-line descent had been established in the Kinki region earlier than other core regions of Yayoi social evolution. That made the chieftains of the Kinki region able to establish their domination over the latter and form the foundation upon which the inter-regional hierarchy, the establishment of which is supposed to have marked the beginning of the Kofun period, was based. However, the available data, the mortuary evidence in particular, suggest the contrary: as far as the contents of the burial of the deceased in individual compound burial groups is concerned, the core regions of Yayoi social evolution throughout western Japan appear to have actually become *homogeneous* around the later half of the Late Yayoi period (Kondo 1983): as briefly illustrated in the previous section, the combination of around four or five adults, both male and female, with a couple of infants, constitutes the commonest content of the graves in the compound burial groups of the Late Yayoi period throughout western Japan, including northern Kyushu, the Inland Sea coast, San'in (Japan Sea coast), and Kinki regions (Figure 4.11) (Mizoguchi 2000b), and the deceased can be inferred to have been members of a chiefly lineage or a chiefly segment of the dominant clan of a regional polity (Tanaka 2000; Mizoguchi 2001).

Besides, the thesis has another serious problem: did the emergence of the segregated resting places for the members of individual chiefly lineages, in the form of the compound cemeteries, reflect the establishment of a system of unilinear male-line descent? Both Takakura and Harunari, as illustrated above, advocate this idea. According to the outcome of Yoshiyuki Tanaka's osteoarchaeological reconstruction of the kin relations among the deceased of some compound burial groups from the Late Yayoi period and the Early Kofun period (Tanaka 1995), though, the adult males and females buried together in individual compound burial groups and in individual burial facilities were not husbands and wives but probably brothers and sisters (Tanaka 1995). Based upon this observation, Tanaka infers that the chiefly family, whose eldest son had the exclusive right to be the chief of a clan-type corporate group, was not fully established at the time; it is more likely that the chieftain of a clan was *chosen* from the male and female members of the dominant household/lineage (Tanaka 1995). In all, Tanaka's study suggests that the system of unilinear male-line descent had not been established at the transition between the Yayoi and Kofun periods.

These observations show that the Kinki core region did not enjoy the advantage over the other regions of establishing the system of unilinear male-line descent earlier than other core regions of Yayoi social evolution. Besides, it turns out that the system

(a)

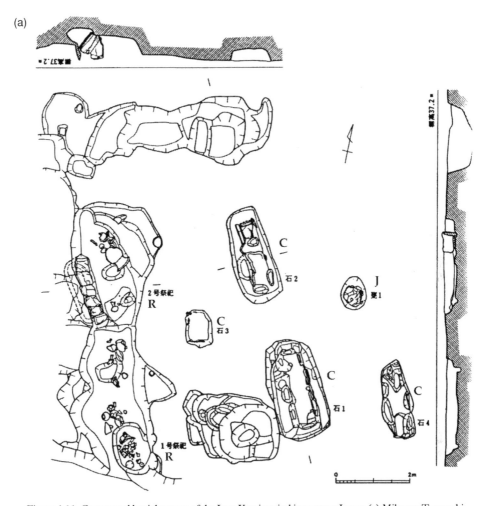

Figure 4.11 Compound burial groups of the Late Yayoi period in western Japan: (a) Mikumo-Teraguchi, Fukuoka Prefecture, Kyushu region (Fukuoka PBE 1983). Key: C: cist, J: burial jar, R: ritual pit. (b) Chusenji tumulus No. 9, Shimane Prefecture, the San'in (western Japan sea coastal) region (Kondo 1972). Key: WCBs: wooden coffin burials. (c) Akasaka-Imai, Kyoto Prefecture, the Tango (mid Japan sea coastal) region (Mineyama TBE 2001). Hatched rectangles represent grave pits.

of unilinear male-line descent had not been established anywhere in the archipelago at the time. Rather, the situation just before the beginning of the Kofun period in terms of the system of descent/kin organisation and mortuary practices as their representation was one of *homogenisation* throughout the wider area later to become almost covered by the distributional horizon of the earliest keyhole-shaped tumuli, i.e., the northern Kyushu, Inland Sea, San'in (the Japan Sea coast), and Kinki regions (Figure 4.11). In terms of social stratification in individual areas within the horizon, it can be said that a chiefly lineage emerged in individual clans, and the relationship between the clans occupying individual floodplain-scale units would have been one

(b)

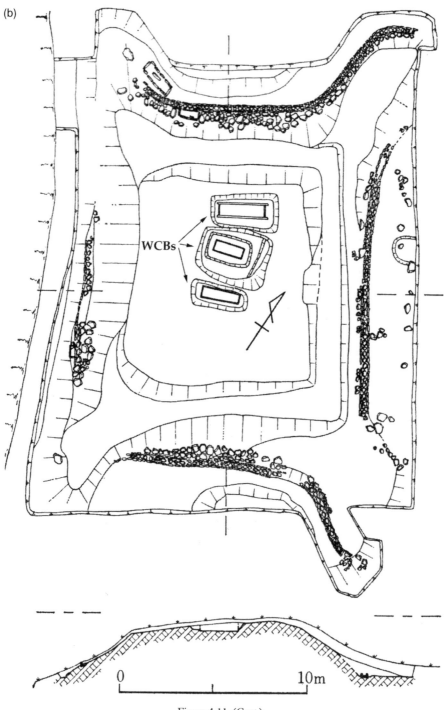

WCBs

Figure 4.11 (*Cont.*)

0   10m

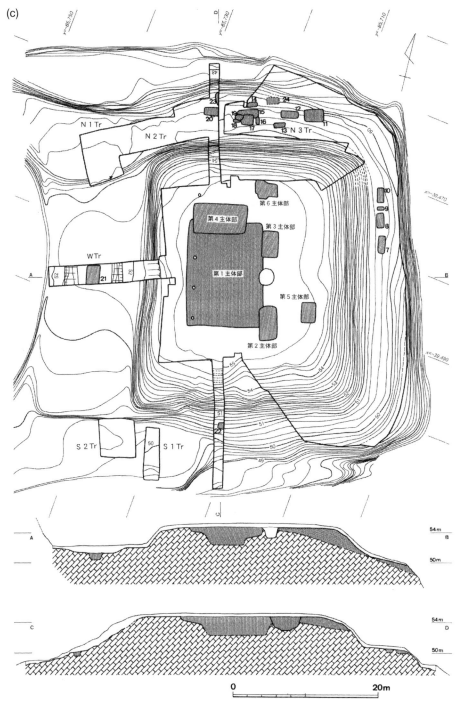

Figure 4.11 *(Cont.)*

of ongoing competition (Mizoguchi 2000b): differences in the quality and quantity of grave goods can be seen between the compound burials in individual floodplain-scale units, and that would have reflected the deepening hierarchisation of inter-clan relationships, but they appear to have often fluctuated through time. It is often the case that the distribution of the earliest keyhole-shaped tumuli of the area did not coincide with that of the rich compound burials of the previous, i.e., the Late Yayoi, period (cf. Mizoguchi 2000b). It appears that the relationship between neighbouring floodplain-scale units also underwent the same process of competition, probably over access to long-distance exchange networks which were being abruptly formed (e.g. Mizoguchi 2000b). Through this competitive process, it seems that larger units of integration, each of which consisted of several floodplain-scale units, gradually emerged throughout the horizon.

The relationship between such larger units of integration appears to have also been one of competition over the exchange of goods and raw materials. It has been strongly contended that the polities of the Kinki core region, the present-day Nara basin and Kawachi plain in particular, secured control over the importation of iron source materials from the Korean peninsula, and that served as an important base upon which the dominance of those polities over other polities throughout the horizon was established (e.g. Tsude 1998). However, progress recently made in the study of iron production technology, the distribution of iron tools, and the process of the replacement of stone equivalents by iron tools has falsified this thesis: in terms of these factors, the northern Kyushu region remained the most advanced throughout the Late Yayoi period, and the Kansai region was the least advanced amongst the regions constituting the distributional horizon of the earliest keyhole-shaped tumuli (cf. Murakami 2000). This strongly suggests that the distributional horizon of the earliest keyhole-shaped tumuli came into being in the midst of ongoing inter-group competition at various levels, contrary to the above-illustrated, widely held thesis that the distributional horizon came into being as a consequence of the *completion* to a certain degree of the hierarchisation of intra- and inter-group/regional relations.

A phenomenon which has recently come to attention appears to further reinforce the picture, that is: the earliest keyhole-shaped tumuli, which initially were believed to have been identical, have turned out to vary in their shape and content (i.e., the trace of the mortuary practices conducted there), in a manner which allows them to be classified into distinct morphological classes (e.g. Hojo 1999). The proto-types/genealogical roots of those categories can be found in Yayoi compound burial groups covered with earthen mounds in areas around the Inland Sea region, and the largest tumulus in the horizon, the Hashihaka tumulus of the south-eastern corner of the Nara basin, is interpreted to have been constructed by selectively putting together characteristics of those prototypes (Hojo 2000). However, as mentioned, the construction of the specimens of these regional types continues, and the Hashihaka-type remained one of the *subtypes* constituting the broad category of the earliest keyhole-shaped tumulus type, although, admittedly, its specimens were distributed widely throughout the distributional horizon of the earliest keyhole-shaped tumuli (Hojo 2000) (Figure 4.12).

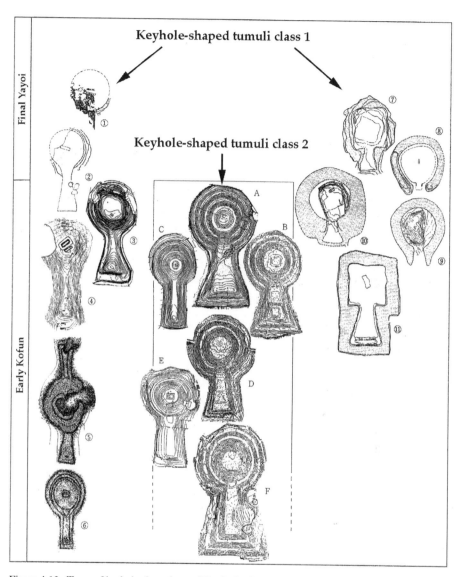

Figure 4.12 Types of keyhole-shaped tumuli in the beginning of the Kofun period (from Hojo 2000). Hojo claims that the keyhole-shaped tumuli class 2 was formed by incorporating attributes of various local tumuli-building traditions which emerged in regions throughout western Japan during the Late Yayoi. These local traditions represented by the tumuli class 1 continued before class 2 eventually became the dominant form for the tumuli of local chiefs having strong ties with the paramount chief residing in the central Kinki region (see also Hojo 1999).

I would argue that the phenomenon can be understood as the formation of a sort of *peer polity interaction sphere*-type horizon (Renfrew and Cherry 1986): competition over the control of exchange networks and competitive emulation mediated, and was mediated by, increasing intra- and inter-corporate/inter-regional group hierarchisation, and through that process the ritualistic custom of burying the dead chiefs in broadly keyhole-shaped mounds would have emerged (Mizoguchi 2000b).

In all, what the foregoing has revealed is that the tumuli marked *neither* the establishment of a hierarchical network of polities in which the polity of the Kinki core region was dominant *nor* the establishment of the system of unilinear male-line descent which is inferred to have served as a prerequisite for the establishement of a stable social hierarchy. Instead, the outcome has suggested a much more complicated picture, in which the hierarchical network of polities centred around the Kinki core region was gradually emerging out of the ongoing process of inter-group competition at various scales/levels when the distributional horizon of the earliest keyhole-shaped tumuli came into being.

The paradox of 'being critical'
A re-examination of the way in which the process towards the beginning of the Kofun period has been studied has revealed that some of the key inferences made for the reconstruction of the social organisation of the time and its transformation have been treated as if they are confirmed facts and do not need verification. To put it more precisely, the problems which I have pointed out above have never been felt to be problematic. In other words, these presuppositions, having turned out to be somewhat erroneous (in what way they are erroneous is a crucially important problem in considering the implications of the issue, and we shall come back to it later) have been recognised as indispensable elements of Kofun archaeology as a communication system. That means that a certain set of expectations have been formed and reproduced concerning the way these elements are connected to a pool of other elements and the image of the Kofun period. In this case, the system–environment boundary, by which what are and what are not the constitutive elements of the communication system are distinguished, appears to be drawn by referring to the most significant characteristic of the present-day emperor system, i.e., its *continuity*.

There is a suggestive case for this: it seems to have been taken for granted that not only the process *after* but also *up to* the beginning of the Kofun period, as the point when the foundation of the imperial genealogy is tacitly regarded to have been established, was an uninterrupted and unilinear one. For instance, Makoto Sahara and Shozo Tanabe once praised the 'creativity' of the Yayoi culture of the Kansai region in comparison with its northern Kyushu counterpart, which they characterised as stagnant and uncreative (Tanabe and Sahara 1966). Their contention was based upon such observations as the form of many of the basic tools of the Early Yayoi period being changed in the Middle Yayoi period in the Kansai region whereas they remained basically unchanged in the northern Kyushu region (Tanabe and Sahara 1966). However, it is obvious that observations of this nature do not necessarily show which region was *more creative*, nor do they indicate which region was *more progressive* and *advanced* in the process towards the achievement of a certain degree of social hierarchy/complexity. An interesting point about Tanabe and Sahara's thesis is that they investigate archaeological evidence and reach the above-mentioned conclusions with the conviction that they are investigating the 'prehistory' of the 'Yamato court' ('*Yamato chotei*') (cf. Tanabe and Sahara 1966, 108), which is the name given to the ancient emperor-led polity residing in the Kinki core region, i.e., the present-day Nara basin and Kawachi plain, in the Kofun period. As long as relevant pieces of information are intentionally put together and holes and gaps in the proposed picture in terms of available archaeological evidence fill in the way which fits the 'guidelines', i.e., to show how *natural* and *logical* it was that the Yamato court was established in the present-day Nara basin and Kawachi plain (where the capitals and the imperial palaces of the ancient state of Japan were later to be situated), any work/models put forward along such guidelines are bound to portray what happened before and after the beginning of the Kofun period as a unilinear evolutionary process, i.e., the unilinear process through which a primitive society transformed itself into a social organisation in which what can be described as a 'court' emerged.

That means that as long as the beginning of the Kofun period is regarded as *marking/coinciding with* the emergence/establishment of a political entity called the Yamato court, it is only too natural that the process towards it is portrayed in a *teleological* manner. It can also be deduced that this teleological tendency would make it difficult to relativise the historical process which the Kansai region went through towards the beginning of the Kofun period by comparing the equivalent process of other regions; the supremacy and dominance of the Kinki core region over other core regions of the Yayoi social evolution is taken-for-granted, rather than the subject of investigation. Therefore, the model (which I would argue to be most viable) that the beginning of the Kofun period was an episode in the ongoing process toward the integration of the regional polities through their competition is hardly acceptable for many.

Let me look into some intriguing implications of the last point, which I regard as of crucial importance for a consideration of the nature of the whole matter. The model which I put forward above would lead to the inference that the spread of the keyhole-shaped tumulus and allied mortuary customs all over western Japan and parts of eastern Japan in an *archaeologically short period of time* resulted from the strategic distribution by the polity of the Kinki core region of a sort of prestige assemblage for achieving and securing its dominance. This inference implies two things: (1) the beginning of the Kofun period did not mark the establishment of the dominance of the Kinki core polity but marked the beginning of the process through which it gradually achieved strategic dominance over other polities, and (2) the dominance of the Kinki core polity, i.e., the so-called Yamato court, was achieved upon historically contingent conditions, such as its securing exclusive contacts with the Wei dynasty of China, which was recorded in the Wei's official chronicle Weiji (see Chapter 4.3).

Both these points, interestingly, dispute the two factors used to legitimise the emperor system, i.e., its continuity and pre-givenness: should the above-mentioned observation be the case, the origin of the imperial genealogy would be inferred to have been historically contingent and its continuity not established for some time after the beginning of the custom of constructing the keyhole-shaped tumulus (many of whose largest examples, as mentioned, are regarded as the tombs of the ancient emperors). In other words, quite intriguingly, the archaeological paradigm concerning the beginning of the Kofun period and the social process towards it conforms to the two factors which are tacitly used to legitimise the emperor system.

What does this intriguing situation in archaeology derive from? I would infer that an archaeological discourse/communication system which reproduces itself by criticising the emperor system needs the *constitutive characteristics of the emperor system to remain intact*. In other words, in order for the study of the beginning of the Kofun period to continue to be a critical discourse of the emperor system, the constitutive elements of the emperor system need to be intact: otherwise, the base upon which the emperor system stands is proven to be shaky, and *the meaning of the existence of the critical discourse of the emperor system itself becomes shaky*. Of course, this, should it be the case, would not be perceived by those who take part in the reproduction of the discourse as such: if the shakiness of the base of the emperor system is made apparent, an objective of its critical discourse is achieved. However, in actuality, this strategy has not been chosen. The foundation of the legitimacy of the emperor system has been left intact, and the strategy of preserving it by describing it as a logical consequence of the historical trajectory has been chosen instead.

Enlightenment and belief in therapy
A significant characteristic of classical Marxist thought as an Enlightenment social philosophy in a broader sense, as illustrated earlier (Chapter 2), is its belief in *Reason*: Reason, if properly shown and appreciated, has power, armed with logic, to lead people to the right decision and the right direction. In this case, the decision and the direction are social ones. Although reason itself is regarded as a universal human faculty/ability, it has to be articulated as long as it is appreciated and followed. A trick, which gives rise to a circular argument, is that reason articulated is bound to be not only appreciated but also followed because reason is a universal faculty of the human being.

The latter half of this circular logic is important for the current consideration. As long as the logic works, once reason or elements of it were articulated, they would have an almost therapeutic effect upon those who suffer from the illogical, i.e., the ills of society. As illustrated earlier in the second section of this chapter, the ills of post-Second World War Japanese society, according to Japanese Marxist thought/archaeology, stem from the surviving emperor system which ideologically concealed and legitimised social contradictions. These characteristics led to the devastation of the war and continue to do damage by ideologically concealing and tacitly legitimising the preserved problems which might lead to a devastation of the same magnitude as that of the Second World War. Accordingly, the ills have to be revealed/articulated properly, and should they be revealed/articulated properly, the whole problem would be solved in one way or another, i.e., in the form of various socio-political changes. In order for the ills to be properly revealed/articulated, as far as the above argument goes, there has to be someone who knows the *proper way* in which they should be revealed/articulated. Those who claim to know the way, including politicians, activists, and scholars, have to identify themselves as such, and in order for them to do so, ironically, the ills have to be there; should the ills be gone, the foundation upon which they identify themselves as those who are in the know would be gone, too, and should their identity be gone, the possibility of a cure for the ills would be gone. In other words, the existential/ontological base of the ills *needs to be preserved* in order for those who claim/regard themselves as specifically qualified to reveal/criticise them to continue to do this job.

The continuation of this peculiarly paradoxical situation has been made possible by the paradigm of taking for granted the existence of those who enlighten and those who are enlightened. This paradigm is in a way a remnant of the hierarchical differentiation (or 'pre-modern' mode) of communication systems in which 'who utters what' determines the way each communication system is structured and reproduced: what those who are ranked higher utter determines the rights and wrongs in a communication (see Chapter 3.6). However, in the functional differentiation (or 'modern' mode) of communication systems, such systems become horizontally located and interconnected to one another, and the hierarchical positionality of the individual becomes increasingly irrelevant to the way a communication system is structured and reproduced. Rights and wrongs in a communication system, or the distinction between the elements and non-elements of that communication system, are not determined by what the higher-ranked utter but instead by referring to the way other communication systems are structured and reproduced. This means that the *interdependence* between communication systems becomes the prerequisite for their existence and continuation in the functional differentiation of communication systems.

This puts any *critical* discourse/communication system in difficulty: in order for any critical discourse/communication system to continue, it needs to preserve what it criticises. Without the subject of the critique, a critical discourse/communication system cannot reproduce itself in functional differentiation. The Kofun archaeology as a critical discourse of modernity/functional differentiation embodies the difficulty of being critical in modernity: the very existence of Kofun archaeology (a critical discourse) helps the reproduction of the discourse of the emperor system (the subject of the criticism).

4.5 Imprisoned in the circularity and paradox of modernity

The Japanese experiences which have been illustrated above show the inevitability of paradox in reproducing archaeological discourses/communication systems in modernity. At the same time, we have seen how the paradox is de-paradoxised, i.e., made invisible or forgotten. In hierarchical differentiation/the pre-modern mode of communication systems, the de-paradoxisation is achieved by referring to who utters what; the rights and wrongs are determined by the social position of the person who utters them. In functional differentiation, this technology of de-paradoxisation no longer works, because the communication systems are organised horizontally. Instead, a communication system has to be de-paradoxised by referring to another communication system such as a political communication system, which is randomly chosen rather than by a universalisable reason. For instance, the Protestant Christian belief used to connect the religious and economic communication systems under the concept of 'calling', but no longer (cf. Weber 1930).

However, what was going on in Japanese archaeology up to the 1960s was the continuation of a pseudo pre-modern situation: reference by the Marxist discourse to that of the emperor system in its (Marxist discourse's) de-paradoxisation was perceived as if it was natural/logical/right. As illustrated, the combination of historical factors, (a) the widely shared experience of the manipulation of the image of the emperor and imperial history during pre-Second World War years, (b) heavy capitalism, and (c) the Cold War equilibrium, made the perception that the critique of the emperor system was the best way to the realisation of a better society widely sharable. Ironically and paradoxically, though, the discourse of the critique of the emperor system needed the continuation of the emperor system for its continuation. In other words, in the uniquely stable context of the post-Second World War years, archaeological discourse/communication systems became interdependent on the discourse of the emperor system through the necessity of their own de-paradoxisation. The critique of something can only be made possible by the existence and continuation of that very something in functional differentiation.

However, this technology was identical to, or rather was actually based upon, the tradition of the way in which the emperor system had been drawn upon as the means with which to de-paradoxise the paradox of the identification of the nation-state of Japan and the Japanese (cf. 4.2 above). In the process of the establishment of the modern nation-state, its contents and domain were in continuous transformation, and the identity of the nation-state and the people could only be acquired and reproduced by continuously revising the perception of similarities and differences between the Japanese and the non-Japanese, and the boundary between them was itself continuously redrawn (see Chapter 4.2). The authority and legitimacy of the emperor system were derived from the narrative of the continuity of the imperial genealogy, and the narrative of the continuity enabled the reproduction of the illusory perception of the stable/unchanged identity of the Japanese and the domain of Japan, both of which, in actuality, were in a process of constant change. And that the emperor system was functioning this way itself legitimised the emperor system. *Circularity and paradox were moblised to conceal and deproblematise themselves*: a typically modern phenomenon.

What is symptomatic about the Japanese experience is that all these discourses which we have seen working, the archaeological, the emperor system, the national body, the Japanese, and so on, depend on one another in terms of their continuation/survival. Their interdependence is historically contingent, and that very contingency makes the interdependence unbreakable. And this unbreakable interdependence between certain discourses/communication systems determines their structure and content. This implies that a critical discourse/communication system needs the discourse/communication system it criticises to continue in order to reproduce itself. In other words, any critical discourse/communication system in functional differentiation/modernity cannot be critical to the extent that the criticised discourse/communication system is terminated. The archaeological communication system is no exception.

What is important to note is that once having become interdependent, the contingency involved in the interdependence between discourses/communication systems continued to be concealed/forgotten until the 1970s. However, since then, the environment surrounding the reproduction of the discourses/communication systems appears to have changed: the contingency behind the interdependence between the discourses/communication systems has become apparent, and the de-paradoxisation of the paradox of a discourse/communication system by referring to another discourse/communication system has become increasingly difficult; it has been revealed that there are a number of equally viable ways to de-paradoxise a communication system. This has led to endless relativisation in discursive space and tremendous difficulty in de-paradoxising discourses/communication systems. In short, *anything goes* has become the dominant feeling, the feeling of reality, about society. This is what some scholars describe as the coming of the post-modern, and the next chapter will consider the difficulties archaeologists have come to be faced with in it.

5

Fragmentation, multiculturalism, and beyond

5.1 Introduction: crisis, hyper-capitalism, and post-processual archaeologies

Crisis, what crisis?

It has been a while since the word 'crisis' began to be uttered in describing the state of Japanese archaeology. An interesting thing about this is that the nature of the crisis itself has never been specified in this 'crisis discourse'; or rather, it seems that the fact that we do not know how to describe/characterise this crisis itself constitutes the core of the crisis. Japanese archaeology was felt to be in a different type of a crisis situation back in the late 1960s and early 1970s. However, Japanese archaeologists apparently felt they not only knew what constituted the crisis but also what was behind the crisis back then. The ever-accelerating pace of the destruction of archaeological sites was truly threatening during those periods (NKK 1971, 1980), and devising strategies to counter it was an urgent task. Meanwhile, archaeologists also knew, or were believed to know, how to *grasp* and *talk about* the crisis, and as a prerequisite for doing so they also felt they knew how the crisis situation had come about/was created. In other words, Japanese archaeologists by the late 1960s and early 1970s had a clearly articulated system of concepts and terms, i.e., a 'theory', a Marxist theory as illustrated in Chapter 4 and to be touched upon later again, to make sense of the situation and with which to decide how to make an intervention in it.

That we have lost our ability to grasp and talk about the crisis which we feel we have been in since then means, concerning the above, that we Japanese archaeologists have lost the theory altogether. Saying this, though, immediately raises a question: have we just forgotten it? It seems rather odd that an established theory in an academic discipline is forgotten in such a relatively short period of time. However, what has happened cannot but be described in this manner. As illustrated in the previous chapter, one of the causes of this 'forgetting' would be that Japanese archaeology has a tendency of not systematically articulating conceptual frameworks for describing, explaining and understanding archaeological evidence, regardless of the degree of abstraction (Mizoguchi 1997). However, as we saw in Chapter 4.2, the tendency appears to have been there well before the above-mentioned crisis situation surfaced. This means that the forgetting cannot simply be explained as a consequence of an inbuilt tendency/a structuring principle of Japanese archaeology as a communication system.

Demise of grand narratives

In attempting to make sense of this phenomenon, the following points seem to be of particular importance. First, this 'forgetting' might be an example of the demise of grand narratives/theories, recognised to have taken place throughout the social and arts sciences in the 1970s and 1980s (cf. Lyotard 1984). When making sense of the crisis situation back in the 1960s and 1970s, i.e., differentiating symptomatic phenomena and articulating explanations as to their cause, Japanese archaeologists referred to the package of thoughts broadly defined as Marxism (see Chapter 4.2), a defining grand theory and narrative framework of the twentieth century. Some elements of Marxist thought maintain their importance in the discursive space of contemporary society (e.g. Jay 1984), but the classical Marxist thesis, claiming that the intrinsic contradiction of the capitalist economy inevitably leads to its self destruction in the form of the proletariat revolution and to its replacement by socialism, and allied remarks on the state of the domains of social totality, lost its appeal as the sense of reality; and what people could think of as a coherent political action programme for the everyday was gone. (We shall return to this point in detail later.) The loss of the sense of reality of not only the classical Marxist thought and programme but also other grand theories and narratives, as Jean-Francois Lyotard famously pointed out, was paralleled with the coming of a social formation sometimes described as the post-modern (Lyotard 1984). Regardless of characterising it as a discontinuous change or the acceleration of an ongoing trend/trends (Luhmann, for instance, took the latter view by seeing it as a phenomenon of accelerating functional differentiation characteristic of modernity: see Chapters 3.6 and 3.7), we seem to be in a situation in which the universal knowledge which we acquire, or we wishfully imagine/believe we acquire, through our *universally shared* experience, which is a fundamental base of *grand* narratives/theories such as classical Marxism, has become inaccessible. The feeling that the knowledge we obtain from our experience can have universality was based upon the perception that our experience of suffering, for instance, derived from the fact that the ideal society (which is, of course, ideal to *everyone else*) had not arrived. That led us to think that we had to strive towards a *common* goal, i.e., realisation of the ideal society, and sharing of this image of the ideal society, a socialist society in the Marxist vision. This made it possible to observe the society we live in and its reality that way, i.e., the problem about society which we felt was *universal*.

Note, again, as we have been doing throughout the volume so far, the circular and paradoxical relationship between the observation of the present and the imagining of the ideal society. The sense of reality of the theory and the sense of validity of the image of the ideal society put forward by the theory mutually supported each other's existence. The circularity and paradox were being solved by chronically *postponing* the realisation of the ideal society; the not-yet-coming of the ideal society enhances the importance and righteousness of the theory for constructing the ideal society itself. However, this mechanism of de-paradoxisation appears to have stopped working sometime in the second half of the twentieth century, sometime between the late 1960s and the 1970s in Japan. And, as a systemic reaction to it, we have begun to adopt an attitude of taking for granted the coexistence of a number of ways of feeling/grasping/describing a thing. This adoption of a pluralistic attitude has, somewhat inevitably, come with the attitude of chronically relativising the validity of one's observation/decision and shifting one's position, and that has led to the rise of chronic *anxiety* and *cynicism* about what we can do with archaeology and what we can gain from practising it. This is quite natural because we have lost our confidence in historical thinking in its classic sense: we are supposed to learn history to learn how to act in the present for the future, but in circumstances such as this, what difference is there between now and the future? What is ahead is only the endless generation of *differences*, or in other words, the endless relativisation of the way we see the world and the way we act in the world (cf. Luhmann 1998).

A parallel transformation in archaeology, albeit with a different outlook, can be recognised as having taken place initially in the UK and then become widespread in the English-speaking world. Let us now turn to that.

Now we are all multiculturalists
A poignant expression of this general social situation is the rise of *multiculturalism* (see Chapter 2.3 for its position in the broad topography of contemporary social philosophy), which, I would argue, has its expression in Anglo-American archaeology in the form of post-processual archaeologies (e.g. Preucel 1991).

This 'movement', rather than disciplinary body of knowledge, as already well argued, has opened up the previously rather closed discursive space of archaeology (although some early attempts to open up archaeology to social issues, albeit not yielding a significant impact, had to be recognised, cf. Clarke 1939) to all sorts of possibilities yet to be articulated, and their articulations are taking place through confronting various contextual realities of doing archaeology in various parts of the contemporary world, most often in the form of recognising the importance of local/indigenous voices previously dismissed/suppressed by the Eurocentric/colonial epistemology of Science (e.g. Gosden 1999, Chapter 8). In that sense, the post-processual-archaeologies movement appears to be reconnecting archaeology to social reality (e.g. Hodder 2003). However, the movement is also leading to anxiety and cynicism, which characteristically accompany multiculturalism. For instance, how is an absolutely value-neutral, and hence universal, i.e., politically correct, language possible as we promote the importance of distinct local knowledges/cultures? Is it not a self-contradiction of promoting both? Or, would affirmative action/prioritising a previously subordinate group not lead to the creation of another structure of domination/discrimination? Suspicion that academic integrity is being compromised by prioritising and privileging 'multivocality' is met with the objection that yearning for academic integrity itself is the uncritical, unconscious endorsement of a western-world biased, colonialistic, male-centric world view, and this objection is further met with the counterargument that the emphasis upon multivocality is the manipulation by interest groups of the past, which is exactly what the proponents of multiculturalism accuse western male scholars of doing. Naturally and logically the argument ends up being a vicious-circular one, because both the opponents and the proponents of the multiculturalist stance share the problem they mutually accuse each other of creating, i.e., prioritising the voice of one interest group/groups or certain epistemic stance over others. And the most viable compromise is to agree that the most important thing is to continue arguing about the issue in order to try to find a better solution/compromise.

Interestingly, a similar kind of anxiety and cynicism albeit with a different appearance is also acutely felt in Japanese archaeology, as illustrated in Chapter 1: there is no common ground upon which to measure the 'value' of a site/a statement about the site and what is possible is only not to close down the discursive space where different interest-laden opinions continuously negotiate each other's positions. It seems we are experiencing a *universal* difficulty in various *regionalised* manners, and the experience of this peculiar mixture of the universal and the regional is ever augmenting the above-mentioned multicultural attitude and its consequences.

Let us look more deeply into the emergence of the post-processual archaeologies movement and its subsequent trajectory of transformation here in order to contextualise the movement and to make a systematic comparison with the Japanese situation possible. The emergence of the post-processual archaeologies movement, retrospectively, was most tangibly marked by the publications of two books, one edited and the other single-authored by Ian Hodder, namely *Symbolic and structural archaeology* and *Symbols in action* (Hodder ed. 1982; Hodder 1982). The former is a collection of papers, and the latter is a monograph of Hodder's ethnoarchaeological fieldwork in Africa, with extensive interpretations and commentaries on the implications for archaeological theory; and they can both be characterised by the premise that material items, both portable and architectural, work/are used as symbolic media for the conduct of various social strategies. The introduction of this to archaeology marked a radical departure from the then dominant perspective (the New/'processual' archaeology, cf. Trigger 1989, Chapter 8) which took for granted that material culture *functioned* as the material media of the working of social subsystems,[1] whose reaction to a change in their environment (including both the intra- and extra-system, natural and cultural environment) was such that the internal equilibrium (stability) and the survival of the system whole consisting of a number of subsystems were made possible (cf. Binford 1962).

The relationship of such material categories as the technomic, socio-technic and ideo-technic (Binford 1962) with subsystems whose working/'functioning' (meaning working for the sustenance of the internal stability of the system whole, as mentioned) they mediated was understood to be one of *mechanistic reflection*. Besides, each subsystem was treated as an anthropomorphic unit, although, in reality, its working was constituted by individual human acts. Therefore, there was no room for intentionality to intervene in the relationship between material culture and human behaviour/society.

Some intriguing similarities with the Japanese Marxist approach can be pointed out about the framework of processual archaeology. The Japanese Marxist approach

---

[1] By 'function', here, I mean the working of something constituting a larger whole in the direction of maintaining/regaining the stable state/'equilibrium' of the larger whole.

also sought the specification of causality, and hence the specification of the u.
cause–effect connections. In the case of Japanese Marxist archaeology, the cause-un.
consisted of the force of production and the effect-unit the ideological components
of society. In the case of processual archaeology, the former consisted of a new
condition in the environment external to a system whole and/or to the subsystems
constituting it, and the latter a new adaptive state of the system and subsystems. Both
frameworks share the belief that *fixed, essential elements* of society, by explaining the
state in which *any* society can be understood, exist. For Japanese Marxist archaeology, the infra- and superstructure constituting the social totality are treated as
such elements, and for processual archaeology they are the hierarchically structured
subsystems constituting the system whole. In Chapter 4.2, I mentioned that the
processualist framework was dismissed by practitioners of Japanese Marxist archaeology as ahistorical and uncritical. However, as far as their logical structures are
concerned, they are akin to one another. We shall come back to the implications
later.

Coming back to the present topic, one of the most significant of Hodder's findings
is that the extension of a spatio-temporal unit within which the condition requiring a
certain *functional* reaction was shared often did not coincide with the spatio-temporal
distribution of the material items which, from Binford's and the processualists'
perspective, were assumed to mediate the working of the subsystems functionally
reacting to it (cf. Hodder 1982, 58–74). In the process of making sense of such
phenomena, Hodder came to realise that material culture was 'meaningfully constituted', by which he meant that material items were used with various intents which
were much more complicated than what could be described as *systemic* reactions to
external factors, and should be made sense of as if reading 'material culture text'.
This meant that material items were mobilised by specific individuals to express some
specific meanings, laden with specific interests and value judgments, as authors did
in writing texts; and hence they can be made sense of as if *reading* them (e.g. Hodder
1986).

That a configuration of material attributes/items/features can be read as if it were a
written text means that, in order to make sense of it, the reader (the archaeologist) has
to try to understand not only the *intent* of those who 'wrote' it (the people/individuals
in the past) but also their *mentality*, i.e., the condition in which they were situated
and how that constituted the way the text was written. The 'reading' is also inevitably
influenced by the way in which the reader/archaeologist is situated in his/her contemporary world, and a good reading has to take into account these two horizons
of situatedness. An awareness of situatedness, past and present, forced proponents
of this idea to seek theoretical sophistication by referring to the theory and method of
hermeneutics, which methodologically formulated the way to move back and forth
between the above-mentioned two horizons in order to reach a better reading by connecting and harmonising their historical implications (cf. Hodder and Hutson 2003,
195–202). It should be noted here that the procedure is bound to be *ever ongoing* and
indeterminant because an inevitable transformation of the state of the situatedness of
the reader in the present inevitably leads to a different understanding of that of the

interpretation of written ...

past and its historical implications. This implies the untestability/unfalsifiability of the interpretations put forward by the proponents of the hermeneutical approach.[2]

At the same time, the realisation of the possibility and potential of *reading material culture* led to the recognition that the relationship between material items and their meanings can be compared to that between signifiers and signifieds. This, together with the introduction of hermeneutic theory and methodology, can be understood to coincide with the 'linguistic turn' which took place widely in social and historical sciences. An origin of this kind of paradigm shift can be traced back to Michel Foucault's influential work (especially *The order of things*, 2001), which revealed that the differentiation/articulation of new concepts/words and the discovery/invention of their referents could not be separated into two separate, temporal–sequential or cause–effect type categories but rather had to be understood to constitute a horizon (*episteme*) in which their cause–effect relationship is constantly reversed and transformed. Drawing upon this recognition, Foucault argued that history could be written as a sequence/stratigraphy of such horizons, and that what historians could do was not to specify the causal connection between concepts and their referents but to describe the structure of each such horizon and its internal dynamics (2001). Foucault's proposition ignited a sea change in the social and historical sciences in which *mutuality* and *interchangeability*, especially that between units/categories of historical investigation, which were previously understood to constitute such distinct categories as cause and effect, infrastructure and superstructure, and so on, became emphasised; and that resulted in the shift of research focus from the *economic/institutional* to the *cultural/mundane*. Again, it should be noted that the emphasis upon mutuality and interchangeability made the investigation indeterminant, because a historical phenomenon cannot be assigned to either the cause or the effect, and that made falsifiable model-building impossible.

The 'linguistic turn' in archaeology, methodologically, took the form of the introduction of structural analysis in which material items/patterned units are arranged into a series of dichotomous pairs such as male : female :: blue : red by their recurrent coexistence in individual contexts. Each such pair is treated as a referent/signifier of the other differentiated pairs, and that means that the cause(s) of the formation of the series itself has to be sought *outside* the series. Such outside factors as power relations of various sorts, the operation of ideologies, and so on, are often designated as the causes by which the series was generated (e.g. Tilley 1991). For instance, a male : female dichotomy is transformed recurrently in everyday life to a number of other dichotomies such as purity : pollution :: culture : nature, and so on whereby the domination by the former over the latter is naturalised (e.g. Hodder 1982, 125–184). However, those factors, i.e., power relations, ideologies, and so on, are also referents of something else, particular world views (such as ideological explanation : systemic explanation :: political left : political right), for instance, and in that sense

---

[2] This point attracted criticism from processualists as a fatal lack of the rigorousness required for any *scientific* endeavour, but this point has no significant relevance to the current argument. What is particularly significant here is that the untestability/unfalsifiability of the interpretations implies uncertainty/indeterminacy in academic communication. We shall come back to it later.

remain indeterminant; why a specific cause, such as the operation of an ideology, can be specified can only be explained by referring to factors, again, *external* to the cause itself. In other words, the signifier of a certain signified is inevitably transformed to the signified of another signifier, and the spiral is logically impossible to terminate; the 'chain of signifiers' continues to grow. Besides, a differentiated/recognised series of dichotomous pairs would never coincide with what was *discursively* grasped by those who left behind the material items from which the series is articulated; it has been well recognised that most daily human acts are conducted in a habituated manner and not discursively articulated or grasped (cf. Giddens 1984, Chapter 1), and that is also the case for the relationship between acts and the material items which mediate their conduct. These factors inevitably make it difficult to give any closure to structural analysis; it is impossible to exhaust possible investigations to verify the findings, because it is we archaeologists who determine the way to give a discursive explanation to the phenomenon which was not grasped by people in the past in a discursive manner. A chain of symbols and their referents can never be exhausted. In other words, it is impossible to impose a closure on the chain of signifiers which is both ever growing and ever differently articulated.

Now we all are obsessed with the body

I would argue that the concept of the body and embodied experience/practice, currently the subject of keen theoretical interest and debate (e.g. Meskell and Joyce 2003), has been introduced in order to solve the above-illustrated, intrinsic problem of the broad interpretive/hermeneutical approach (another possible cause of a sudden increase in interest in the body will be touched upon later). The intrinsic nature of the body as the closest and most intimate environment of the working of our mind, mediating our engagement with the world by enabling and constraining our physical movement, makes the body the unit which can be assumed to constitute, albeit partially, the situatedness past and present in an identical manner. For instance, the sensory experience we have when we walk around one of the well-preserved henge monuments of the British Isles can be assumed to have been reasonably similar to that of those who built it and conducted activities within it, though the way of talking about it would never coincide (cf. Barrett 1994). In that sense, the body, in the attempt to hermeneutically make sense of the past through the reading of material culture, can work as the *de-paradoxisation device* (for the concept of de-paradoxisation and its theoretical implications for the argumentation throughout the volume see Chapter 3.6 above); by referring to bodily experience (constrained as well as constituted by a specific architectural structure, for instance) to which a series of dichotomous pairs can be connected (e.g. going in and coming out of a henge circle might have been perceived as crossing the boundary between ritual and mundane, and hence to mark such dichotomies as culture : nature :: sacred : profane, and so on), we can impose a closure on the above-illustrated uncontrollable indeterminacy/ growth of the chain of signifiers by claiming that a specific bodily engagement with a certain material being in the past world which generated the series of dichotomous pairs can be re-experienced by us archaeologists, which makes it possible to understand the original meanings generated through the experience as well. In other words, the possibility of re-experiencing can solve the 'indeterminacy problem' by securing inter-subjective consensus *across time*.

This theoretico-epistemological position, 'somatised archaeology', has been formulated and refined by incorporating ideas and methods from the philosophical tradition of phenomenology, and has been particularly influential in Britain (cf. Tilley 1994; Thomas 1996; amongst many others). However, the position has been subject to some severe criticism, one of which, quite relevant to the current argument, is to claim the perception of the body and the bodily experience to be multiple and fluid, and to criticise the phenomenological approach's tendency to focus solely on the *universality* of the bodily experience (e.g. Hodder and Hutson 2003, Chapter 6, Meskell and Joyce 2003). It is claimed that by assuming the universality of the bodily experience, the experience of the present and its description is privileged, prioritised and made dominant, and the possibility of different bodily experiences and perceptions in the past tends to be ignored (Hodder and Hutson 2003, 119).

The problem of this criticism is that the similarity or difference of the present bodily perception or experience from the past can only be assessed if they are differentiated and articulated to discursive expressions; the experience is surely there, but unless the feeling is talked about or written down, it cannot be compared or scrutinised. In that sense, this type of criticism, except for some uniquely successful cases from Ancient Egypt and the classical Maya, by fully utilising the advantage of having abundant documents and iconographic depictions concerning different bodily perceptions and experiences from what we can conventionally imagine (cf. Meskell and Joyce 2003), brings back the indeterminacy problem; by urging us to assume the multiplicity of bodily experience and perception, which is *not* itself necessarily problematic, the critics ask us to be aware of the *unknowable*, and hence urge us to accept indeterminacy. Putting it tactically and cynically, doing the above also makes it considerably easier to produce new accounts concerning the issue; an article can be written by merely criticising the endeavours attempting to reach something sharable by saying that such efforts fail to take into account something probable, i.e., the multiplicity and fluidity of the perception and experience of the body, but unknowable, i.e., undiscursivised. It should be added that claiming something probable but unknowable makes one's position *uncriticisable*, because the probability of the claim itself can never be checked because it is unknowable. In that sense, the probable-but-unknowables such as the multiplicity of bodily experience have a *transcendental nature* of a sort, as we saw in Chapters 3 and 4; the multiplicity and fluidity of the perception and experience of the body as tangible as a conceptual construct but intangible as a concrete, sharable being at the same time.

The spurt of interest in the body and the bodily experience/perception appears to mirror what is going on in the realm of self identification in contemporary society. It is widely recognised that concern about the body has lately been increased and intensified in various ways. Concern about health, appearance, how to alter it, and so on are preoccupations of most of us today. The cause, no doubt, is multifaceted (e.g. Turner 2003), but it seems that the single factor ultimately shared by all the possible causes is the fixity and uninterchangeability of the body. The body is the inescapable material frame in which the subject is situated.[3] In that sense, as all other things in the world, ranging from thoughts through perceptions to the material, can be both signifiers and signifieds at the same time and hence replaceable/transformable/interchangeable, the causal-connectedness between the body and the subject is irreplaceable, untransformable, and uninterchangeable, although the *relationship* between the body and the subject is dual and mutual, and the way it is *perceived* is often fluid and changeable from one social context to the next (cf. Meskell and Joyce 2003; Fowler 2004, Chapter 2). That means that anything which the subject does to the body can be fixed and specified as to its *causality*, albeit temporarily, and hence provides the subject with the feeling of being 'in control'. Otherwise, the subject, in the circumstance illustrated above, is not ever able to acquire such a feeling. In other words, the body functions as *the* fixed/fixable point[4] with which to impose a closure, *albeit temporarily*, to the ever expanding chain of signifiers which the subject generates and has to cope with at the same time.

The increasing awareness of the body, from the above viewpoint, can be understood as an attempt to enhance this fixity and to secure the feeling in the subject of being in control of the world through the mediation of the body. If this were the case, the parallelism with the implications of the introduction of the notion of the body/phenomenological experience to the post-processual interpretive/hermeneutical archaeology, 'somatisation of archaeology' (Meskell 1996) would be quite apparent; both the subject and the hermeneutical archaeologist, situated in late-/high-/post-modernity, need the tool with which to secure the imposition of a closure to the world/phenomena it deals with in order to acquire the feeling of being in control and in order to make the interpretation coherent and sharable.

In addition, exactly the same can be applied to the rising popularity of so-called 'Cognitive archaeology'. I do not intend to make as extensive a critical summary of this genre as of somatised archaeology, the cases in which different modes of wiring the brain can be causally connected to the different cognitive or behavioural patterns of species in genus homo (e.g. Mithen 1996) are most successful and best exemplify the structural similarity of the genre's recent popularity to that of somatised archaeology; the generation of meanings can be causally connected to the working and structure of the brain, and the indeterminacy of meanings in the reproduction of communication systems can be solved or forgotten, though, in reality, connecting the generation of meanings to the work and structure of the brain itself does not tell us anything at all about the contents of meanings and their social significance.

The coming of the multivocal

As the above-illustrated attempt at *taming* the uncontrollable expansion of the chain of signifiers has become a vogue, the attitude of abandoning the possibility of containing the uncontrollable expansion of the chain of signifiers but of positively

---

[3] Although its material extension/boundary can be (perceived to be) blurred and transformable, particularly through the mediation of material culture (cf. Hodder and Hutson 2003, Chapter 6; Meskell and Joyce 2003).

[4] I should immediately emphasise here that the body *as an entity* is not a fixed, stable unit but a fluid entity with its ever-changing perceived contents and boundary, cf. Meskell and Joyce (2003).

allowing it without worrying about making the acquisition of coherent and fixed interpretations/understanding impossible has also become rife. This trend is intricately related to the demands of multivocality.

Archaeology was destined to become aware of its importance when archaeologists started listening to informants in order to make sense of the intentions and meanings behind material culture patterns (cf. Hodder 1982). When they encountered intentions, systems of meanings, and the involvement of practical consciousness not discursively expressed but only articulated through problematisation in the constitution of material culture patterns, archaeology became destined to be confronted with this demand; when interpretive ethno-archaeologists such as Hodder began to listen to the narratives of indigenous populations on their material cultures and their meanings, what was certain to become obvious was the fact that indigenous voices had been ignored just as their cultures and ways of life had been dismissed, suppressed and silenced as primitive, barbaric, and irrelevant to *scientific* endeavour (cf. papers in Ucko 1995). Therefore, listening to indigenous voices became a methodological requirement in ethno-archaeological practice, and the realisation of the above led to the conscious attempt not only to listen to indigenous voices but also to involve indigenous peoples in the practice of archaeology as stakeholders (Ucko 1995; Hodder and Hutson 2003, 217–233).

In that sense, the conscious incorporation of multivocality into archaeology was meant to positively expand the horizon of archaeological practice which previously had silenced indigenous voices, past and present. However, the post-processual archaeologies movement, increasingly locating emphasis on multivocality, ironically, has ended up forming a 'negative paradigm', a paradigm based upon the epistemological stance that the knowledge that *no unified/definite knowledge of the world is possible* is the only knowledge which is sustainable. In other words, the attempt to promote multivocality has allowed relativism to come in by the back door.

It has to be noted, again, that no one would deny the role played by post-processual archaeologies in igniting various debates about the relationships between archaeological knowledge production and society (e.g. Hodder 1999). However, one also cannot deny the rise of the feeling that this relativistic 'deconstruction' of belief in the unified knowledge of the world has also resulted in the destruction of the discursive space for critical and constructive *dialogue* and, ironically, led to the erosion of the epistemological base for mutuality/mutual understanding between different voices/stakeholders that the movement is meant to promote. The majority of practitioners of post-processual archaeologies would argue that what they are after is quite the contrary: opening up an increasing number of discursive spaces for freer, critical dialogue. However, what we are actually witnessing appears to be the creation of *mutually segregated*, even sometimes hostile, discursive spaces/fields which do not communicate with one another.

And quite ironically, if situated in this broad picture, the rise of somatised archaeology, illustrated above, is a part of, as well as a reaction to, this ongoing process of fragmentation in archaeological discourse; an attempt at expanding the horizon of our perception and opening up a sharable framework, accompanied by the introduction of a new type of indeterminacy and segregation in the form illustrated above.

Fragmentation and the paradox of the hyper-capitalist economy

The operation of such mutually isolated discursive spaces, i.e., an ever-increasing number of self-claimed *new* approaches/stances under the banner of post-processual archaeologies, can be compared to the operation of the hyper-capitalist economy (Bauman 2000b, Chapter 2). Acquiring universality and homogeneity by showing the masses the impossibility of obtaining universality and homogeneity is the fundamental, paradoxical characteristic of hyper-capitalism; one's desire to be different can only be fulfilled by purchasing something different from what the majority of people have, but that something is itself bound to be a mass product. In that sense, it is impossible to be genuinely 'unique' and 'different' in this world. Otherwise the growth of capital stops when everyone comes to think they are all unique and different. Meanwhile, everyone tacitly knows that it is impossible to be genuinely unique and different, and everyone knows that this is the only universal truth in the world of capitalism, symbolised by the proliferation of pop-art (Jameson 1991). This is a game rather than what we can comfortably call life, and the feeling of playing an endless game is inevitably accompanied by cynicism.

The celebration of differences by the practitioners of post-processual archaeologies (cf. Hodder 1999), I would argue, is structurally parallel to this. No one appears to truly believe that what he or she is saying about the past is genuinely unique and different. No one truly wants to be genuinely unique and different, either because, if it were the case, he or she would be ignored or treated as not being an archaeologist or because doing so might disturb the continuation of the communication he or she is involved in. Here, we see a parallel between the working of capitalism and the working of post-processual knowledge production. There is always the thirst for uniqueness and difference, but everyone knows too well that it will never be quenched. Or rather, no one wants to be genuinely quenched. One wants to put forward a *unique* and *different* idea, but one also wants one's unique and different idea to be accepted as *ordinary* and *similar* as well.

What would result from the rise of this paradoxical, hyper-capitalistic, *anti-discourse* discourse? I would argue that it is mutual indifference and/or 'illogical' hostility against those who reproduce other discourses. In order to have one's 'unique' and 'different' idea accepted as ordinary and similar, one tends to form a small circle of colleagues who share an identical epistemic framework. Such a circle, sharing a 'miniature paradigm' so to speak, has to be large enough to provide one with the feeling of being accepted by others but small enough to provide one with the feeling of being unique and different from other such circles. By an epistemic framework in this context, I mean a framework which makes one comfortable with a specific way of communicating with others and making sense of the world. The framework consists of the way one moves one's body, the way one feels things, the way one expresses one's feelings, and so on. The framework has to be able to make relationships among the members of a circle as intimate as possible, to make them feel they are unique and different from others, and to that end the epistemic framework shared by the members of such a circle has to be not easily understandable to the members of other circles. A session in a British Theoretical Archaeology Group (TAG) conference might serve as a good example of such a framework and miniature paradigm at work.

Celebrations of uniqueness and differences: are they really good?
Cultures/ethnic groups which celebrate their uniqueness and difference can be compared to such discourses. Together with the inception of hyper-capitalist social formation, the end of the Cold War has been behind this phenomenon. The Cold War brought a state of equilibrium to international relations in which the politico-militaristic tension between the United States and the Soviet Union functioned as a systemic regulator. Conflicting interests and tension between groups of various sorts such as nation-states, culture groups, ethnic groups, economic classes, and so on, were suppressed by the ultimate conflict between the US and the USSR; under militaristic domination by these two countries, with the genuine threat of a thermonuclear war, there was no room for internal conflicts in individual nation-states to surface. This politico-militaristic dichotomy between the western versus the eastern blocks also gave rise to a parallel dichotomy in the epistemic landscape, i.e., liberalism versus socialism. In these circumstances various causes of discontent were attributed to either of the two 'world views', simplified, and solved externally, i.e., making people think that any social problem and suffering was caused by the bad deeds of the opposing block and its constituent nations (see Figure 4.5) (cf. Huntington 1998).

Concerning the above, the sudden cropping up of the claims by various, predominantly ethnic affiliation-based groupings, which had been silenced during the Cold War era, of their suppressed rights and emancipation, and post-processual archaeologies' alliance with these, most often indigenous, voices can be understood to have resulted from the end of the Cold War. That implies that the validity of the claims put forward by these formerly silenced groups and their voices cannot be taken for granted by right but has to be scrutinised just as other dominant grand narratives of the Cold War era have to undergo critical re-examination. We shall tackle this issue later in this chapter. However, the above-mentioned problem with the micro-discourses generated by the alliance between various interest groups and post-processual archaeologies has to be critically examined here.

These micro-discourses tend to focus solely on their unique contextualities and the way they have been historically constituted. It might be added that the memory of suffering tends to make their tone self-righteous and defensive. However, without a conscious attempt to understand the logic and mechanisms behind the operation of other cultures and without a deliberate attempt to create a sharable discursive space between them, cultures/ethnic groups cannot coexist peacefully. And such a sharable discursive space has to be supported not only by the knowledge of how these cultures have been formed and why, but also by the knowledge that peoples cannot attain satisfactory mutual understanding in any straightforward manner: they only know they are in a state of being able to believe that they understand one another through the continuation of dialogue (see Chapter 3.3–3.7).

The ultimate importance of historical and historicised knowledge comes in here; knowing how the counterpart has come to behave the way s/he behaves enables one to tolerate any unexpected action from the counterpart that disturbs the continuation of dialogue. However, a paradoxical characteristic of the post-processual discourse prevents historical, long-term investigation from being fully conducted: on the one hand, the discourse emphasises that any human action is historically constituted, but on the other hand, it claims that any historical experience is unique as occupying an unrepeatable moment in the flow of time. It encourages the *thick description* (Geertz 1973) of the *synchronic* networking of contextual factors surrounding the experience in a specific temporal horizon rather than the *diachronic* description of the way the condition of a particular historical experience came about over a certain period of time.

What I wish to illustrate in this chapter is that the above-illustrated tendencies in the post-processual discourse, the increasing segregation of various inward-looking discourses, accelerated indeterminacy in archaeological interpretations, and increasing interest in the body, are not only structurally parallel to the operation of hyper-capitalism but also interconnected with it in a *systemic* manner. This suggests that this tendency, i.e., the tendency epitomised by multiculturalism and the post-processual archaeologies movement, might be a *global phenomenon*, meaning the same type of tendencies can be seen in place outside the sphere of the strong influence of the Anglo-American post-processual movement, because now the hyper-capitalist economy is the global/globalising economy, although the form of its representation varies from region to region and from country to country. The Japanese experience will prove that this is the case.

5.2 Paradox and confusion: the case of Japan

Past for the future

We have already seen the trajectory of modern Japanese archaeology since the Meiji restoration up to the 1970s in Chapter 4.2 above. That trajectory coincides with the Japanese experience of classical modernity: it witnessed the hasty introduction and intensive endeavour to firmly install a package consisting of the essential ingredients of modernity:

(a) industrialisation,
(b) rationalisation,
(c) commodification,
(d) bureaucratisation,
(e) citizenship,
(f) deconstruction of kinship/local ties,
(g) secularisation,
(h) institutional segmentation and specialisation.

Among them, (e) the foundation of citizenship was the most difficult because the disembedment of people from their kinship/local community-based ties, which took place as a long and slow-moving process in the west, had to be carried out in an extremely short period of time in Japan; besides, the disembedment and re-embedment of people to integrate them as a nation had to be achieved as a unified process. As we saw in Chapter 4.2, it was the emperor and the notion of the national body, in which the emperor was the embodiment of the nation and the father and the people the organic parts of that body and the children of the emperor, that were invented to accomplish this extremely difficult task. As a *modern* scientific discipline with the unique character revealed in Chapter 2.2, archaeology, from the beginning, was destined to be mobilised to support this conceptual construct in the form of tracing the historical roots of the genealogy of the emperor and the boundary forma-tion and concretisation of the national body (see Chapter 4.2). In that sense, as long as the notion of the national body survived, this conceptual construct continued to function as the ultimate axis of the structuration and reproduction of the discursive space of Japan in general and that of archaeology in particular. Being for or against the notion determined one's attitude to the socio-political economic/cultural for-mation of the society. The coming of the late-/high-/post-modern in Japan, in that sense, was marked by the fading from the public psyche of the notion of the national body and by the coming of the conditions which led to that fading. In order to trace this process, i.e., the process toward the coming of the post-modern in Japan, and in order to examine how archaeology was transformed through this process, we have to go back to the end of the Second World War (parts of the following arguments in this section are from Mizoguchi 2005a).

The post-war years, particularly between 1945 and the 1950s, saw the rise of various movements criticising the mobilisation of the past for the legitimation of the abuse of the political system which resulted in the devastation, colonial expan-sion and aggression of neighbouring countries in the years before and during the Second World War. However, the critique itself was conducted by drawing upon a conception identical to that which history and archaeology in the pre-war years drew upon: presupposing and taking for granted the existence of uninterrupted continuity between the past and the present (see Chapter 4.3 and 4.4). By drawing upon this conception the critique of the present was conducted by pointing out that its ills 'originated' in the past.

Traditional Marxist frameworks, the introduction of which to archaeology in Japan took place during the pre-war period (see Chapter 4.2), fitted the exercise particularly well. Marxism as a version of evolutionist thinking presupposes that the historical trajectory of an attribute of a given social formation can be traced back through time as if the original form of an organ of a given species can be found in its predecessors in the process of biological evolution. This means that factors which led Japan to the devastation of war must have had their evolutionary roots in the past. The study of the past, in that sense, is also regarded as offering the possibility of verifying the Marxist critique of the present: the validity of Marxist interpretations proven through the study of the past can also verify Marxist claims about the present because present factors must have had their primitive expressions in the past. There, again,

exist *circularity* and *paradox* in this strategy of unifying the critique of the present
and the past: the former is valid because it is proven through the study of the past, and
the latter is right because it is proven through the critique of the present. How, then,
were the circularity and paradox solved, i.e., hidden/de-paradoxised? The paradox,
it seems, was de-paradoxised by claiming that the validity of the claims about the
past and the present would be proven *in the future* in the form of the realisation of
a socialist social formation in Japan. Through chronically *postponing* the realisation
of an ideal society, a socialist Japan, the circularity was transformed in the realm of
conception to a *cause–effect relationship* in which the cause lay in the past and its effect
constituted the present and future, which is yet to come.

Anxiety and the fear of being mature

It was only too natural that a feeling of uncertainty and inexplicable fear began to
spread when the pattern of post-war capitalist economy and Cold War equilibrium
began to show signs of change in the 1970s. The changes, as illustrated below, took
the form of a slow but steady erosion of the political reality of the Marxist programme for the better future. In archaeology, the change was gradually leading to
the fragmentation of the discursive space of, and the effective coming of multivocality in Japanese archaeology (see Chapter 1). Fragmentation, in this case, means the
coexistence of an increasing number of distinct sets of expectations which archaeologists draw upon to reproduce their discourses. In other words, it is fragmentation
in the *aim* of archaeological practice: a majority opinion no longer exists about what
archaeology is for (previously it was for the construction of a better future through
the implementation of a Marxist programme), and what we are up to with archaeology. A serious consequence of the fragmentation is the generation of a discourse of
'discourselessness'/'aimlessness' and the parallel rise of the *narrative of the extreme,*
i.e., of the *oldest* and the *largest,* and that of *continuing local identity from the most
distant past.* As illustrated below, this fragmentation and related phenomena can be
understood as *systemic* reactions to a deepening 'functional differentiation' in social
formation (Luhmann 1995; and see Chapter 3.6 above).

The initial phase of the fragmentation, on the surface, took the form of the demise
of the Marxist programme itself. This was a typical example of the cessation of the
reproduction of a discourse caused by the transformation of its environment. As illustrated in Chapter 3, a communication system/discourse is reproduced through the
reproduction of its boundary, by which the constitutive elements of the discourse are
differentiated from those that are not. The differentiation goes on in a self-reflexive
manner. By 'self-reflexive manner' I mean that the differentiation is conducted by
drawing upon the memory of previous differentiations. The memory constitutes a
set of expectations, the expectations of what reaction an act executed in a certain
way would evoke in a certain person, and they would change as the occasion of their
being unfulfilled/betrayed increased. The change of the set of expectations by which
a discourse is structured and reproduced, in that sense, takes the form of a structural change in the experience of those who take part in the discourse of the domains
outside the discourse itself, i.e., the environment of the discourse; each individual's
attitude to the way the discourse operates is changed through his/her experience of

Marxist 1970s (handwritten)

change in the environment of the discourse, and that would result in the increase of the occasion of one's expectation being unfulfilled/betrayed in the discourse itself.

Bearing the foregoing in mind, let us examine the change which took place in the environment of Marxist discourse. As a persuasive political programme, Marxist-led socialism had lost its appeal in Japan by the mid/late 1970s, and this was well reflected by the decline of labour and union movements. The transformation of the condition and structure of workplaces, from collective to more segregated conditions in the factories for instance, gradually destroyed the locales in which workers had maintained their day-to-day contact and shared experiences, which generated a coherent and collective 'working-class spirit' and working-class 'habitus'. The decline of Japanese coal mining, ship building, steel industries and so on, symbolically coincided with this process (Tomoeda 1991). Concurrently, the annual income level of ordinary citizens rose sharply, and the feeling of 'belonging to the middle class' became widespread. This feeling was partly, but strongly, supported by the fact that workers became able to buy such commodities as colour TV sets, refrigerators, washing machines and so forth (e.g. Tomoeda 1991). Factory workers could not buy them easily in the early 1960s, but by the end of the 1970s they were owned by more than ninety percent of households and were purchased not for their functional necessity/cost performance but for their stylistic differences (Tomoeda 1991, 142). A crucial incentive for labour and union movements, a desire to make the conditions of workplaces and daily living better by making changes in employer–employee relations, was replaced with claims for and an interest in pay rises, as was the case in other industrialised countries (Bauman 1988: 71–88). The self identity of factory workers, which had been acquired by sharing homogeneous workplace conditions, such as coal-mining pits, and fighting for a cause, such as liberating themselves from relentless capitalist exploitation, was now acquired by purchasing commodities with certain 'style' and 'taste' (Bauman 1988). The detachment of the masses from sharable experiences/face-to-face encounters situated in particular time–space settings, and the disappearance of physical/experiential constraints upon the living condition of the masses, came hand-in-hand. Zygmunt Bauman describes it as the transformation from 'heavy' to 'light' capitalism (Bauman 2000b).

In such social circumstances and the mental/material conditions constituted in them, from a pragmatic political point of view, it would have seemed pointless and meaningless to carry on talking about issues such as the emergence of class-based inequality and social contradictions in the past in order to make changes in the present. The enthusiasm behind the investigation of these issues, as illustrated in the previous section, had been supported by the feeling that these things had causal connections with the ills of the present. The feeling which can be described as that of *causal-connectedness* to the past was gone just as the collective feeling of common injustice and the collective yearning for a common goal, i.e., the realisation of socialist democracy, were gone. A foundation of the *reality* of Marxist discourse resided in the belief that archaeological practice could have a pragmatic impact upon Japanese politics: by revealing from a Marxist point of view how Japanese prehistoric societies evolved, it was believed that the archaeologist could both verify the party policy of

the communists and enrich the party's programme for the future
389–395). This foundation of a sense of reality in archaeological
as well.

What has to be emphasised here is that these changes stemmed f
complexity in the capitalist social formation in which the increasing ...gmentation
and differentiation of new domains of social interaction and expertise became the
norm of social reproduction and the time–space organisation of social life, and the
constitution of self identity underwent a drastic transformation as a systemic reaction
to it. The articulation and institutionalisation of cultural resource management,
becoming a principal domain of Japanese archaeological practice, can be understood
as a reflexion of such a process.

Due to the drastic increase in large-scale development, cultural resource management units, usually attached to local education boards, began to be organised, and
archaeology became a stable 'job'/a domain of expert knowledge. This resulted in the
rise of *professionalism*, in which 'pragmatic' concerns, i.e., how to retrieve as much
information as possible in rescue contexts rather than how to consider and describe
the character and the importance of a site from a wider, theoretically informed perspective, were given priority. Gone were the days when such 'communal excavations'
as the excavation of the Tsukinowa tumulus in Okayama Prefecture were not only
possible but also enthusiastically welcomed as a form of realistic endeavour to transform society for the better. The excavation initiated by and involving the residents
of the small mining town of Yanahara in the Chugoku mountain range yielded a
concrete political outcome in the form of the strong showing of the candidates of
left-wing/reform-oriented parties in the local elections (Tsukinowa kofun kanko kai
1960). Now, a rescue excavation was quietly processed as a public service provided
by a local government, in which neutrality, political or otherwise, was an absolute
requirement in order to serve the community.

Each rescue context requires strong personal commitment, which is often challenging physically as well as mentally. At the same time, it creates a sense of deep
personal attachment to the site and the unique local circumstances in which the
site is being rescue-excavated, and makes the narrative created out of the excavation inevitably 'local', 'personal', and 'different'. The officers who conduct a rescue
excavation have to identify and dig features and artefacts belonging to various periods over the (often very long) duration of the site, have to maintain good human
relations among diggers, and have to complete the excavation on time: they have
to be ruthless managers as well as being extremely knowledgeable archaeologists.
Many of them have a hard time oscillating between these two 'social persona', the
ruthless manager and the knowledgeable archaeologist, and they inevitably resort to
the sincerest solution: to excavate the site which they are digging in the best possible
way and *nothing more than that*.

This means that one just concentrates on *everyday details* and stops thinking about
wider and *abstract* issues, such as the political, which the outcomes of the excavation
may be able to address, and the Tsukinowa excavation well exemplifies. This has
led to the erosion of the mentality of doing archaeology for the future, for the good

of future society. That 'future-oriented' inclination used to unify the intentions of the individuals who worked in the domain yet to be professionalised, and which was hence unorganised and fragmentary. Professionalisation, ironically, has replaced the future-oriented mentality with the present/everyday-oriented one, and led to the fragmentation of archaeology as a field of practice/praxis (see Figure 5.2).

It is also important to note that the Marxist programme placed too much emphasis upon the reconstruction of the *totality* of society, and did not enable the rescue archaeologist to give meaning to the minute detail of the features he or she recorded in terms of how the detail was meaningful in the study of past society. For instance, as mentioned above (see Chapter 4.4), an important objective of Japanese Marxist prehistoric archaeology was to trace the developmental stages through which egalitarian agrarian communities evolved to an early state. In examining the process, settlement sites and cemeteries were classified into settlement/cemetery *types*, which were assumed to *reflect* the way the communities were organised in each developmental stage in a straightforward fashion. What was most important in this framework of examination was the *taxonomy* of sites (e.g. Takakura 1973; also see Chapter 4.4 above), not necessarily the *detail* of the configuration and the contents of the features which constituted individual settlement/cemetery sites and which were recorded with the utmost care and sincerity. This intrinsic characteristic of the Marxist programme, i.e., its totalising tendency, made the programme not only unattractive but also irrelevant to the everyday concerns of the rescue archaeologist.

Fragmentation and the re-emergence of the transcendental
The increasing complexity and fragmentation in capitalist social formation took the foregoing form in archaeology, and resulted in the fragmentation of the *identity* of the archaeologist: the segmentation and differentiation of each excavation site as a field of life–world experience made the spatio-temporal extension of the domain for self identification, within which existed a set of expectations, which is drawn upon in the reproduction of a discourse/identity, very small.

It is natural for the fragmented self to seek *transcendental* entities with which to regain a sense of unity/oneness (see Chapter 3.8), and the inflation of the narratives of the extremes such as the oldest and largest in archaeological discourse since the 1980s can be understood as such a move. By referring to something (felt to be) transcendental, to which one can assume that everyone belonging to a social category/group feels attached, one assures oneself that one can communicate with and understand the other in that group (Chapter 3.8). The articulation of such a group is influenced by various socio-economic/political/cultural factors, and the relationship between the creators and the receivers of the narrative of the transcendental being is one of interdependence.

Let me take the discursive formation surrounding the Jomon settlement site of Sannai-Maruyama, Aomori prefecture, as an example of the generation of such a transcendental archaeological entity. In order to fully understand the implication of the generation of the 'Sannai-Maruyama discourse', we have to begin by investigating the positionality of the Jomon discourse, the 'prehistory' of Japan in the discursive space of pre-Second World War archaeology (see Chapter 4.2, esp. Table 4.1), in relation to that of the Yayoi discourse, the initial phase of the 'history' of the Japanese and the 'national body'.

The Jomon period began around 12,000 bp and ended around 500/400 BC (Takahashi, Toizumi, and Kojo 1998). Despite its enormous length in time (reputed to be the longest single archaeological age in world prehistory), the Jomon period has since before the Second World War been predominantly conceived by its culture, not its society or history (see Chapter 4.2). The concept of culture, in this case, is interchangeable with 'lifeways.' How the Jomon hunter-gatherers acquired their foodstuffs, attired themselves, buried their dead, and prayed for good fortune to natural spirits and ancestors by using material items mysterious to our eyes have been the subjects of detailed, and importantly synchronic, 'reconstruction' (e.g., Izumi 1996). Despite its furiously detailed pottery-based typochronology, the period has never quite been *historicised*, except for a few attempts at describing the transformation and the causality behind it of the Jomon society (e.g., Imamura 1996; Habu 2004). Rather, the Jomon period tends to be treated in a tacit way as the 'timeless past,' either before the dawn of history of the 'Japanese' and 'Japaneseness' or where the authentic essence of Japaneseness was born, and there lies a complex of historical factors behind it (parts of the following argument of this section are from Mizoguchi 2002, Chapter 2).

The image of the timeless, static Jomon derives from two factors. First, the pace of social change and transformation in the Jomon period was much slower and more gradual than that in the Yayoi and Kofun periods as far as stylistic change in the material culture in general is concerned. Second, the positionality of Jomon archaeology in the general discursive space of Japanese archaeology, which has been formed through the history of the modernity of Japan, as briefly illustrated in Chapter 4.2, makes it seem so in contrast to the historical Yayoi and Kofun. Let us begin by examining the former.

The formal contents and structure of the basic assemblage remained almost unchanged from the later part of the Initial (Earliest) Jomon to the Latest Jomon period, although of course there were numerous stylistic changes over such an exceedingly long period of time (e.g. Suzuki 1984). However, we have to ask ourselves: what do we mean by saying that the tempo of change in the Jomon material culture was 'slow' in the first place? One can assess something as slow only by comparing its rate of change with that of others, and a case for the slow Jomon can be made only by comparing the Jomon with the 'rapid' Yayoi and Kofun. In fact, a drastic acceleration in the pace of social change since the adoption of wet rice agriculture up to the emergence of the Japanese early state is often emphasised in contrast to the length of time that elapsed between the introduction of farming and the formation of the state-society elsewhere in the world (e.g., Sahara 1987, 328–330). The comparison might appear objective and valid because it adopts a universal measurement, i.e., the length of time that elapsed between two events which took place almost globally. However, in purely logical terms, there is no universal reason to use this length of time as the yardstick for recognising the slowness or quickness of change in any time period; without prioritising the two events defining the length of time, i.e., the introduction/beginning of agriculture and the foundation of an ancient state, the measurement cannot claim its universality, because such events as the emergence of tribal social organisation are no less significant in the history of the human being. It can be deduced, in this case, that what is tacitly implied, or taken for granted unconsciously, is that history after the invention/introduction/adoption of agriculture is true history (see Chapter 4.2, esp. Table 4.1); the history which we can make sense of/we feel relevant, can be prioritised, even if Sahara himself did not mean this. In that mental landscape, such equally significant events in the history of human beings as the emergence of tribal social organisation have no *universal* relevance. In that sense, the comparison between the slow Jomon and the rapid Yayoi and Kofun (Sahara 1987) is made possible by recognising the pace of change in the process from the invention/introduction/adoption of agriculture through the emergence of 'civilisations'/ancient states as a universal standard which legitimises the attitude of treating the Jomon as timeless or historyless in comparison with the rapidly changing, hence historical, Yayoi and Kofun.

It has been shown that the Jomon sequence was in fact punctuated by 'historical' episodes suggesting significant changes in the way society was organised and structured: the beginning of a sedentary way of life, reflected by the emergence of stable, substantial settlements with a distinctive circular layout with traces of long-term occupation (later Initial Jomon); and the emergence of social integration of a certain scale and complexity, reflected by the formation of regional ritual centres located at roughly equal intervals through wide areas of the archipelago (late Early/Middle/Late Jomon), among others, vividly illustrate the dynamism of Jomon history (see Anzai 2002 for a new attempt at writing Jomon histories). However, investigations into these episodes have so far tended to stop short of situating them in their unique historical contexts or in a long-term transformational perspective. Instead, ranges of characteristics and traits are extracted from each of these historical phenomena, given niches in a synchronic system of meanings, and treated as the essence of Jomonness, and hence, in some cases, as the essence of Japaneseness. For instance, Michio Okamura characterises Jomon 'culture' by the traits which he regards as significant in comparison to the 'traditional Japanese way of life' (Okamura 1996, 77–80). Jomon culture is in this case tacitly recognised as the root of the traditional Japanese way of life and characterised as a timeless entity. The cover slip of Okamura's recent book also bears the phrase: 'the roots of our life reside here' (Okamura 2000). 'Our life' is the traditional Japanese way of life, and 'here' is (the synchronic discursive space of) the Jomon. This synchronisation of traits, originally embedded in a diachronic process and in constant transformation, constitutes one of the significant principles on which the reproduction of the discursive space of Jomon archaeology draws. It has to be noted that this synchronisation tendency is more obvious in the literature itself, whose main readership is intended to be the general public. And, interestingly, the scholars who should be fully aware of the necessity of overcoming this tendency, and express that in their academic writing, often adopt a different approach and write a synchronic history compartmentalising things into different categories of lifeways and describing each of their contents in an often evocative narrative style (e.g. Kosugi 2003). This suggests that there undeniably exists a communication system in which to communicate about the Jomon as the *dehistoricised* entity is the norm for its continuation, and that this particular communication system is perceived to be for the general public and, hence, the major communication system about the Jomon.

This habituated ignorance of history, in other words the dehistoricisation of the Jomon period, also derives from the perception which originated in the pre-Second World War period that a new population, which was to become the ancestors of the imperial family and the Japanese people, came from outside the archipelago and either replaced or assimilated the aboriginal population (cf. Oguma 1995, Chapter 5; Teshigawara 1995, 47; also see Chapter 4.2). The population, inferring from the mythological description of the imperial chronicles 'Kojiki' and 'Nihon-shoki' (cf. Aston 1972), brought with them agriculture and other developed technologies, including metallurgy. Therefore, the 'stone age' people who left behind Jomon cultural remains were recognised as the aboriginal population of the land, and the study of Jomon 'culture'[5] was naturally the study of both the *pre*history (in the sense the period being *before* the foundation of the imperial genealogy) of the land and that of the aboriginal population. This implied that the Jomon culture/period was excluded from the subject of *historical* research, i.e., the reconstruction and study of the sequence of events/the stages of development. Besides, the Jomon culture, in that paradigm, was the culture of the *Other* as that of the subsequent periods was the *Same* as the traditional, i.e., rice agriculture-based, Japanese culture. This perception further enhanced the tendency for the Jomon culture/period to be excluded from the subject of historical investigation, the investigation of the imperial genealogy and the Japanese people (see Chapter 4.2, esp. Table 4.1).

These factors can be arranged into sets of dichotomies which draw the boundary separating the discursive space of Jomon archaeology from that of the subsequent Yayoi period, thus: static/timeless Jomon and dynamic/historical Yayoi, the Jomon as the prehistory of the Japanese and the Yayoi as the history of the Japanese, the Jomon as the Other and the Yayoi as the Same and familiar, and the Jomon as Nature and the Yayoi as Culture. The Yayoi period, as the period which witnessed the introduction and establishment of the rice agriculture-based lifestyle, has long been regarded as the period when the basic elements of the Japanese way of life and the essence of the Japanese mentality were formed (e.g., Watsuji 1951, 47–56; Takakura 1995, 13–15). This perception, in addition to the factors mentioned above, has enabled the Jomon period to be treated as the 'pre'-history of the Japanese, and hence as a pool of non-historic, i.e., *cyclical/repetitive*, hence *natural*, matters such as domestic and shamanistic activities.

The ways in which the symbolic items of Jomon material culture are described are predominantly to do with their domestic and shamanistic character, and their connection with sex, nature, and so on; in contrast to their Yayoi counterparts, whose functions are always connected with something 'political', 'economic', and 'social.'

[5] Before the establishment of the nation-wide pottery chronological system in the 1930s (cf. Teshigawara 1995, 134–143) the Jomon 'culture' was believed to have continued at least as late as the end of the Kofun period/culture on the fringe of the latter's 'expansion' (see Figure 4.2) (Teshigawara 1995, 139).

The clay figurines, whose mysterious appearance makes them a type of artefact regarded typically as constituting Jomonness, are understood to have been mobilised in rituals for the *fertility* and *regeneration* of subsistence resources by metaphorically referring to the childbearing ability of the female (Isomae 1987). However, in a number of cases vast quantities of figurines were amassed, deliberately smashed and deposited in ceremonial gatherings (e.g., Yamagata 1992). A phenomenon such as this would lead to the articulation of various interpretations and narratives, which would certainly include thus: rituals regularly conducted by mobilising clay figurines at what appear to have been regional ceremonial centres had *socio-political* as well as shamanistic/religious purposes: the mobilisation of clay figurines would have enhanced, structured, and reproduced intra- and inter-communal ties somewhat unintentionally through the mediation of ritual communication among those who gathered from a wider domain than that of daily encounter.

Yayoi ritual items, such as bronze bells, which from our modern conception are as mysterious in their appearance and usage as Jomon clay figurines, are in the majority of cases interpreted as having functioned as 'political items'; they are understood to have been *strategically* mobilised, that is displayed at politico-ceremonial occasions, for instance (e.g., Fukunaga 1998, 236–239), and deposited for the maintenance and enhancement of hierarchy, power and intra- and inter-communal ties (Kobayashi 1961, 208–235).

It should also be noted that the clay figurines are often analyzed as generally depicting female figures (e.g., Isomae 1987; Imafuku 1999, 90), despite the fact that many of them cannot be sexed (Kobayashi 1990, 15–16). What is contrasted to the strategic nature of the Yayoi knowledge here is the Jomon ritual knowledge which is literally 'embodied' by the sexed body of the figurines. Together with the fact that a tangible category of Yayoi symbolic items are weapon-shaped, and hence easily connected to male activities, further sets of dichotomies like those below might be formed: Jomon : Yayoi :: female : male :: figurines : bronze (weapon-shaped) ritual items :: domestic/shamanistic : political :: *embodied* knowledge : *strategic* knowledge.

Various symbols of the sexes existed in the Jomon period, many of which depicted the male sexual organ (so-called 'stone clubs/rods', *sekibo* in Japanese, for instance. See Yamamoto 1995). Some of them depicted male and female sexual organs in one artefact. By referring to these facts, some might say that it goes too far to say that the dichotomies between Jomon and Yayoi and between female and male constitute the boundary of Jomon discursive space. However, it appears undeniable that much more attention has been placed upon Jomon clay figurines in the representation of the Jomon in various media than on other Jomon symbolic items depicting sexual organs or sexable characteristics and that this attention has, to a considerable extent, been stimulated by the sex/gender of the figurines. Even if the contribution of the dichotomies between Jomon and Yayoi and between female and male to the boundary formation of Jomon discursive space were rejected, it would be accepted that the dichotomies between Jomon and Yayoi and between embodied and strategic knowledge/experience significantly constitute the boundary of Jomon discursive space. In that sense, it might be more appropriate that the boundary is drawn along the dichotomy between the Jomon as the sexually embodied and the Yayoi as characterised by male socio-political decision making. If it were the case, it can easily be transformed to the dichotomy between the Jomon as Nature and the Yayoi as Culture.

If we shift our focus to spatiality, Jomon and Yayoi discursive spaces form distinct 'stations' in the daily life of contemporary Japanese people. These stations are not only bounded by material media/residues of the practice of people in those periods and the images attached to them, but also by actual spatial differences in contemporary society. While the majority of major Jomon sites with either monumental structures or reconstructed features, including the Sannai-Maruyama, are located in eastern Japan, most of the major Yayoi sites, such as the Yoshinogari (see Chapter 1), are located in western Japan. This, to some extent, is related to real differences in the socio-historical processes which structured the society of those periods, but the fact in contemporary Japan that visible/visualised (by site reconstruction) traces of the life of the Jomon and Yayoi periods mark such a clear division between eastern and western Japan constitutes a firm base for the reality of the boundary between those stations. This reality constitutes an epistemological base for the significance which these stations have in the self identification of contemporary Japanese people.

These interconnected discursive layers of the Jomon–Yayoi division are, particularly importantly for the current discussion, embedded in the east–west division constituted by the uneven distribution of wealth and social capital of modern Japan. The east, Tohoku (north-east) region in particular, has suffered from a lack of investment in commerce as well as production industries and from the long-term decline in rice agriculture which is, quite ironically (considering that rice agriculture is the definitive trait of the Yayoi socio-cultural complex), the main source of wealth in the region. In addition to that, the nature of the Tohoku region has been endangered by the Japan Nuclear Fuel Ltd (JNFL) reprocessing plant situated by the state in Rokkasho Village, to begin operation in 2006, where five tons of fissile plutonium will be produced annually for the running of MOX (uranium and plutonium mixed-oxide fuel)-fuelled nuclear power stations to be constructed throughout Japan (www.japannuclear.com/nuclearpower/moxprogram). It is because of the mixture of the economic desperation of the region and the state strategy of initiating a project inevitably subject to a public outcry and opposition in a remote place in the mental map of the majority of the Japanese, from which, again, Tohoku suffers, as the embodiment of the Nature side of Japan and its history in the perception of the Japanese. The chain of signifiers, Tohoku, Nature, the Jomon, suffering from political decisions made by male politicians, is formed and reinforced.

As the economic success of post-Second World War Japan has come to a halt, it is only natural that the somewhat *systemic* interdependence between these discursive spaces should be changing. This is influenced by the profound changes occurring to the value attached to the experience of these discursive spaces as well as to the discursive spaces themselves (cf. Akasaka 1996). In the above-mentioned mutually interconnected existence of the Jomon and Yayoi discursive spaces, which are situated in and constitute the contemporary Japanese topography of identities,

Jomon-related items/characters, regardless of material or imagery, have been negatively valued, while positive meanings have been attached to their Yayoi counterparts. It is widely accepted that the Japanese have toiled to achieve success in the post-Second World War topography of international relations and the distribution of wealth by acquiring technologies and ideas from abroad, refining them, and exporting them back. Economic success, which the majority of the Japanese regard as characterising post-Second World War Japan as a nation-state, is widely believed to have been achieved by the intrinsic diligence and hard-working nature of the Japanese people long nurtured through their involvement in labour-intensive rice paddy-field agriculture and by, again diligently, copying and refining ideas of foreign origin (cf. Sahara 1987, 328–330, esp. 329). A parallel between this and the characterisation of the Yayoi period, constituted through the reproduction of the Yayoi discursive space, is obvious: the Yayoi discursive space has been the space in which the economic success of post-Second World War Japan is assigned a cause and in which both good and bad consequences of the success are made sense of, all in all, in a positive manner.

Currently, though, the picture is changing. The kind of Jomon image currently gaining popularity is, in a way, the *reverse image* of post-Second World War Japan. Many traits such as those mentioned above, long regarded as constituting the backbone of the success of post-Second World War Japan, have become subject to serious doubt under the prolonged economic difficulties, and many of these traits have often been connected to the characteristics of Yayoi culture. The appeal of Jomonness, signified by those on the opposite side of their Yayoi counterparts in the above-illustrated dichotomies, is currently on the increase. Jomon : Yayoi :: Eastern Japan : Western Japan :: something we have forgotten/neglected : something driving us/having driven us mad :: nostalgia : despair.

An interesting element of the rise of interest in the Jomon period and Jomonness is that this phenomenon is related to a change in the attitude of the general public to the *body* and the *mind*. When Jomonness is depicted in such media as exhibition brochures and popular books (e.g., OCJW 1996), it is the *embodied* nature of Jomon knowledge and technology which is repeatedly emphasised. The *embodied* nature of Jomon knowledge and the foreign, hence discursive (because it has to be translated), hence *modern* (because modernity was brought into Japan from abroad in the wake of the Meiji restoration in 1868) nature of Yayoi knowledge are rarely subject to explicit contrast, but the embeddedness of Jomon subsistence activities in the *body* of nature, often tacitly connected to the image of Jomon clay figurines like the Japanese 'mother goddess' (see, e.g., Isomae 1987), is often contrasted with the destructive intervention in the body of nature by Yayoi agriculturists.

Like the fact that colonial encounters were often depicted as an encounter between a fully attired male figure and a naked female figure (see, e.g., Gregory 1994, 124–133), Jomonness, it seems to me, has begun to be connected to the female body, into which Yayoiness, which has traditionally been connected to male images, has penetrated. Interestingly, one of the prominent theories on the process of the advent of the Yayoi agrarian society argues, to put it simply, is that a group of male individuals brought a wet rice agriculture-related socio-technological complex from the Korean peninsula and married Jomon women. The theory argues that this is why many traits of Jomon pottery survived and were passed on to the pottery assemblage of the Initial/Early Yayoi (because pottery making is a female labour; see Komoto 1982 for an example). This, as it stands, means that a new layer of gender-related dichotomous contrasts (this itself is a unique occurrence in the discursive space of traditional modern Japan, in which masculinity plays such an important role) has been added to the archaeology-related discursive space of modern Japan; Jomon : Yayoi :: Eastern Japan : Western Japan :: (female) body : (male) mind :: (mother : father) (?) :: idyllic : evil :: nostalgia : despair :: remedy for modernity : ills of modernity.

It is quite striking that this series of dichotomies articulated in the high-, late- or post-modernity of Japan forms an almost complete parallel to what we have seen happening in contemporary western archaeology in the form of somatised archaeology: the (unconscious) attempt to impose a closure to the uncontrollable expansion of the chain of signifiers relies upon the fixity and controllability of the *body*, and the move has been stimulated by *feminist* scholarship focusing on the way the body and its perception are mutually constituted and their connection transformed (see Chapter 5.1; and Meskell and Joyce 2003). The increasing emphasis on the left-hand side of the dichotomies above, I would argue, is what constitutes the epistemic background against which the Sannai-Maruyama discourse has emerged; the discourse is firmly embedded in the condition comparable to that in which contemporary western archaeology is situated.

The Sannai-Maruyama is widely regarded as the core settlement of a regional unit (OCJW 1996; Habu 2004, 108–134). The structure and functions of the regional core settlements of the Later Jomon phase (cf. Mizoguchi 2002, 102–105) have been revealed increasingly of late, and the circular concentric layout of a mortuary area, a residential area with a number of pit dwellings, and a storage area with storage pits, situated from the centre to the outside respectively, has been recognised in a number of core-settlement sites (Mizoguchi 2002; Habu 2004, Chapters 4 and 5). In the core settlements, the members of a number of larger, non-residential corporate groups (such as clans) are inferred to have got together regularly, and would have exchanged goods and people and reconfirmed their ties through the mediation of ancestral and natural spirits (Mizoguchi 2002, 102–105). The function of the core settlements as the node of social interactions and relations at multiple levels, it is inferred, made them longer-lived and more stable than the ordinary, 'satellite', settlements (which might have been visited and occupied during a particular season or seasons of the year) and material remains and traces of these activities, including the long-distance chaining of exchanges, wider-ranging and conspicuous (Mizoguchi 2002).

The Sannai-Maruyama, whose occupational history spans from the Early to Middle Jomon periods, fulfilled all such criteria of the core settlements of the Later Jomon phase as above. In that sense, the site is important as an exemplary example of the core settlements. What makes the site distinct, though, is the fact that no other core settlement of the Later Jomon phase has been subject to such a large-scale excavation at one go as the Sannai-Maruyama (OCJW 1996; Habu 2004, 108–134, esp. Figure 4.17). The construction of a baseball stadium uncovered the heart of the site, and the quality as well as the quantity of the artefacts and features exposed by a series of rescue excavations surprised experts and the general public alike. However, the magnitude of the hype surrounding the discovery and the subsequent generation of a discourse, which deserves to be called the Sannai-Maruyama discourse, defied convention. The discoveries of items from sources of distant origin were connected to such inferences as the existence of Jomon 'merchants' and Jomon 'trade'. The tentative calculation of population size, made by referring to a range of indicators, such as the number of pit dwellings coexisting at one phase, highest estimates being around 500, led to the famous description, 'the Jomon town' (OCJW 1996). In all, almost every inference made within the discursive field had a tendency to be exaggerated in the direction of recognising the site as a trait of an advanced developmental stage in the evolutionary sense. Yoshinori Yasuda even went as far as describing the stage as a 'civilisation' (Umehara and Yasuda 1995).

That the palimpsest of the artefacts and features of a number of site formation phases of a core settlement was exposed to the public gaze at once was, as was the case at the Yoshinogari, illustrated in Chapter 1, an important factor contributing to the generation of the discourse and the hype. However, such phenomena as persistently emphasising that a certain trait of the site was what had previously been recognised to have been achieved thanks to the *introduction of agriculture* makes it highly likely that, without this change in the configuration/positionality of the Jomon and Yayoi discursive spaces, the generation of hype and discourse might never have happened, or would have taken place to a much lesser extent: the boundary of the discursive space was marked by such keywords/concepts as 'embodied knowledge' and 'the roots of our/the Japanese culture', and almost all of them, as can clearly be seen, can be articulated to the domains of Jomon discourse, whose positional value has risen as that of their Yayoi counterparts has sunk.

This coupling between the changing positionality of the Jomon discursive space and the Sannai-Maruyama discourse is, as suggested above, further connected to the mentality of seeking the transcendental. By characterising the site as a Jomon *urban* site, a representative trait of so-called Jomon *civilisation* (cf. Umehara and Yasuda 1995), for instance, and by ignoring the outcome of previous research into the organisational characteristics of the Later Jomon phase and effectively decontextualising the site itself (see Habu 2004, 108–134), the *meaning content* of the Sannai-Maruyama discourse was effectively undermined and instead the *quantifiable* elements of the discourse, such as the largest and the oldest of such and such, were exaggerated to various degrees, circulated, and enthusiastically promoted (cf. Habu 2004).

What is worthy of note is that, here again, the discrepancy between the scholarly communication and that for the general public has been exposed. For instance, a reconstructive drawing by Shuzo Koyama, formerly the professor at the National Ethnological Museum, of the central area of the site depicted the two midden areas as if they were carefully shaped like altars despite the fact that they were formed through the cumulative deposition of discards consisting mainly of potsherds but including symbolic items such as clay anthropomorphic figurines over a long period of time (Habu 2004, 118–120). It is highly unlikely that Koyama himself genuinely believes that those middens were actually shaped like altars equipped with steps and other facilities for ritualistic activities. It can be inferred that they were depicted that way in order to illustrate in a supposedly accessible manner to the general public an inferred function of the middens as facilities for or focal points of religious activities of some sort. The inference is based upon the fact that not only an enormous number of potsherds continued to be discarded in the same spots in the site but also the symbolic items mentioned above were deposited in the middens. In that sense, the inference itself can at least be verified/falsified with concrete evidence. What is quite disputable here is to visually explain the function of those features by depicting them in an easily understandable but clearly false manner. That a respected academic figure dared to do it suggests that the mentality and norm existed which prioritised approachability over accuracy in presenting the outcomes of scientific investigations. And approachability would be recognised as the key to get the interest of the general public in the site going and growing.

In other words, the continuation of the discourse for the general public is subtly but consciously perceived by archaeologists to depend upon how well its structuring principle, by which meanings given to finds are determined, conforms to public desire for the past to take the form of the popular image of the Jomon illustrated above. We have to admit that this is inevitable because the general public, particularly the residents of not only the local area but also the entire Tohoku region, constitute an important stakeholder group. Thanks to their enthusiasm, driven by their feeling that the site and its past provide them with something with which they reidentify themselves and regain their pride which has been suffering not only from socio-economic degradation but also from the position they and their past have been given in the mental topography of the Japanese past illustrated above, the preservation and the reconstruction of the site have become possible. However, the way the site has actually been presented and promoted, i.e., by either packaging its image in an approachable but false manner or emphasising its greatness in quantifiable attributes, may well betray the way people want to connect themselves to the significance of the site.

The mentality of packaging the image of the site in an approachable manner is identical to that of those who attempt to engineer society by enlightening the unenlightened through education (see Chapter 4.3). The belief that society can be engineered through education is based upon the perception that the way the unenlightened think and act can be moulded through a specific manner of communication. I have argued in Chapter 4.3 that it is the sense of sameness that tends to be mobilised when the past is called upon in order to engineer the way people make sense of society and act upon it. In the case of the Sannai-Maruyama, depicting the middens to be like altars, or as Habu suggests, like the Mississippian mounds in Cahokia (Habu 2004, 119), can be inferred as an attempt to evoke a sense of familiarity whereby to engineer the way the general public makes sense of the site and the site-related narrative. This 'narrowing-down' of the range of possible images about the past, even if conducted with good intentions, not only impoverishes the imagination of, and hence disempowers, the general public but also unwittingly serves to promote a rather parochial attitude to the past as the other.

Also, emphasising the 'greatness' of the site in terms of scale, including the recon-structed scale of the population (c. 500), the number of potsherds and other artefacts excavated, and so on, not only makes the past relativisable by increasingly painting the picture in a quantifiable manner but also makes the past alienable, and that exactly contradicts the desire of people who are fed up with the relentless pursuit of economic gains, the backbone of the economic success of post-Second World War Japan, which alienates many from the life–world whose function as a stable source of a sense of security has increasingly been eroded by hyper-capitalistic profit-making through the endless generation of differences and relativisation. In fact, the focus of interest expressed by the local population in the outcomes of the excavation has been on the detail of the lifestyles vividly reconstructed from well-preserved artefacts and ecofacts (e.g. Okada and NHK 1997, 189–234), rather than the 'greatness' of the site. People feel close to the Jomon people by seeing similarities in their contempo-rary equivalents of such mundane artefacts as culinary remains and a small basket affectionately called the Jomon 'pochette' (cf. OCJW 1996).

Even if the unconscious desire of creating the transcendental out of the site suc-ceeded momentarily, it is bound to fail. Sannai-Maruyama discourse, after all, is a local discourse, or comes sooner or later to be perceived as a local-interest-driven discourse, and can effectively and easily be relativised: in other words, the discourse is too *concrete* to be genuinely transcendental (see Chapter 3.8). It is ironic that the Sannai-Maruyama discourse, which is tacitly implied to derive its strength from antipathy to the established discourse of seeking the origin of the Japanese way of life/Japaneseness in the Yayoi period and at the beginning of the rice paddy-field agriculture-based way of life, has ended up seeking the same in a different socio-cultural/technological complex, that is the Jomon. As fully illustrated above, the Yayoi and the Jomon discursive spaces draw their boundaries not only with abstract symbolic traits but also with concrete traits such as differential site distribution. In that sense, again, the creation of the transcendental out of the Sannai-Maruyama discourse is bound to fail; the discourse is based upon its spatio-temporal base, which is inevitably concrete and bound to be *compared* with the other potential bases upon which transcendental images are created. Hence, many competing, 'would-be' transcendental discourses continue to come out: the oldest and largest still remain the constitutive traits of many of them. And, an emerging trend in the generation of the narrative of the oldest is particularly suggestive in predicting the future of transcendental narratives.

For instance, the calibrated carbon-14 dates taken from carbonised residues on the surface of pots dating from the earliest typo-chronological phase of the Yayoi have attracted huge media coverage, public interest and controversy (Harunari et al. 2003). These dates are 400–500 years before the date (500–400 BC) which was given from cross-dating connecting the relative-dated artefacts from the archipelago and artefacts in the Korean peninsula and mainland China, whose absolute dates can be inferred with a certain feasibility (e.g. Okazaki 1971). The point which is of particular relevance to the current argument is that solely the antiquity of the dates was given attention in the initial coverage, and it was associated with such phrases that the textbook entry had to be amended even before the proper peer, scientific re-examination of the dating had begun. Interestingly enough, the calibrated carbon-14 dates allegedly putting back the date for the beginning of the Kofun period were also released to the media a short time later (newspaper articles: see *Gekkan bunkazai hakkutsu-shutsudo joho* (The monthly buried cultural property-related excerpts from newspapers), July 2003 issue). What we can see here, it seems to me, is the surfacing of a tacit desire for the elimination of meaning content in constructing a new transcendental archaeological entity: instead of factors which have residual meaning content, hence causing controversy, such as the largest and oldest site, purely quantifiable factors such as the outcomes of scientific dating are now coming to the fore.

No way out?

The situation and trends like the above, if continued unchecked, would no doubt further accelerate the thirst for yet more transcendental discourses, and would lead to further fragmentation of the self and identity of archaeologists and the general public alike. Needless to say, this leads to the endless relativisation of one's standpoint and *nihilism*.

However, the generation of nihilism is not confined to the realm of the circulation and consumption of created archaeological narratives. The generation of nihilism of a self-reflexive kind plagues an important locale at the interface between the archaeologist and the general public, where the source of archaeological knowledge creation is obtained: the excavation.

5.3 The late-/high-/post-modern condition and archaeological practice: rescue archaeology and site protection in Japan

The rescue context as the node of late-modern problems

As illustrated above, the rise of nihilism and the narrative of the extreme/transcendental are two sides of the same coin: a reaction to the radicalisation of functional differentiation, and the fragmentation of the general discursive space driven by hyper-capitalism. How does the phenomenon express itself in the interface between the archaeologist and the general public? Let us investigate it by examining rescue archaeology and site protection, together constituting a significant discursive space where the archaeologist and the general public meet as 'stakeholders', as we briefly saw at the beginning of Chapter 1.

In Japan, as elsewhere in the world, the vast majority of excavations are conducted under rescue circumstances. In that sense, the excavation can be perceived as a problematisation in contemporary society of socio-economic issues; negotiations over issues such as who covers how much of the cost, how much time can be 'spared' for it, and so on, take place routinely, as we saw in the examples of the rescue excavation and subsequent preservation of the Yoshinogari, and a mutual understanding of a *professional and pragmatic kind* between developers and 'rescuers', taking the form of situational tacit knowledge, is often developed. However, what I would like to focus on here is something deeper, i.e., what is behind the socio-economic issues articulated and discussed through the process of the negotiation and what structures the way they are articulated and discussed (cf. Notomi 1997). To put it in a more concrete manner, what I would like to analyse is a set of 'binary codes', along which the boundary of the rescue and site protection-related discursive space is reproduced, and which structure the way the discussion goes by differentiating what is desirable from what is not for the excavation and, particularly, the protection/preservation of the site.

The binary codes, in this case, obviously, are constituted by reducing the complexity constituted by a matrix of innumerable interconnected factors which are drawn upon in the aforementioned negotiation, and the economic factors amongst them played a particularly significant role in the interconnection of these factors. However, it has to be noted that socio-cultural factors, as illustrated in the portrayal of the Yoshinogari and the Sannai-Maruyama discourses, significantly influence the way a distinction is made between what is and what is not 'economic', and it is this socio-culturally determined distinction that constitutes a significant axis along which the binary codes defining the discourse of rescue excavations are laid.

By 'economic' in this case I mean to *make money well-spent*: this includes the decision to spend money for a long-term 'profit' for the institution(s) concerned by knowing that the expenditure will not yield any short-term return; should gaining short-term profit be the absolute priority, and perceived by the majority of the general public to be so, the preservation of the site would not be an agendum. The recognition/definition of long-term profit, in this case, is interconnected with various socio-cultural concerns, such as the preservation and use of local cultural heritage, or the trace of the great deeds of the ancestors, and these concerns are often articulated through the experience of difficulty in acquiring stable self identity in contemporary society as the Sannai-Maruyama case well exemplifies (Chapter 5.2). This difficulty, however, appears to be experienced differently by the archaeologist and the general public, and it can be expected that the difficulty is dealt with differently, by the former as the *provider* of the narrative of the past and by the latter as its *consumer*. This discrepancy may well hold the key to understanding the mechanism of the generation of the site-excavation-based narratives of the extreme, and hence deserves a careful examination.

Self identification and discursive formation from rescuing
Let us begin from a constitutive characteristic of functionally differentiated society (see Chapter 3.6). The spatio-temporal path/movements of individuals in the scales of social life, i.e. the everyday, medium (monthly, yearly, etc.), and lifetime scales, differ spectacularly from one individual to another in industrialised countries in modernity, in contemporary society in particular. It means that we cannot rely in communication on the belief of shared experience, which is based upon homogeneity in the spatio-temporal path/movement in those scales. This implies a range of suggestions for the consideration, from the perspective of the spatio-temporal constitution of social life, of the nature and character of contemporary society, that have already been touched upon earlier in this volume, but what is of particular importance for the current argument is the fact that sharing *biographical knowledge* cannot normally be hoped for on the occasion of communication in this circumstance. This means

that those who communicate with one another do not know how the other has come to be what s/he is/appears or how s/he behaves and they have to presuppose that in communication.

This leads to the following consequences. *First*, one is chronically under pressure to *reidentify* what one is on each occasion of communication. *Second*, this also makes one feel it is possible/easy to become someone else. In fact, to become someone else by changing one's life-course, which was unimaginable/difficult in pre-modern and classical-modern societies, is now possible. *Third*, through the experience of chronically reidentifying oneself, the changing/reinventing chronically of what one is itself becomes the aim/meaning of one's life. The economic system of contemporary society, i.e., hyper-capitalism, fully utilises this phenomenon and continues to profit, as illustrated (see Chapter 5.1).

Bearing in mind this broad picture of life in contemporary society, if we shift our focus to the everyday life of those who are involved in the excavation and protection of sites in Japan, some striking, and potentially significant, contrasts to the ordinary general public can be found. The average everyday life of rescue excavation officers in Japan is full of fixity and biographic experience which life in contemporary society commonly lacks, or is perceived to lack. The majority of rescue excavation officers in Japan are attached to the education boards of local governments. They are public office workers. Their social status is, in the public's perception, fairly high, although a widespread mistrust of the public servant at all levels from a surge of corruption charges scandalously covered by the media (including some incidents in which excavation reports which have been stated as published on paper with certain public expenditure have not yet been published) has tarnished it substantially, and their expected life-course in terms of career advancement is highly stable. The main content of their work, excavating sites and managing allied administrative matters, is also highly routinised. The methodology of, and techniques/equipment used in, the excavation are highly standardised, and training courses for the rescue officers are run by a semi-governmental agency, Nara Cultural Properties Research Institute (cf. www.nabunken.go.jp). In all, once settled, both the everyday life and the life-course of Japanese local government-attached excavation officers are stable and predictable, particularly in terms of the spatio-temporal organisation of their movements. The movement of an officer working for a small township education board would be very much confined to the inside of the township border for the duration of his/her career, moving between the home, the office and the sites, which often makes their knowledge on various local matters truly encyclopedic.

The stability, fixity and predictability of life in the profession often attracts media attention: the everyday life and biography of the officer in charge of a site yielding a 'media-worthy' artefact/feature or two, such as the Yoshinogari and Sannai-Maruyama, are often depicted with a sense of curiosity, sympathy, admiration and tacit ridicule of his/her often lifetime commitment to local archaeology, which does not bring anything profitable but self-satisfaction, and his/her 'pre-modern' lifestyle, i.e., a lifestyle full of stability, repetition, and predictability which appears totally different from that of the masses (e.g. Okada and NHK 1997; Notomi 1997). Media interest obviously derives from the fact that it is the traces of the life of

Rescue archaeology

'our ancestors', the epitome of stability, fixity and predictability, which we believe/are made to believe the ancestors enjoyed and we have lost, that they excavate every day. Naturally, the tone of the narrative which the media tries to set is that which emphasises the lost stability, fixity and predictability which can only be revisited through the mediation of the archaeologist who him/herself lives a relatively stable, fixed and predictable life in a contemporary society which is characterised by its fluidity and unpredictability (Bauman 2000b, Chapter 2).

Meanwhile, the rescue archaeologists also share the *subjective topography* of contemporary society with the general public, whose spatio-temporal path of movement in the aforementioned scales is not so fixed and stable, and has become less so as the prolonged economic recession has led to the adoption of 'flexible', i.e., short-term contract-based, employment styles. This increasingly accelerates the radicalisation of functional differentiation, in which we come to realise that there is no longer anything stable and universal with which we can identify ourselves. A common reaction is the widespread adoption of the technology of self identification unique in contemporary society: chronically reinventing/reidentifying one's identity, as illustrated earlier in this chapter. In circumstances in which you cannot rely on a shared horizon when communicating, what you can do is to monitor the situation and decide how to act on each occasion of communication, and that, as mentioned, inevitably involves the reidentification of oneself. Through such an experience of chronically reidentifying who one is, the chronic reidentification of the self itself becomes the aim of one's life in order to reduce the stress caused by the contingency of communication. The shortening of fashion cycles, the explosion of Internet culture, etc., can be explained as chronic attempts by the mass to reidentify themselves (Bauman 2000b). Even if rescue archaeologists live relatively fixed, stable lives, they cannot escape the reality of contemporary society. They are pressurised to be 'someone else' by breaking their 'routine'. Serious ethno-methodological research (Garfinkel 1984) needs to be conducted to verify this thesis, which is based upon my limited personal communication with colleagues working as rescue excavators, but the explosive increase in the number of local archaeological journals emphasising their interests in the fiendishly minute detail of local sites, the artefacts they yield and their informal/unconventional character, and of activities in cyberspace, seems to me to reflect the situation well; these media offer a discursive space in which individuals can competitively express often very minute *differences* from one another in their opinions by either ignoring, or intentionally choosing to be different from, pre-existing disciplinary codes.

The encounter with a site which yields a number of 'important' findings is certainly an occasion for rescue archaeologists in which the sleepy routine can be broken; the excavation will be covered by the media and the excavation officer(s) and concerned academic/nonacademic archaeologists will start considering the possibility of preserving the site by having it scheduled by the Agency for Cultural Affairs (www.bunka.go.jp/). It is this kind of situation in which a distinct discursive space emerges and starts reproducing itself as if it is an autonomous entity. It is this discursive space of the preservation of the site and its nature and character to which we now turn.

To preserve or not to preserve: the discursive space of the preservation of the site

The discursive space of the preservation of the site, as a communication system (see Chapter 3), reproduces itself as a series of discussions and negotiations, and the issues specifically raised in this discursive space range from (a) how important the site is, through (b) who covers how much of the cost of repurchasing the land from the developer(s), to (c) what benefit to the local economy/general welfare can be extracted from the preservation? All the issues are obviously interconnected as at the same time each of them constitutes a sub-discursive space in which a unique set of 'binary codes' structures the way the discussion goes by tacitly differentiating what is desirable from what is not for carrying on the discourse towards a desirable agreement. For instance, the binary codes for the reproduction of the sub-discursive space (b) would consist of payment : non-payment, how much to pay : how little to pay, and so on, and that for the reproduction of the sub-discursive space (c) would consist of beneficial (for whom) : unbeneficial (for whom), how beneficial (for whom) : how unbeneficial (for whom), and so on. However, it is the sub-discursive space (a) that determines the 'tone' of the way in which the entire discursive space works, i.e., the tone set by the sub-discursive space (a) determines the extent to which both those who *support* and those who *oppose* the preservation feel able to *compromise*. In that regard, I wish to focus on the set of binary codes that structures the discourse/discursive space of the *importance/value* of a site.

Three *forces* of discursive formation come in and draw up the set of binary codes: the *academic*, the *media* and *administrative/financial* forces. As far as common-sensical thinking goes, the academic force would be expected to play the decisive role in the discussion of the importance of a site. However, in actuality, the media force of discursive formation plays a determinant role, and that seems to me to imply/create some serious problems.

Let me illustrate the operation of the media force of discursive formation and interpret the source of its significance/dominance in the reproduction of the discursive space of the importance, and hence the preservation, of the site. In order to do so, let us go back to the nature and characteristics of the spatio-temporal organisation of social life in contemporary society. The lack of fixity, stability and predictability sets the background against which, it has been argued, the unique technology of the self identification of contemporary society, described by late-/high-/post-modernity, is created: the chronic reinvention/reidentification of the self. At the same time, the stress caused by chronically reinventing/reidentifying oneself necessitates the creation of the virtual reality/narrative of a life full of fixity, stability and predictability. Sometimes it takes the form of making the excessive care of the body, in which the floating mind having to make sense of floating meanings can be fixed, a dominant routine in one's life, as touched upon earlier in this chapter. In many cases, though, it takes the form of the virtual reality of *nostalgia* for the past in general in which either everything is fixed because everything has already happened and hence cannot/need not be changed or everything is primitive and ruled by tradition and hence one does not have to make any decision but follow the routine. Both of these somewhat 'systemic' reactions by the self to the experience of the spatio-temporal organisation of contemporary society, characterised by functional differentiation and fragmentation, are mediated and fulfilled by the media force.

Exposure to the media is an occasion for the individual to become 'someone else' other than the 'routinised' self. The media constitute a discursive space in which the chronic creation of differences, i.e., gathering and distributing the news, is the norm of conduct. Meanwhile, the media sell themselves by regularly featuring items evoking the image of a long-gone fixity, stability and predictability and a sense of nostalgia, and their coverage of the discovery of an 'important' new site, whose importance is based upon the media's saying the site is important (circularity, a constitutive characteristic of modernity, again!), constitutes an important part of their evocation of nostalgia for the increase of their profit, e.g., the sales and circulation figure of the newspaper. Why is this the case, and why is it not the academic force of discursive formation which determines the importance of the site? Obviously the cause is multifaceted, but I would argue it is the ontological desire of the rescue excavators to become someone else, as illustrated above, that plays a significant role in their creating and telling narratives which exactly conform to what the media want to hear from them. That is the narratives of (x) the oldest, (y) the emergence of a tradition which had survived over an incredible number of years before being destroyed during the post-Second World War economic development of modern Japan, and (z) the emergence of the early agrarian state to which the ancestry of the imperial line is thought to be traced back that conforms, in one way or another, to the mental topography shared by the Japanese of their past, as illustrated earlier. Examples of (x), (y) and (z) will be given later.

It is often rumoured/heard in Japanese archaeologists' conversation that some 'white lies' have been told by the excavation officer to the media in order to create an 'atmosphere' in which the financial/administrative force can be persuaded to back down. It is true that the recognition/valuation by the media force of the importance of a site gives an incentive to the administrative/financial force to consider the preservation of the site and the payment of the necessary cost because the administrative/financial force knows that at times the halting of the project and preservation of the site can benefit them financially in the long run: the administrative/financial forces, as well as the academic force of the discursive formation, recognise that the media force plays a very significant role in shaping the sense of reality in contemporary society, and if skilfully packaged, that which fits it can bring considerable profit. In that sense, a preserved and 'reconstructed' site, as a number of examples such as the Yoshinogari and Sannai-Maruyama show, can bring as much money and economic benefit to the region as the development project does (Figure 5.1), particularly when its importance is recognised by the media to be attractive enough to its audience to bring profit to them by advertising and promoting its importance. In that regard, the relationship between the media and the administrative/financial forces is mutual and circular, i.e., the sites which make profit for the media make profit for the local government and the local economy, and vice versa.

However, the academic force, at least, can try to influence the way the media force of the discursive formation of the preservation of the site operates in order to control

Figure 5.1 Popularity and economic benefits of the reconstructed sites: the Yoshinogari (photographs by the present author).

the way 'white lies' are told, or to avoid the telling of them altogether. Nevertheless, the endeavour of illustrating problematic implications of the aforementioned narratives (x), (y), and (z), and of telling the media what they (rescue archaeologists and/or academics) think significant, rarely appears to take place. At times it even appears the case that it is the media force which determines the way the academic force operates in the discursive formation of the preservation of a particular site (cf. Notomi 1997, 102). For instance, at the Sannai-Maruyama, Habu pointed out that the site is characterised by its uninterrupted occupation by a large number of people in academic papers as well as popular writings/media coverage despite the fact that significant transformations of the intra-site structure and population size have been well recognised (2004, 120–121). It can be said that those academic papers and public presentations sticking to the misleading thesis constitute pseudo-science, but the point is that those who have written are regarded as scholars and their work is regarded as academically credible, despite their self-contradiction.

The consequences which the domination of the media force leads to are sometimes bizarre, and yield damaging implications concerning the position of the discursive space of the past, in which archaeology is supposed to play a dominant role, in the general discursive space of contemporary society. We Japanese archaeologists have witnessed a number of cases lately, such as the thesis claiming the Sannai-Maruyama as a *town* of the Jomon hunter-gatherer *civilisation* (see Chapter 5.2). In these cases, highly problematic comments, often contradicting the knowledge achieved by the scholarship but confirming what the media force wants to hear, are aired by the excavators and university academics concerned.[6] These comments are, quite ironically, subsequently criticised by the media for either exaggeration or misrepresentation of the information. The operation of circularity, a determinant characteristic of modernity and functionally differentiated social formation, again, can be seen here: put cynically, the media create the cause of the misrepresentation of archaeological evidence and exaggerated interpretations and pick them up and accuse the archaeologists, in order to make profit.

This exaggeration/misrepresentation, in most cases, is made towards the direction of *over*-conforming what the media force wants to hear/is supposed by the academic force to want to hear, i.e., the aforementioned narratives (x), (y), and (z). Therefore, a set of binary codes is in operation in the reproduction of the discursive space of the preservation of the site in which the discovery of something to do with (x) the 'oldest',[7] (y) the emergence of a tradition which had survived over an incredible number of years before being destroyed during the post-Second World War development of modern Japan (such as various rice agriculture-related habits reconstructed from wooden implements shaped like those which were widely used in rural areas before the 1960s), and (z) the emergence of the early agrarian state to which the ancestry of the imperial line is thought to be traced back (the 'Yamatai' discourse, see

---

[6] E.g. the hunting-gathering community of the Sannai-Maruyama settlement having been 'class-divided' (Okada and NHK 1997, 210).

[7] Such as the forged, and now discredited, lower Palaeolithic sites claimed and widely and excitedly reported by many newspapers to date from 500,000 bp, (see NKK 2003 for details).

Chapter 4.3), are regarded as good for the continuation of dialogue for the preservation of the site, and in which other implications of the findings, regardless of their character, i.e., factual, interpretative, falsifying the established thesis, and so on, are regarded as 'irrelevant' for the continuation of dialogue for the preservation of the site and, hence, regarded as the subjects of *academic indulgence* by all three forces of the discursive formation concerned. For instance, though in a slightly different situation, at the Yoshinogari, those who criticise the way the reconstruction has been carried out (see Chapter 1) in terms of its unfalsifiability and over-reconstruction are accused of being irresponsible for not coming up with alternatives, despite the obvious fact that the critics are arguing the *impossibility* of proposing anything scientifically responsible (Notomi 1997, 99–100, 115): here, taking an academically responsible stance is regarded as irresponsible.

The at times emotionally charged over-enthusiasm of the academic force in confirming the above set of binary codes, I suspect, can be understood to derive from the aforementioned ontological desire of those who constitute the academic force, i.e., rescue archaeologists and/or academics, and this thesis, I think, can be supported by the following fact: most of the voices criticising the aforementioned situation are heard in journals of private study/research groups for limited, like-minded audiences or the chat rooms, bulletin boards and web logs of individual websites. These media exactly confirm the attributes of the technology of the self identification of contemporary society: these media offer a space in which individuals can competitively express their often very minute *differences* from one another by ignoring pre-existing disciplinary codes in order to acquire a virtual sense of chronically reinventing/reidentifying themselves. Regardless of whether one is for or against the way in which the discursive space of the preservation of the site is reproduced, archaeologists, like the general public, adopt the technology of the self identification of contemporary society. In other words, both those who are for and against telling 'white lies' for the preservation of sites and those who are for and against maintaining scientific responsibility by sacrificing threatened sites are equally under pressure of chronically reconfirming and renewing their identity, and they have to cope with the situation in one way or another.

We might end up being indifferent to everything
If the technology of our being ourselves, i.e., the technology of self identification, itself causes problems such as those I have illustrated in contemporary society, the first step in solving them would be to grasp the background of the emergence and the reproduction of the technology, the way the technology is employed in each context of our everyday life, and the consequences the employment of the technology brings about.

As illustrated, the reproduction of the structure of the discursive space of the preservation of the site is dominated by the media force of discursive formation, and the way the academic force of discursive formation, which is supposed to critically counter the media force's domination, reproduces itself is so fragmented that it is unable to critically assess the state which it is in. The way the academic force

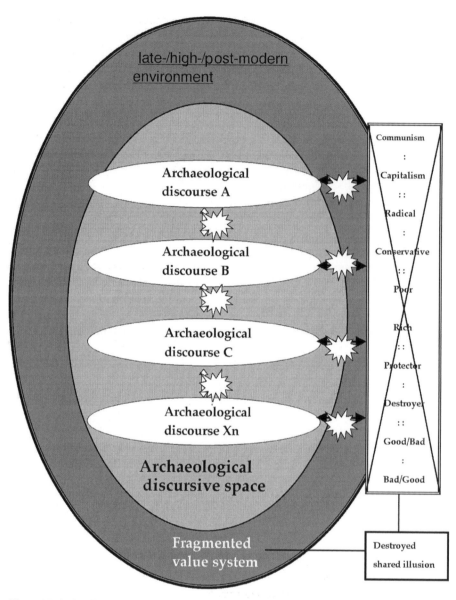

Figure 5.2 Archaeological communication system and its 'late-/high-/post-modern' environment. Compare with Figure 4.5.

reproduces itself is fragmented in terms of its spatio-temporal structure: the space for the internal debate has been shifted from established journals with a wider circulation to privately published journals for limited, like-minded audiences or, to a much smaller extent, to the chat rooms and web logs of individual websites. As argued, I think they are archaeologists' systemic responses to the *radicalisation* of the nature of contemporary social formation which is described as late-/high-/post-modernity

(Figure 5.2). The trend itself cannot be blamed because the trend is, as argued above, a systemic reaction to the ever-enhanced nature and character of modernity: what I find problematic is that we Japanese archaeologists appear to have lost the integrated discursive space in which the modes of our individual discursive formations can be *critically compared and mutually assessed*. This, I would argue, constitutes the main cause of our not even being bothered with the social implications of our uncritically cooperating with the reproduction of the narrative of the extreme, i.e., (x) the 'oldest', (y) the emergence of a tradition which had survived over an incredible number of years before being destroyed during the post-Second World War development of modern Japan, and (z) the emergence of the early agrarian state to which the ancestry of the imperial line is thought to be traced back.

A fear is that we would all end up being indifferent to everything but differentiating ourselves from all the others in various ways, and the discipline of archaeology, the only discursive space in which the history of the human being before the invention of writing can be talked about, would end up being dominated by the attitude of *anything goes*. And, in such an atmosphere, the only thing that matters is not to violate each other's pursuit. Now we have reached full circle; the stakeholders of the Yoshinogari, as we saw at the beginning of this volume, were operating with the shared principle of not disturbing the reproduction of the site-specific discursive space as pursuing each person's own interest. However, this peculiar equilibrium led to the narrative line unwittingly conforming to a variant of the narrative of the extreme touched upon above, i.e., the narrative of Queen Himiko and the Yamatai-koku polity as the origin of the Japanese ancient state, which helps newspapers and other types of the media to sell themselves well and which made the preservation of the site and the promotion of the preserved site possible. In this late-/high-/post-modern world seemingly dominated by cultural concerns epitomised by multiculturalism, economy, after all, may still determine the way things go in the last instance.

5.4 Fragmentation, relativisation and second-order observation

As illustrated by using the 'post-processual archaeologies' movement and what is happening to Japanese archaeology, it seems that archaeologists, at least in the 'developed countries', are now situated in a condition in which virtually every discursive formation is bound to be fragmented and relativised.

As fully illustrated in Chapter 3, the society we live in is, according to the German sociologist Niklas Luhmann, a functionally differentiated society. The functionally differentiated society is not a stratified society. In the stratified society, the identity of the individual is acquired through his or her class affiliation. In the functionally differentiated society, individuals have to identify themselves differently from one locale to another in the spatio-temporal path they move through every day. For instance, a person is an archaeologist at the site and the laboratory, an enthusiastic supporter of a certain football team at the stadium and in front of the TV set, a connoisseur at the restaurant, a critic in a political discussion, and so forth. Each individual has to cope with shifts from one setting to another by drawing upon different sets of expectations and different binary codes with which to determine what is suitable and what is not suitable for each situation and setting.

This means that one cannot stick to any one set of principles with which to decide how to act and how to rationalise, i.e., make sense and accept, the outcomes of his/her acts. It also means that one cannot draw on any universal value system such as class affiliation or religion, even if one wanted to do so; the spatio-temporal structure of contemporary society and the psyche constituted in it make it impossible to cling to the illusion of universal experience. However, we have to decide how to act in a given situation in one way or another anyway, and decisions can only be made by drawing upon certain value systems. Value systems are like *the blind spot*. Without the blind spot, we cannot see. By referring to value systems, we judge, but we never observe them at the moment when we make the judgment about things by drawing upon them. Having lost the illusion of their universality, or having lost the condition upon which the illusion of the universality is sustained, the true nature of value systems, which was concealed by the illusion of the universality of experience, e.g., the suffering of a social class, has been revealed: value systems are the blind spot. We cannot observe them at the very moment we use them, and that is the only occasion when they surface. Therefore, unless we *consciously* monitor the way we make judgments about things, we are never able to approach value systems. And, even if we manage to approach them, the approach itself inevitably has to be conducted by drawing upon a certain value system: we can never eliminate value systems, as we cannot see things without the blind spot.

The rise of 'multiculturalism', the 'post-processual' discourse, as I argued, is its archaeological expression, and can be argued to be a systemic response to this. The seemingly endless relativisation of one's epistemological base in making sense of the world leads to the acceptance of plurality on the one hand and the mutual ignorance of each other's stances on the other. A symptom of the phenomenon is, as mentioned, that it makes the reproduction of a critical dialogue very difficult, and this is also the case for the practitioners of 'post-processual archaeologies' who claim to open up new discursive spaces for self-critical enquiries into the past.

It is ironic that post-processual archaeologies themselves appear to have become an established genre and, despite their claim of devotion to plurality, the discourse reproduced by the practitioners appears at times to be exclusive rather than inclusive and its contents homogeneous rather than productively heterogeneous. The discourses which they put forward are, despite their different outlooks, almost without exception, about the technology of self identification through the embodiment of recursive daily experiences, and power and dominance generated by the working of the technology. They are also homogeneous and united in their dismissal of frameworks concerning social totality and evolution.

One can say that this is inevitable. One might well say it is because the coming of post-modern conditions has made the body and self identity the most important issues of all because there is hardly anything other than the body and self identity of which we feel we are in control (see Chapter 5.1 above). However, one can easily see, thanks to the sophistication of the mass media (ironically one of the very causes of the fragmentation and nihilism in Japanese archaeology as illustrated above, which constitute a crucial part of post-modern conditions) that this is not universally the case. In many countries where the exploitation by multinational conglomerates of an unprotected labour force (which has accelerated since the collapse of the Cold War equilibrium of world systems) is the cause of the most serious social injustice, historical materialism as a grand evolutionary narrative which offers an image of a just society and the way towards it retains its reality (cf. Chapman 2003).

An irony is that, as touched upon above, this arrogant dismissal by the post-processualists of modern grand narratives derives from the belief that evolutionism – or general systems theory-oriented discourses – can do nothing but harm those whom post-processualists regard as the oppressed. However, it must be of interest to many how the majority of today's oppressed are a modern creation and have been created by waves of globalisation (including the colonial expansion of Europe as well as the ongoing one) and the working of international capitalism and its need to continuously exploit the uneven distribution of capital by drawing and redrawing the boundary between groups of various sorts which are made to hate and discriminate against one another, and not only the study of the way in which already created inequalities are internalised and perpetuated at a specific time in history but also the study of the way in which the conditions upon which those inequalities are based came about in the first place must be of interest to many. And it seems undeniable that refined versions of evolutionism – or general systems theory-oriented discourses – are better suited to the investigation of such an issue (e.g. Kristiansen and Rowlands 1996; Chapman 2003).

In other words, there is bound to be a number of ways with a sense of reality in which to make sense of and talk/write about the world, as the historical trajectory which regions of the world has been through varies. Besides, any attempt at making sense of talking/writing about the world in functional differentiation/modernity is destined to be exposed to the scrutiny of the way the world is made sense of and talked/written about because, as repeatedly pointed out and emphasised throughout the foregoing, we cannot rely on sharable/universal values when doing it. Therefore, the observation of the way in which an observation is made is inevitably subject to scrutiny, and that scrutiny, as an observation, again, is subject to an observation of the way the scrutiny is made because the selection of the value system employed in one observation is bound to be contingent rather than inevitable and hence is bound to critically examine the reason. Logically speaking, this chain of observations, the *second-order observation*, never ends.

What the discourse of post-processual archaeologies is effectively about is to dismiss the inevitability of second-order observations and to give *privilege* to a certain value system which is felt to be real to the advocates, many of whom live in industrialised countries in the conditions which have been described so far. What is actually happening is the *silencing* of those who feel reality with the discourses with which the advocates of post-processual archaeologies do not feel to be reality. It is another paradox in contemporary archaeology: the post-processual project of making archaeology more sensitive to the voices of the oppressed is made possible by effectively *silencing* the oppressed. And this trend is accelerated by the fact that post-processual writings constitute an established genre in the western publishing world, which

dominates the world in terms of circulation, packaging and advertisement, the last two of which emphasise nuances, and care for differences and related aesthetics; the *post-processualisation* of the practice of archaeology is a part of the march of hyper-capitalism, silencing other voices in the form of homogenising through *selling more*.

It should also be added that how much care is taken of the ethical implications is adopted as an important criterion with which to measure the quality of archaeological practices. Allowing as many 'stakeholders' (Hodder 2003, Chapter 16) as possible to have a say is an effective way to clear the criterion (Hodder 2003). Another frequently adopted strategy is to allow the 'indigenous voice(s)' specifically relevant to the project to have maximum say. Both of these stances equally intend to impose a certain closure, albeit temporary, to the potentially endless chain of argumentation whereby to prevent the practices from sinking into complete relativism, i.e., anything goes.

However, it should be quite clear from the argumentation of the volume so far (that of Chapter 5 in particular) that this strategy does not work in the way it is intended. The indigenous voice is, after all, also a specific way to observe what happened in the past and what is going on in the present, and hence subject to criticism and other socio-cultural commentaries, i.e., observations of the observation, from those who do not share the world view/epistemology. And any of these observations, i.e., second-order observations, can be subject to further criticism, i.e., observations of the observation of the observation. The process is bound to be endless. Besides, the reaction by the designated stakeholder whose claim is prioritised *a priori* to any criticism can be *hostile* and, hence, *unfruitful* because of the fact that the stakeholder's position is promised by the individual/group in charge of the project to be prioritised and any criticism violates that sense of artificial security. The situation might result in, again, ironically, the silencing of the very indigenous voice which is supposed to be deliberately given a platform because of the hostility and resentment possibly generated from the fact that the indigenous voice is being *unfairly* prioritised: perceived to be unfair particularly in the current politico-economic condition in which the majority and formerly privileged come to feel vulnerable to the acceleration of the hyper-capitalistic trend of relentless cost-cutting by downsizing and the rapid and frequent relocation of factories to the cheapest labour market at the time. This is one of the most serious difficulties multiculturalism faces, particularly in many industrialised nations (Semprini 2000), and if the above argument were the case, any attempt at 'empowering' previously/tending to be suppressed minority/ indigenous voices would be met with more intensely hostile reactions than their not being empowered (*contra* Hodder 1999, Chapter 9).

Besides, multiculturalism, quite ironically, has the intrinsic tendency of silencing voices other than its self-claimed advocates. Multiculturalists operate/communicate, as those who are not multiculturalists do, by differentiating what do and do not conform to be as they are/should be (see Chapter 3, especially 3.5 on communication and the role of boundary formation). The multiculturalist position advocates the view that there are uncountable equally valid ways to make such differentiation in order to identify what one is. In that sense, this position is, on the surface, supposed to be the most tolerant and inclusive (and hence 'universally valid') of all social philosophies. However, the position, in actuality, can be the most *intolerant*. The advocates of the position tend to forget that the position itself is made possible by the differentiation, i.e., by excluding, dismissing and criticising those views which claim that there are *different degrees of validity* between different ways to identify what one is and, in that sense, not exactly tolerant and inclusive. However, belief in its own tolerance and inclusiveness makes the advocates blind to this self-contradiction. In other words, believing themselves to be tolerant and inclusive in a transcendental way by excluding those views which they recognise to be intolerant and exclusive, makes them believe that their position constitutes a universal value system. On the contrary, the multiculturalist belief in its own universal validity makes it most intolerant to views which it recognises to be intolerant, that quite often is not the case. That explains the self-righteousness which characterises the way multiculturalists criticise other views/social philosophies.

What we can do about the contradiction and paradox, it seems to me, is not to attempt to create/cling on to a false sense of the possibility of setting up yet another universal value system/stance such as the multiculturalist, with which we archaeologists might come to believe we can halt the endless self-reproduction of the chain of observations in the form of acquiring not a *universal applicability* but a *universal legitimacy* (justice to the oppressed!) to the claim. As we saw, this is not only impossible but quite ironically it might also be harmful in that it might promote intolerance.

Reconciling different value systems, a fashionable choice lately, such as reconciling different cultural value systems, reconciling processualism and post-processualism, and so on, is not an answer, either, because the way to reconcile them is also bound to be subject to critical scrutiny, i.e., observation. Besides, that might make what is at issue blurred and lead to a dangerous accumulation of frustration/stress from *leaving indeterminacy uncared for*, which might make resorting to over-simplification of the matter such as resorting to the narratives of the extreme (see Chapter 5.2 and 5.3 above) an attractive choice.

What we can do is to observe the consequences of an observation all the time, and at the same time to invent and reinvent a better technology to maintain the *continuation, with minimum stress*, of the chain of observations which takes the form of a continuously rearticulated archaeological dialogue. This is not to plunge into bottomless relativism: we can at least observe the relationship between a specific observation and the condition upon which it is made. In other words, the way in which an observation is made is also the way the condition upon which the observation is made is made sense of. By continuing to do this we can at least better prepare ourselves, albeit each in our own way, for the possible risks which our archaeological communication, regardless of whether culture-historical, functional, systemic, processual, or post-processual, may entail; we can at least know and bear in mind that any communication, even guarded by a critical self-consciousness, inevitably blinds us to the stance, which might be harmful to some, as illustrated above by using the silencing of the voice of the 'oppressed', in which we utter about information the moment we utter it. In other words, the *immunisation* of the way we continue to communicate from chronically generated risks, i.e., to build in the mechanism of reminding us of the intrinsic tendency of the communication in the functionally differentiated society illustrated throughout the volume, is vital.

And, in doing the above, we have to carry on producing images of the past with which people anchor their self identities in one way or another in this world of indeterminacy and multicultural frustration. After all, we cannot carry on communicating without de-paradoxising the inevitable and intrinsic paradox of communication (see Chapter 3), and the runaway expansion of the chain of signifiers, encouraged and accelerated by hyper-capitalism, cannot be halted without the imposition of a closure by using something perceived to be fixed and determined, such as the *past*. In that sense, we *need* the past in order to live in the contemporary world maintaining sanity, calm, thoughtfulness and tolerance to the other, others also having their own ways to connect themselves to the past. An important task of archaeologists is not only to carry on persuading people to be aware of the dangers and problems but also to carry on producing many *pasts* that are all equally coherent, responsible to data, and relevant to people.

6

Conclusion: demands for problematising and explaining one's position all the time

Throughout the volume, we have examined the way archaeology as a communication system is situated and reproduced in the *functionally differentiated social systems* of contemporary society. *Modernity*, a different name for functionally differentiated social formation, has been in need of sophisticated *de-paradoxisation devices*, because the intrinsically paradoxical nature of communication, which was previously de-paradoxised by taking for granted the hierarchical ordering of the world in which the god, the king, the monarch, or something of that nature ultimately determined what was good and right and what not, has to be dealt with in one way or the other without referring to/relying upon *transcendental value systems*. How to de-paradoxise the operation of communication systems, i.e., how to prevent them from stopping their operation because of their indeterminacy, without relying upon their hierarchical configuration, in that sense, has been one of the most significant and determinant themes of life in modernity, and the discipline of archaeology has been mobilised to that end in different ways through time as modernity has matured and transformed. By tracing this co-transformational process of modernity and archaeology, we have revealed the nature of the crisis we are currently in and how it has come about.

This undertaking has made it painfully clear that to seek a way out of this crisis is no simple task. We might even be mistaken in hoping that we *can* seek a way out because, as illustrated throughout the volume, the crisis is a *consequence* of modernity, and we are forced by the reality of the *maturation*, not the *transformation* to a new social formation, of modernity to change our way of observing what is going on around ourselves, as we did in this volume. As argued in Chapter 5, multiculturalism, a form of *post-modern* thinking, does not reflect a drastic change in social formation. Instead, its emergence has marked the fact that to communicate by assuming the existence of universally shared values is *no longer possible*. Multiculturalism is a form of our various attempts to cope with this harsh reality.

The volume has also revealed that just accepting and celebrating differences, an attitude proliferating under the banner of multiculturalism, and of the post-processualism in archaeology, is no answer. Rather, it has been argued, the celebration and promotion of differences might lead to some paradoxical consequences such as that the promotion itself results in the prevention of differences being accepted by the very group, i.e., the dominant majority, which the attempt targets to persuade to accept (see Chapter 5.4). Multiculturalism, epitomising the atmosphere of the hyper-capitalist present, celebrating and promoting differences, it has also been argued, can promote intolerance to those who believe there are *different degrees of validity* to *different ways to identify oneself in the contemporary world*, because the sense of universal validity multiculturalists have about the position, which we saw in the previous chapter was proven to be logically false, makes advocates self-righteous in criticising those who do not share their position: see the vicious tone adopted by some post-processualists in their critique of *other archaeologies.*)

The remedy, obviously, does not lie with such strategies as simply reinstalling a grand universal/universalising communicative framework such as Marxism. Rather, what we shall strive for/what we can reasonably hope to achieve is (1) to *contain* the existing risks which the irreversible process of the fragmentation of archaeological communication has already yielded, (2) to minimise the potential risks which it may be yielding, and (3) to imagine and create ways to carry out these objectives and ways to carry on discussing how to implement, in the most effective way, these objectives. We have already come to know that regulation by referring to grand narratives/universal values of the horizon of choices which our communication inevitably opens up all the time is impossible. Instead, we have to start by asking what the problems are. Grand narratives and universal values used to tell us what the problems were: they emerged as obstacles to the achievement of an ideal society and/or as deviations from morality, but no longer.

A profound difficulty in undertaking the above is that the experience of the successful continuation of communication is a foundation of self identity, and a critical examination of the mechanism of the reproduction of and the actual indeterminacy of communication in fragmented micro-discursive spaces might be met with an unexpectedly violent reaction or denial, which might cause the termination of the dialogue altogether. As Harold Garfinkel's ethno-methodology suggests (1984), if the boundary of the internalised core of the experience of the (successful) continuation of communication (practical knowledge/consciousness in Anthony Giddens's terminology, 1984, Chapter 1) was violated, people would react in a somewhat violent manner *without logical explanation* even for themselves (Garfinkel 1984; Heritage 1984). And that would certainly constitute a major obstacle to the objectives.

The so-called post-processual archaeologies/discourse can be characterised as the project of sensitising this intrinsic interdependence between self identity and the routinisation (/the accumulation of the experience of the successful continuation) of communication. The project has put its analytical focus upon the coupling of those interdependent factors with power, and has been elaborating the way to capture the process through which the uneven distribution of authoritative as well as allocative resources was/is incorporated to the constitution and reproduction of self identity in the present as well as in the past (e.g. Shanks and Tilley 1987). What the project has yielded, the positive and negative, has already been well elucidated, and a broad consensus is that the project has transformed the discipline of becoming self-critical to the same extent as other related disciplines such as history, anthropology, and sociology. However, the consideration and argument of this volume suggest that archaeology has *not become self-critical enough*. The post-processual project has not fully grasped how and why the project itself came into being in the first place (however see Hodder 1999, Chapter 9). By ignoring the fact that the generation of post-processual discourse is itself a form of reaction to the progression of function differentiation in communication systems/the intensification of the condition of modernity, the discourse effectively puts itself in the position of the *transcendental*: criticising other discourses as being unaware of/uncritical about the negative elements and consequences of modernity and as uncritically adopting theories and the methods reflecting them, but forgetting that it itself also derives from the self-reflexive fragmentation of communication systems, which leads to a wide range of problems, some of which have been the subject of investigation in this volume.

The experience of failed communication by relying on the taken-for-granteds of 'classic' modernity, i.e., Reason, grand narratives such as Marixism, universal values/goals for humanity, and so on, were accumulated to such an extent that the manner of communication and the old expectations one had about it had to be abandoned. Instead, the strategy of reducing the stress and uncertainty of discommunication by confining oneself to a micro-discursive space in which everyone feels they share a certain set of values has been adopted. Micro-paradigms coexisting under the broad umbrella of post-processual archaeologies can be understood as such micro-discursive spaces. As long as the strategy continues, the sincerest attitude to the residents of discursive spaces other than one's own is to accept the existence of other values and not to intervene in the way others communicate.

We have also recognised an important implication of the proliferation of such micro-paradigms, that being the proliferation has been connected to the multiculturalistic demand of multivocality and empowering minority/indigenous voices. It has been argued that the promotion of multivocality and the prioritisation of minority/indigenous voices may lead to consequences contrary to what is intended; in the situation in which the relativity of every possible epistemic stance is well recognised artificially prioritising particular groups would almost certainly be met with hostile, at times even violent, reactions due partly but importantly to the accumulation of frustrations from endless relativisation.

Our investigation of the consequences of the proliferation of this type of attitude to communication in general has revealed that not only has this attitude accelerated the pace of the fragmentation of the general discursive space and the accumulation of stress and hostility against those who are deliberately 'empowered' (one of the most serious problems which multiculturalism currently faces: see Semprini 2000), but it has also led to such harmful reactions as the conscious creation of a universalising, pseudo-transcendental narrative, which I have termed above the *narrative of the extreme*, in order to regain in the realm of perception the false sense of universal communicability. The consequences would be either the further deepening of fragmentation- and discommunication-related nihilism – or the increasing possibility of political manipulation. What is going on in Japan is a mixture of both, and they constitute a mutually enhancing vicious circle.

The conclusion of this volume, bearing this in mind, is rather simple in writing, but would inevitably be complex in implementation: we need a kind of theory which constantly reminds us of the necessity of, and supports, communication across the boundaries of segmented micro-discursive spaces. To this end, we need a theory which is *ontological* in the sense that it enables us to relate our mundane archaeo-logical practice to the mechanism of the constitution of contemporary society. We should avoid theoreticism in constructing the theory because that would make yet another source of nihilism/sense of irrelevance, but we should neither be worried about nor avoid explicit theorisation. The fundamental function of the theorisation is the creation of a continuously rearticulated set of *guidelines* to achieve and maintain the continuation, as non-stressful as possible, of archaeological communication; only the endless cycle of discursively confirming what the ego and the alter really mean and explicitly criticising the implications of their utterances can get over the endless generation of nihilism, the cause and consequence of uncertainty, related stress and the generation of extreme measures such as the invention of transcendental narra-tives. In that sense, conciliatory gestures, which have been repeatedly pointed out as coming to characterise contemporary archaeology, may be rather harmful. Vague-ness in the content of an opinion/thesis/utterance makes a commentary on/criticism of it rather difficult and raises the stress of coping with the uncertainty and allied risks illustrated throughout this volume. Such a theory has to be one which prepares us to cope with self-generating/articulating uncertainty and risks by illustrating the mechanism behind the continuous regeneration of uncertainty and risks, and pre-vents us from hastily resorting to easier-looking, but in actuality riskier and more harmful, choices/solutions such as the invention of, and resorting to transcendental narratives.

What I hope such a theorisation will lead to is to open up a sort of *public dis-cursive domain*. However, this should be different from the Habermasian concept of the ideal speech situation (Habermas 1987). In the ideal speech situation, anything with the potential of distorting understanding of what is uttered, deriving from the uneven distribution of various resources ranging from the command of language through one's biographical background to actual allocative resources, is eliminated. In our project, on the contrary, we begin by accepting that the realisation of the ideal speech situation is *impossible*. Not only the diversity of our biographic expe-riences but also the fragmentation in the way we articulate reflexive commentaries to them in this high-/late-/post-modernity make impossible even the agreement of what to eliminate as obstacles to the realisation of the ideal speech situation. Instead of clinging to the illusion that we can eliminate the possibility of the intervention of external (distorting) factors in the reproduction of communication systems, our attempt would take the form of imagining a different way to appreciate the meaning, tendency and potential of archaeological communication. We have to prepare our-selves not only for the range of risks which we have already unintentionally created through our archaeological communication but also for the range of risks which our *future* communication *may* generate. However, unless we actually create risks, we can neither see them nor prepare ourselves for them. The fragmentation of archae-ological discursive space and our confining ourselves to individual micro-discursive spaces have given us comfort by reproducing the illusion that the indeterminacy of communication can be overcome and that risks can be avoided. However, they also make us blind to the risks which our communication is inevitably creating. The only thing we can do is to urge ourselves to get across the boundaries of segmented micro-discursive spaces and communicate, observe what risks are created, and articulate further communication on them.

Not the *tolerance* of, or deliberate attempt of empowering, different stances but only the *mutual, endless demand* for the explicit articulation of problematique, i.e., the horizon of choices/issues for debate, can secure the productive and creative *continuation* of archaeological communication and endow us with the imaginative problematisation of new issues relevant to the present, at the same time avoiding falling into the problem of post-modernistic nihilism/endless relativisation and the unconscious generation of intolerance.

REFERENCES

Akasaka, Norio. 1996. *Tohoku-gaku he (Toward the Tohoku region studies)*, *Vol. 1* (in Japanese). Tokyo: Sakuhin-sha.

Akazawa, Takeru. 1983. *Saishu-shuryo-min no kokogaku (An archaeology of hunter-gatherers: an ecological approach)* (in Japanese). Tokyo: Kaimeisha.

Anderson, Benedict. 1991. *Imagined communities: reflections on the origin and spread of nationalism*. London and New York: Verso.

Anzai, Masahito. ed. 2002. *Jomon shakai ron (Papers in the study of Jomon society)*, *Vols. 1 and 2*. Tokyo: Dosei-sha.

Ariès, Philippe. 1965. *Centuries of childhood: a social history of family life*. New York: Random House.

Aston, W. G. 1972. *Nihongi: chronicles of Japan from the earliest times to AD 697*. Tokyo: Charles Tuttle Co.

Balibar, Etienne and Wallerstein, Immanuel. 1991. *Race, nation, class*. London: Verso.

Barrett, John C. 1994. *Fragments from antiquity: an archaeology of social life in Britain, 2900–1200 BC*. Oxford: Blackwell.

Bauman, Zygmunt. 1988. *Freedom*. Milton Keynes: Open University Press.

2000a. *Globalization: the human consequences*. Cambridge: Polity.

2000b. *Liquid modernity*. Cambridge: Polity.

Beck, Ulrich, Giddens, Anthony and Lash, Scott. 1994. *Reflexive modernization*. Cambridge: Polity.

Binford, Lewis R. 1962. Archaeology as anthropology. *American Antiquity*, 28 (2): 217–225.

Bradley, Richard. 2002. *The past in prehistoric societies*. London: Routledge.

Chapman, Robert. 2003. *Archaeologies of complexity*. London: Routledge.

Clark, J. Grahame D. 1939. *Archaeology and society*. London: Methuen.

Clarke, David L. 1978. *Analytical archaeology* (2nd edn). New York: Columbia University Press.

Diaz-Andreu, Maria and Champion, Timothy. (eds.) 1996. *Nationalism and archaeology in Europe*. London: UCL Press.

Fowler, Chris. 2004. *The archaeology of personhood: an anthropological approach*. London: Routledge.

Foucault, Michel. 1977. *Discipline and punish: the birth of the prison*. London: Penguin.

2001 (1967). *The order of things*. London: Routledge.

Fuji, Naomoto, Inoue, Kaoru, and Kitano, Kohei. 1964. *Kawachi ni okeru kofun no chosa (Report of the excavation of the ancient burial mounds in Kawachi county)* (in Japanese with English summary). Osaka: The Institute of Japanese History, Osaka University.

Fujitani, Takashi. 1994. *Ten'no no pejento (Emperor, nation, pageantry)* (in Japanese). Tokyo: NHK.

Fukunaga, Shin'ya. 1998. Dotaku kara dokyo he (From bronze bells to bronze mirrors) (in Japanese). In *Kodai kokka ha koshite umareta (The emergence of the Japanese ancient state)* (ed. by H. Tsude), pp. 217–275. Tokyo: Kadokawa.

2002. *Yamatai-koku kara Yamato-seiken he (From the Yamatai-koku to the Yamato political organisation)* (in Japanese). Toyonaka: Osaka University.

Fukuoka PBE. 1983. *Mikumo-iseki IV (The excavation report of the Mikumo site, Vol. 4)* (in Japanese). Fukuoka: Fukuoka Prefectural Board of Education.

Fukuyama, Francis. 1992. *The end of history and the last man.* New York: Free Press.

Gamble, Clive. 2001. *Archaeology: the basics.* London: Routledge.

Garfinkel, Harold. 1984. *Studies in ethnomethodology.* Cambridge: Polity.

Geertz, Clifford. 1973. *The interpretation of cultures.* New York: Basic Books.

Gellner, Ernest. 1983. *Nations and nationalism.* Oxford: Blackwell.

Giddens, Anthony. 1984. *The constitution of society: outline of the theory of structuration.* Cambridge: Polity.

1990. *The consequence of modernity.* Cambridge: Polity.

Gosden, Chris. 1999. *Anthropology and archaeology: a changing relationship.* London: Routledge.

Gregory, Derek. 1994. *Geographical imaginations.* Oxford: Blackwell.

Habermas, Jurgen. 1987. *The theory of communicative action: Vol. 2, lifeworld and system, a critique of functionalist reason.* Cambridge: Polity.

Habu, Junko. 2004. *Ancient Jomon of Japan.* Cambridge: Cambridge University Press.

Hamada, Seiryo. 1918. *Kawachi-koku Kou sekki-jidai iseki hakkutsu hokoku (The report of the excavation of the Kou site, Kawachi district): Kyoto teikoku daigaku bunka daigaku koko-gaku kenkyu hokoku (Archaeological research report from Faculty of Letters, the Kyoto Imperial University), Vol. 2* (in Japanese). Kyoto: Kyoto University.

Hara, Hidesaburo. 1972. Nihon ni okeru kagakuteki genshi- kodai-shi kenkyu no seiritsu to tenkai (The establishment and the development of the social-scientific study of Japanese pre and protohistory) (in Japanese). In *Nihon genshi kyousan sei shakai to kokka no keisei (Primitive communism and the formation of state in Japan)* (ed. by H. Hara), pp. 343–409. Tokyo: Asakura Shoten.

Harunari, Hideji. 1984. Yayoi jidai hokubu kyushu no kyojyu kitei (Postmarital residential rules of the northern Kyushu region in the Yayoi period) (in Japanese). *Kokuritsu rekishi minzoku hakubutsukan kenkyu hokoku (Bulletin of the National Museum of Japanese History)* 1:1–40.

1985. Yayoi jidai Kinai no shinzoku kosei (The kin organisation of the Kinai region in the Yayoi period) (in Japanese). *Kokuritsu rekishi minzoku hakubutsukan kenkyu hokoku (Bulletin of the National Museum of Japanese History)* 5:1–47.

Harunari, Hideji, Fujio, Shin'ichiro, Imamura, Mineo and Sakamoto, Minoru. 2003. Yayoi jidai no kaishi nendai (The absolute date for the beginning of the Yayoi period) (in Japanese). In *Nihon kokogaku kyokai dai 69 kai sokai happyo-yoshi (Abstracts for the 69th annual meeting of the Japanese Archaeological Association).* Tokyo: the Japanese Archaeological Association.

Harvey, David. 1989. *The condition of postmodernity: an enquiry into the origins of cultural change.* Oxford: Blackwell.

Hashiba, Yusuke. 1889. Some results obtained from the comparative study of cordmark potteries. *The bulletin of the Tokyo Anthropological Society,* 37(4): 231–238.

Hayashi, Kensaku. 1979. Jomon jidai no shuraku to ryoiki (Settlements and their territories in the Jomon period). In *Nihon kokogaku wo manabu (Studying Japanese archaeology), Vol. 3* (eds. by H. Otsuka, M. Sahara and M. Tozawa), pp. 102–119. Tokyo: Yuhikaku.

Heritage, John. 1984. *Garfinkel and ethnomethodology.* Cambridge: Polity.

Hobsbawm, E. J. 1990. *Nations and nationalism since 1780: programme, myth, reality.* Cambridge: Cambridge University Press.

Hodder, Ian. 1982. *Symbols in action.* Cambridge: Cambridge University Press.

1986. *Reading the past: current approaches to interpretation in archaeology.* Cambridge: Cambridge University Press.

1991. Postprocessual archaeology and the current debate. In *Processual and postprocessual archaeologies: multiple ways of knowing the past* (ed. by R. Preucel), pp. 30–41. Carbondale: Center for Archaeological Investigations.

1999. *The archaeological process: an introduction.* Oxford: Blackwell.

2003. *Archaeology beyond dialogue.* Salt Lake City: University of Utah Press.

Hodder, Ian (ed.) 1982. *Symbolic and structural archaeology.* Cambridge: Cambridge University Press.

(ed.) 1991. *Archaeological theory in Europe: the last three decades.* London: Routledge.

Hodder, Ian and Hutson, Scott. 2003. *Reading the past: current approaches to interpretation in archaeology* (3rd edn). Cambridge: Cambridge University Press.

Hojo, Yoshitaka. 1999. Sanuki-gata zenpo-koen-fun no teisho (Introducing the notion of the Sanuki type keyhole-shaped tumulus) (in Japanese). In *Kokka keisei ki no kokogaku (The archaeology of state formation period in Japan)* (ed. by Department of Archaeology of Osaka University), pp. 205–229. Osaka: Department of Archaeology, Osaka University.

2000. Zenpo-koen-fun to Wa-oken (The keyhole-shaped tumulus and the Wa polity) (in Japanese). In *Kofunjidaizo wo minaosu (Social structure and social change in the formative phase of the mounded-tomb period of Japan: a new perspective)*, pp. 77–135. Tokyo: Aoki.

Hudson, Mark. 1999. *Ruins of identity: ethnogenesis in the Japanese islands.* Honolulu: University of Hawaii Press.

Huntington, Samuel. 1998. *The clash of civilizations and the remaking of world order.* New York: Simon and Schuster.

Ikawa-Smith, Fumiko. 1982. Co-traditions in Japanese archaeology. *World Archaeology,* 13: 296–309.

Imafuku, Rikei. 1999. Jomon bunka wo taigen suru daini no dogu (Jomon non-functional tools as the symbols of the Jomon culture) (in Japanese). In *Saishin Jomon-gaku no sekai (Latest outcomes of Jomon studies)* (ed. by T. Kobayashi), pp. 84–95. Tokyo: Asahishinbunsha.

Imamura, Keiji. 1996. *Prehistoric Japan: new perspectives on insular East Asia.* Honolulu: University of Hawaii Press.

Isomae, Jun'ichi. 1987. Dogu no yoho ni tsuite (The usage of *Dogu* clay figurines) (in Japanese). *Kokogaku kenkyu (Quarterly of Archaeological Studies)* 34 (1): 87–102.

1998. *Kiki-shinwa no meta hisutori (A meta-history of the myths featured in the Kojiki and Nihon-shoki imperial chronicles)* (in Japanese). Tokyo: Yoshikawakobunkan.

Iwanaga, Shozo. 1986. Hoko-gata saiki (Japanese bronze spearhead-shaped implements) (in Japanese). In *Yayoi-bunka no kenkyu (Studies in the Yayoi culture),* Vol. 6: *Dogu to gijutsu (Tools and technologies)* (ed. by H. Kanaseki and M. Sahara), pp. 113–118. Tokyo: Yusankaku.

Izumi, Takura, ed. 1996. *Jomon doki shutsugen (The emergence of the Jomon pottery)* (in Japanese). Tokyo: Kodansha.

Jameson, Fredric. 1991. *Postmodernism: or, the cultural logic of late capitalism.* London: Verso.

Jay, Martin. 1984. *Marxism and totality: the adventure of a concept from Lukcs to Habermas.* Berkeley and Los Angeles: University of California Press.

Kan, Sanjun. 2001. *Nashonarizumu (Nationalism)* (in Japanese). Tokyo: Iwanami.

Kensetsu-sho. 1997. *Kokuei Yoshinogari rekishi-koen tatemono to fukugen kento chosa houkokusho (The report of the reconstruction of the buildings of the Yoshinogari site for the display at the Yoshinogari National Historical park)* (in Japanese). Kanzaki: Kensetsu-sho Kyushu chiho kensetsukyoku kokuei Yoshinogari rekishi-koen koji jimusho.

2000. *Kokuei Yoshinogari rekishi-koen seikatsu fukugen tenji kihon sekkei houkokusho (The report of the reconstruction of the lifeways of the residents of the Yoshinogari site for the display* at the Yoshinogari National Historical park) (in Japanese). Kanzaki: Kensetsu-sho Kyushu chiho kensetsukyoku kokuei Yoshinogari rekishi-koen koji jimusho.

Kiyama-machi Iseki hakkutsu chosa-dan. 1983. *Sendoyama iseki (The Sendoyama site)* (in Japanese). Kiyama: Kiyama-machi Iseki hakkutsu chosa-dan.

Kobayashi, Tatsuo. 1990. Jomon-sekai no dogu (The *Dogu* clay figurine of the Jomon world) (in Japanese). *Kikan Kokogaku (Archaeology Quarterly)*, 30: 14–16.

Kobayashi, Yukio. 1961. *Kofun-jidai no kenkyu (A study of the Kofun period)* (in Japanese). Tokyo: Aoki.

Kohl, Philip and Fawcett, Clare. 1996. *Nationalism, politics and the practice of archaeology.* Cambridge: Cambridge University Press.

Komori, Yoichi. 2001. *Posutokoroniaru (Postcolonial)* (in Japanese). Tokyo: Iwanami.

Komoto, Masayuki. 1982. Yayoi bunka no keifu (Sociocultural ancestory of the Yayoi culture) (in Japanese). In *Noko bunka to kodai shakai (Agrarian culture and ancient society)*, 48–56. Tokyo: Yusankaku.

Kondo, Tadashi, ed. 1972. *Chusenji kofungun (Chusenji tumuli)* (in Japanese). Matsue: Shimane Prefectural Board of Education.

Kondo, Yoshiro. 1983. *Zenpo-koen-fun no jidai (The age of the keyhole-shaped tumulus)* (in Japanese). Tokyo: Iwanami.

Kondo, Yoshiro. ed. 1991. *Zenpo-koen-hun shusei (The corpus of keyhole-shaped tumuli), Chugoku-Shikoku hen (The Chugoku and Shikoku districts)* (in Japanese). Tokyo: Yamakawa-shuppan.

Kondo, Yoshiro and Sahara, Makoto. 1983. Kaisetsu (Commentary) (in Japanese). In *Omori kaizuka (Shell mounds of Omori)* (by E. S. Morse 1879, translation and commentary by Y. Kondo and M. Sahara), pp. 185–219. Tokyo: Iwanami.

Kono, Isamu. 1935. Kanto-chiho ni okeru Jomon-shiki sekki jidai bunka no hensen (Temporal changes in Jomon style Stone Age culture). *Shizen-gaku zasshi (Journal of Prehistoric Studies)*, 7 (3): 1–63.

Kosugi, Yasushi. 2003. *Jomon no matsuri to kurashi (The ritual and lifeways of the Jomon period)* (in Japanese). Tokyo: Iwanami.

Kristiansen, Kristian.1998. *Europe before history.* Cambridge: Cambridge University Press.

Kristiansen, Kristian and Rowlands, Michael. 1996. *Social transformations in archaeology.* London: Routledge.

Lechner, Frank and Boli, John. eds. 1999. *The globalisation reader.* Oxford: Blackwell.

Lucas, G. 2001. *Critical approaches to fieldwork: contemporary and historical archaeological practice.* London: Routledge.

Luhmann, Niklas. 1995. *Social systems.* Stanford, CA: Stanford University Press.

1998. *Observations on modernity.* Stanford, CA.: Stanford University Press.

Lyotard, Jean-François 1984. *The postmodern condition: a report on knowledge.* Manchester: Manchester University Press.

Meskell, Lynn. 1996. The somatization of archaeology: institutions, discourses, corporeality. *Norwegian Archaeological Review*, 29: 1–16.

1999. *Archaeologies of social life: age, sex, class et cetera in ancient Egypt.* Oxford: Blackwell.

Meskell, Lynn and Joyce, Rosemary. 2003. *Embodied lives: figuring ancient Maya and Egyptian experience.* London: Routledge.

Mineyama TBE, ed. 2001. *Akasaka-Imai funkyubo dai san-ji hakkutsu chosa gaiyo hokoku (Akasaka-Imai tumulus: the preliminary report on the 3rd excavation)* (in Japanese). Mineyama: Mineyama Township Board of Education.

Mithen, Steve. 1996. *Prehistory of the mind: the cognitive origins of art, religion and science.* London: Thames and Hudson.

Mizoguchi, Koji. 1995. Fukuoka-ken Amagi-shi Kuriyama iseki C-gun boiki no kenkyu (A reexamination of location C of the Yayoi cemetery site of Kuriyama, Amagi City, Fukuoka

Prefecture) (in Japanese with English summary). *Nihon kokogaku (Journal of the Japanese Archaeological Association)*, 2: 69–94.

1997. The reproduction of archaeological discourse: the case of Japan. *Journal of European Archaeology*, 5 (2): 149–165.

2000a. Kofun-jidai kaishi-ki no rikai wo meguru mondaiten (Some problems concerning the beginning of the Kofun period): Yayoi-bosei kenkyu-shi no shiten kara (as seen from the history of the study of Yayoi period mortuary practices) (in Japanese). In *Kofunjidaizo wo minaosu (Social structure and social change in the formative phase of the mounded-tomb period of Japan: a new perspective)*, pp. 27–48. Tokyo: Aoki.

2000b. Bochi to maiso-koi no hensen (The transformation of the cemetery structure and mortuary practices of the Yayoi period) (in Japanese). In *Kofunjidaizo wo minaosu (Social structure and social change in the formative phase of the mounded-tomb period of Japan: a new perspective)*, pp. 201–273. Tokyo: Aoki.

2001. Yayoi jidai no shakai (Society of the Yayoi period) (in Japanese). In *Gendai no kokogaku (Contemporary archaeology)*, Vol. 6: sonraku to shakai no kokogaku (The archaeology of settlements and societies) (ed. by R. Takahashi), pp. 135–160. Tokyo: Asakura.

2002. *An archaeological history of Japan, 30,000 BC to AD 700*. Philadelphia: University of Pennsylvania Press.

2005a. Identity, modernity, and archaeology: the case of Japan. In *A Companion to Social Archaeology* (ed. L. Meskell and R. Preucel), pp. 396–414. Oxford: Blackwell.

2005b. Genealogy in the ground: observations of jar burials of the Yayoi period, northern Kyushu, Japan. *Antiquity*, 79 (304): 316–326.

Mizuno, Masayoshi. 1969. Jomon jidai shuraku kenkyu no kisoteki sosa (A basic procedure for the study of Jomon settlements) (in Japanese). *Kodai bunka (Ancient Culture)*, 21 (3 and 4): 1–21.

Murakami, Yasuyuki. 2000. Tekki seisan ryutsu to shakai henkaku (Iron production and exchange and social transformation) (in Japanese). In *Kofunjidaizo wo minaosu (Social structure and social change in the formative phase of the mounded-tomb period of Japan: a new perspective)*, pp. 137–200. Tokyo: Aoki.

Naito, Masanori. 2004. *Yoroppa to Isuramu: kyosei ha kano ka (Europe and Islam: is coexistence possible?)* (in Japanese). Tokyo: Iwanami.

Nakaya, Jiujiro. 1934. Nihon Sekki-jidai ni okeru tairiku-bunka no eikyo (The influence of the culture of mainland Asia on the Japanese archipelago during the stone age) (in Japanese). *Kokogaku (Archaeology)*, 5 (4): 91–103.

Nihon Daiyon-ki gakkai, Ono, Akira, Harunari, Hideji, and Oda, Shizuo, eds. 1992. *Zukai Nihon no jinrui iseki (Atlas of Japanese Archaeology)* (in Japanese). Tokyo: Tokyo University Press.

Nishikawa, Nagao. 1995. Introduction: Nihongata kokumin-kokka no keisei (The formation of the Japan-type nation state) (in Japanese). In *Bakumatsu Meiji-ishin ki no kokumin-kokka keisei to bunka henyo (The formation of the nation-state and cultural transformation in the final Edo and Meiji eras)* (ed. by N. Nishikawa), pp. 3–42. Tokyo: Shin'yo-sha.

NKK (Japanese Archaeological Association), ed. 1971. *Maizo bunkazai hakusho (A report on the protection and destruction of buried cultural properties)* (in Japanese). Nihon Koko-gaku Kyokai (Japanese Archaeological Association). Tokyo: Gakuseisha.

1981. *Dai niji Maizo bunkazai hakusho (The second report on the protection and destruction of buried cultural properties)* (in Japanese). Nihon Koko-gaku Kyoka (Japanese Archaeological Association). Tokyo: Gakuseisha.

2003. *Zen-cyuki Kyusekki mondai no kensho (Inspection of the Early and Middle Palaeolithic problem in Japan)* (in Japanese). Tokyo: Nihon Koko-gaku Kyoka (Japanese Archaeological Association).

Notomi, Toshio. 1997. *Yoshinogari iseki: Hozon to katsuyo eno michi (The Yoshinogari site: toward the preservation and public use)* (in Japanese). Tokyo: Yoshikawa-kobunkan.

Obayashi, Taryo. 1977. *Yamatai-koku* (in Japanese). Tokyo: Chuokoron-sha.

OCJW. 1996. *Jomon no tobira (The Jomon world '96)*, Tokyo: Organizing Committee of the Jomon World '96.

Oda, Fujio. 1990. Yayoi shuraku iseki no chosa to hozon mondai (The rescue excavation and failed preservation attempt of a Yayoi site) (in Japanese). *Kobunka Danso: Journal of the society of Kyushu prehistoric and ancient cultural studies*, 22: 215–224.

Oguma, Eiji. 1995. *Tan'itsu-minzoku shinwa no kigen (The myth of the homogeneous nation)* (in Japanese). Tokyo: Shin'yo-sha.

1998. *Nihon-jin no kyokai (The boundaries of the Japanese)* (in Japanese). Tokyo: Shin'yo-sha.

Okada, Yasuhiro and NHK Aomori Hoso-kyoku. ed. 1997. *Jomon toshi o horu: San'nai-Maruyama kara gen-Nihon ga mieru (Excavating the Jomon town: seeing prehistoric Japan from the Sannai-Maruyama site)* (in Japanese). Tokyo: NHK Shuppan.

Okamura, Michio. 1996. Jomon bunka toha nandaroka (What is the Jomon culture?) (in Japanese) In *Jomon no tobira (The Jomon world '96)* (ed. by Organizing Committee of the Jomon World '96 Exhibition), pp. 72–81. Tokyo: Organizing Committee of the Jomon World '96.

2000. *Jomon no seikatsu-shi (The life of the Jomon people)* (in Japanese). Tokyo: Kodansha.

Okazaki, Takashi. 1971. Nihon kokogaku no hoho (The methods of archaeology in Japan) (in Japanese). In *Kodai no Nihon (Japan in the ancient times)*, Vol. 9, pp. 30–53. Tokyo: Kadokawa.

Okubo, Tetsuya, Fuchinokami, Ryusuke and Yoshitaka, Hojo. 2005. Ryobo mondai 2004 (Issues and problems related to the 'imperial mausolea' in the fiscal year of 2004) (in Japanese). *Kokogaku kenkyu (Quarterly of Archaeological Studies)*, 51 (4): 1–7.

Osawa, Masachi. 1998. *Sengo no shiso kukan (The discursive space of post-Second World War Japan)* (in Japanese). Tokyo: Chikuma-shobo.

2002. *Bunmei no uchinaru shototsu (The internal clash of civilisations)* (in Japanese). Tokyo: Chikuma-shobo.

Parsons, Talcott. 1951. *The social system*. London: RKP.

Preucel, Robert. ed. 1991. *Processual and postprocessual archaeologies: multiple ways of knowing the past*. Carbondale: Center for Archaeological Investigations, Southern Illinois University.

Rekishi-gaku kenkyu-kai. ed. 1951. *Rekishi-gaku no seika to kadai, Vol. 2 (Annual review of the study of history: the outcomes and issues in historical studies 1950)*.

Renfrew, Colin. 1984. *Approaches to social archaeology*. Edinburgh: Edinburgh University Press.

Renfrew, Colin and Cherry, John. 1986. *Peer–polity interaction and socio-political change*. Cambridge: Cambridge University Press.

Ruoff, Kenneth J. 2001. *The people's emperor: democracy and the Japanese monarchy, 1945–1995 (Harvard East Asian Monographs, No. 211)*. Cambridge, MA: Harvard University Press.

Saga PBE. 1979. *Futatsukayama* (in Japanese) Saga: Saga Prefectural Board of Education.

1994. *Yoshinogari* (in Japanese). Saga: Saga Prefectural Board of Education.

1997. *Yoshinogari iseki: Heisei Ni-nendo~Nana-nendo no hakkutsu-chosa no gaiyo (A preliminary report on the excavation of the Yoshinogari site: 1990~1995 field seasons)* (in Japanese). Saga: Saga Prefectural Board of Education.

2000. *The Yoshinogari site: Japan's largest site of an ancient moat-enclosed settlement*. Saga: Saga Prefectural Board of Education.

2003. *Saga-ken Yoshinogari iseki: Nihon saidai no kango-shuraku ato (The Yoshinogari site: Japan's largest site of an ancient moat-enclosed settlement)* (in Japanese). Saga: Saga Prefectural Board of Education.

Sahara, Makoto. 1987. *Taikei Nihon no rekishi 1: Nihonjin no tanjo (A new history of Japan, Vol. 1, The birth of the Japanese)* (in Japanese). Tokyo: Shogakukan.

— 2003. *Gishi-Wajinden no kokogaku (An archaeology of Gishi-Wajinden)* (in Japanese). Tokyo: Iwanami.

Sakai, Naoki. 1996. *Shizan sareru Nihon-go, Nihon-jin (Japanese language and the Japanese as stillborn)* (in Japanese). Tokyo: Shin'yo-sha.

Schnapp, Alain. 1996. *The discovery of the past: the origins of archaeology.* London: British Museum Press.

Semprini, Andrea. 2000. *Le Multiculturalisme.* Paris: Presses Universitaires de France.

Shanks, Michael and Tilley, Christopher. 1987. *Re-constructing archaeology: theory and practice.* Cambridge: Cambridge University Press.

Smith, Anthony. 1986. *The Ethnic Origins of Nations.* Oxford: Blackwell.

— 2001. *Nationalism.* Cambridge: Polity.

Sokolovskii, S. and Tishkov, V. 1996. Ethnicity. In *Encyclopedia of Social and Cultural Anthropology* (ed. by A. Barnard and J. Spencer), pp. 190–193. London: Routledge.

Sørensen, Marie Louise S. 1996. The fall of a nation, the birth of a subject: the national use of archaeology in nineteenth-century Denmark. In *Nationalism and archaeology in Europe* (ed. by T. Champion and M. Diaz-Andreu), pp. 24–47. London: UCL Press.

Suzuki, Kimio. 1984. Nihon no shinsekki jidai (The Neolithic period of Japan) (in Japanese). In *Koza nihon rekishi (Seminars in Japanese history)*, Vol. 1 (ed. by Rekishi-gaku kenkyu kai and Nihonshi kenkyu kai), pp. 75–116. Tokyo: Tokyo University Press.

Takahashi, Kenji. 1914. Kida hakase no 'Joko no funbo' wo yomu (Comments on Dr. Kida's 'Tumuli of the ancient times') (in Japanese). *Kokogaku Zasshi*, 4(7): 29–36.

Takahashi, Ryuzaburo, Takeshi Toizumi, and Yasushi Kojo. 1998. Archaeological studies of Japan: Current studies of the Jomon archaeology (in English). *Nihon kokogaku (Journal of the Japanese Archaeological Association)*, 5: 47–72.

Takakura, Hiroaki. 1973. Funbo kara mita Yayoi jidai no hatten katei (The process of social development in the Yayoi period as seen from the burial and cemetery) (in Japanse). *Kokogaku kenkyu (Quarterly of Archaeological Studies)* 20 (2): 7–24.

— 1995. *Kin'in kokka-gun no jidai: Higashi Ajia sekai to Yayoi shakai (The age of the golden seal polities: golden seals issued by the Han empire of China)* (in Japanese). Tokyo: Aoki.

Takesue, Jun'ichi. 1990. Murasaki-gawa no Yoshinogari: Kitakyushu-shi Kamitokuriki iseki (A site comparable to the Yoshinogari: Kamitokuriki site, near the river Murasaki, Kitakyushu City). *Kobunka danso: Journal of the Society of Kyushu Prehistoric and Ancient Cultural Studies*, 23: 25–34.

— 2002. *Yayoi no mura (The settlement of the Yayoi period)* (in Japanese). Tokyo: Yamakawa.

Taki, Koji. 1988. *Ten'no no shozo (The portraits of Emperor Meiji)* (in Japanese). Tokyo: Iwanami.

Tanabe, Shozo and Sahara, Makoto. 1966. Kinki (The Kinki region) (in Japanese). In *Nihon no kokogaku (Japanese archaeology)*, Vol. 3: *Yayoi jidai (The Yayoi period)* (ed. by S. Wajima), pp. 108–140. Tokyo: Kawade-shobo-shinsha.

Tanaka, Yoshiyuki. 1995. *Kofun-jidai shinzoku kozo no kenkyu: hone kara mita kodai shakai (A study of the kinship structure of the Kofun period: an osteoarchaeological approach to the ancient society)* (in Japanese). Tokyo: Kashiwa.

— 2000. Bochi kara mita shinzoku kazoku (Kin- and family-groups as seen from the cemetery structure) (in Japanese). In *Kodaishi no ronten (Arguments in the study of ancient Japan)*, Vol. 2 (ed. by H. Tsude and M. Sahara), pp. 131–152. Tokyo: Shogakkan.

Teshigawara, Akira. 1991. Shin kyokasho to koko-gaku (New school textbooks and archaeology) (in Japanese). *Kokogaku Kenkyu (Quarterly of Archaeological Studies)*, 38 (3): 4–9.

— 1995. *Nihon kokogaku no ayumi (A history of Japanese archaeology)* (in Japanese). Tokyo: Meicho Shuppan.

Thomas, Julian. 1996. *Time, culture and identity: an interpretive archaeology*. London: Routledge.

Tilley, Christopher. 1991. *Material culture and text: the art of ambiguity*. London: Routledge.

1994. *A phenomenology of landscape: places, paths, and monuments*. Oxford: Berg.

Toma, Seita. 1951a. Eiyu-jidai (The ancient heroic age) (in Japanese). In *Rekishi-gaku no seika to kadai*, Vol. 2 (*Annual review of the study of history: the outcomes and issues in historical studies 1950*) (ed. by Rekishi-gaku kenkyu-kai), pp. 16–20. Tokyo: Iwanami

1951b. *Nihon minzoku no keisei (The genesis of the Japanese nation)* (in Japanese). Tokyo: Iwanami.

Tomoeda, Toshio. 1991. Kozo to hendo (Structures and their changes) (in Japanese). In *Shakai gaku no kiso (An introduction to sociology)* (eds. by T. Imada and T. Tomoeda), pp. 121–149. Tokyo: Yuhikaku.

Trigger, Bruce. 1989. *A history of archaeological thought*. Cambridge: Cambridge University Press.

Tsuboi, Shogoro. 1887. Koropokgru seems to have inhabited Hokkaido. *The Bulletin of the Tokyo Anthropological Society*, 2 (12): 93–97.

Tsude, Hiroshi. 1998. Soron: Yayoi kara Kofun he (Introduction: from the Yayoi to the Kofun period) (in Japanese). In *Kodai kokka ha koshite umareta (The emergence of the Japanese ancient state)* (ed. by H. Tsude), pp. 8–50. Tokyo: Kadokawa.

Tsukinowa kofun kanko kai. 1960. *Tsukinowa kofun (The Tsukinowa tumulus)* (in Japanese). Yanahara: Tsukinowa kofun kanko kai.

Turner, B. 2003. Foreword. In *Embodied lives: figuring ancient Maya and Egyptian experience* (by L. Meskell and R. Joyce), pp. xiii–xx. London: Routledge.

Ucko, Peter J. ed. 1995. *Theory in archaeology: a world perspective*. London: Routledge.

Umehara, Takeshi and Yasuda, Yoshinori. ed. 1995. *Jomon bunmei no hakken: Kyoi no San'naimaruyama iseki (The discovery of the Jomon civilization: the amazing Sannai-Maruyama site)* (in Japanese). Tokyo: PHP.

Wada, Sei and Ishihara, Michihiro. (trans.) 1951. *Gishi Wajinden, Gokanjo Waden, Sojo Wakokuden, Zuisho Wakokuden* (in Japanese). Tokyo: Iwanami.

Wallerstein, Immanuel. 1974. *The modern world system: capitalist agriculture and the origins of the European world economy in the sixteenth century*. New York: Academic Press.

Watabe, Yoshimichi, et al. 1936, 1937. *Nihon rekishi kyotei (Seminar in Japanese history)*, Vols. 1 and 2 (in Japanese). Tokyo: Hakuyo-sha.

Waters, Malcolm. 1999. General commentary: the meaning of modernity. In *Modernity: critical concepts* (ed. by M. Waters), pp. xi–xxiii. London: Routledge.

Watsuji, Tetsuro. 1951. *Shinko Nihon kodai bunka (Japanese ancient culture (new edition))* (in Japanese). Tokyo: Iwanami.

Weber, Max. 1930 [1904]. *The protestant ethic and the spirit of capitalism*. New York: Charles Scribner's Sons.

Wiwjorra, Ingo. 1996. German archaeology and its relation to nationalism and racism. In *Nationalism and archaeology in Europe* (ed. by T. Champion and M. Diaz-Andreu), pp. 164–188. London: UCL Press.

Yagi, Shozaburo and Shimomura, Misokichi. 1893. Report on the exploration of a shell-mound lately discovered at Shizuka, Hitachi. *The Bulletin of the Tokyo Anthropological Society*, 8 (87): 336–389.

Yamagata, Mariko. 1992. The Shakado figurines and Middle Jomon ritual in the Hofu basin. *Japanese Journal of Religious Studies*, 19 (2/3): 129–138.

Yamamoto, Teruhisa. 1995. Sekibo (Stone club/rod) (in Japanese). In *Jomon bunka no kenkyu (Studies in the Jomon culture)*, Vol. 9 (ed. by S. Kato, T. Kobayashi and T. Fujimoto), pp. 170–180. Tokyo: Yusankaku.

Yamanouchi, Sugao. 1937. Jomon doki no taibetsu to saibetsu (The establishment of the phases and regional sequences of the Jomon pottery) (in Japanese). *Senshi kokogaku kenkyu (Studies in prehistoric archaeology)*, 1 (1): 29–32.

Yamao, Yukihisa. 1986. *Shinban Gishi-wajin-den* (in Japanese). Tokyo: Kodansha.

Yasuda, Hiroshi. 1998. *Ten'no no seiji-shi (The political history of the reign of the emperors Mutsuhito, Yoshihito, and Hirohito)* (in Japanese). Tokyo: Aoki.

Yoshida, Akira. 1972. Dorei-sei kenkyu no shomondai (Issues in the study of the slavery stage in the social evolutionary process of Japan) (in Japanese). In *Rekishi-kagaku taikei (Studies in historical sciences)*, *Vol. 2* (ed. by A. Yoshida), pp. 297–320. Tokyo: Azekura Shobo.

1995. *Himiko no jidai (The era of Queen Himiko)* (in Japanese). Tokyo: Shin'nihon shuppan.

CAMBRIDGE STUDIES IN ARCHAEOLOGY

Titles in series

The Archaeology of Class in Urban America
STEPHEN A. MROZOWSKI

Archaeology, Society and Identity in Modern Japan
KOJI MIZOGUCHI